Food Security in Asia

ACADEMIA STUDIES IN ASIAN ECONOMIES

General Editor: Sheng-Cheng Hu, *Director, Institute of Economics, Academia Sinica, Taiwan*

Titles in the series include:

Economic Efficiency and Productivity Growth in the Asia-Pacific Region
Edited by Tsu-Tan Fu, Cliff J. Huang and C.A. Knox Lovell

Food Security in Asia
Economics and Policies
Edited by Wen S. Chern, Colin A. Carter and Shun-Yi Shei

Economic Analysis of Substance Use and Abuse: The Experience of
Developed Countries and Lessons for Developing Countries
Edited by Michael Grossman and Chee-Ruey Hsieh

The Economics of Health Care in Asia-Pacific Countries
Edited by Teh-Wei Hu and Chee-Ruey Hsieh

Food Security in Asia

Economics and Policies

Edited by

Wen S. Chern
Professor, Department of Agricultural, Environmental and Development Economics, The Ohio State University, Columbus, USA

Colin A. Carter
Professor and Chair, Department of Agricultural and Resource Economics at the University of California, Davis, USA

Shun-Yi Shei
Research Fellow, Institute of Economics, Academia Sinica, Taipei, Taiwan

ACADEMIA STUDIES IN ASIAN ECONOMIES

Edward Elgar
Cheltenham, UK • Northampton, MA, USA

Published by
Edward Elgar Publishing Limited
Glensanda House
Montpellier Parade
Cheltenham
Glos GL50 1UA
UK

Edward Elgar Publishing, Inc.
136 West Street
Suite 202
Northampton
Massachusetts 01060
USA

A catalogue record for this book
is available from the British Library

Library of Congress Cataloguing in Publication Data

Food security in Asia: economics and policies / edited by Wen S. Chern, Colin A. Carter, Shun Yi-Shei.
    — (Academia studies in Asian economies)
    "This book contains the selected papers in the 'Taipei International Conference on East Asian Food Security Issues in the 21st Century', held in Taipei, Taiwan April 16–17, 1998."
    Includes index.
    1. Produce trade—Government policy—East Asia—Congresses. 2. Food industry and trade—Standards—East Asia—Congresses. 3. Food adulteration and inspection—Government policy—East Asia—Congresses. 4. Food supply—Government policy—East Asia—Congresses. 5. Free trade—East Asia—Congresses. I. Chern, Wen S. II. Carter, Colin Andre. III. Shei, Shun-yi. IV. Taipei International Conference on East Asian Food Security Issues in the 21st Century (1998) V. Series.

HD9016.E182 F66 2000
363.8'095—dc21   00–037675

ISBN 1 84064 441 9

Printed and bound in Great Britain by MPG Books Ltd, Bodmin, Cornwall

Contents

List of contributors   vii
Acknowledgements   xiii

1. Introduction   1
    Wen S. Chern, Colin A. Carter and Shun-Yi Shei
2. Food security: fallacy or reality?   11
    Yujiro Hayami
3. The urban–rural income gap in China:
    implications for global food markets   19
    Colin A. Carter
4. Rice and food security in Asia: a long-term outlook   35
    Mercedita A. Sombilla and Mahabub Hossain
5. The implications of the ASEAN free trade area on
    agricultural trade between Taiwan and the ASEAN   61
    Ching-Cheng Chang, Deng-Shing Huang and
    Chia-Hsun Wu
6. Assessment of demand-side factors affecting global
    food security   83
    Wen S. Chern
7. Economic development and food security issues in Japan
    and South Korea   119
    Toshiyuki Kako
8. A policy choice of the rice import issue in Taiwan   141
    Min-Hsein Yang and Yu-Hui Chen
9. Rice import competition and demand allocation in
    Hong Kong and Singapore   163
    Tsorng-Chyi Hwang
10. Food security issues in Singapore: implications for East
    Asian economies undergoing agricultural trade
    liberalization   185
    Gwo-Jiun Mike Leu
11. Demand for food safety in Taiwan   205
    Tsu-Tan Fu, Chung L. Huang and Kamhon Kan

12. Forces shaping Asia's demand for vegetable oils and
    protein meals   229
    Alan J. Webb and Mad Nasir Shamsudin

Index   259

Contributors

Colin A. Carter is currently Professor and Chair of Agricultural and Resource Economics at the University of California, Davis, USA. Carter obtained a PhD in Agricultural Economics from the University of California, Berkeley in 1980. His research work has investigated problems related to agricultural policy and trade, with a focus on grain markets. He has co-authored several books, including two on China's grain markets and one on US agricultural policy. From 1986–89, Carter held a three-year fellowship in international food systems with the Kellogg Foundation. Carter has received several research awards from professional associations for published research, including the 1998 Distinguished Policy Contribution award from the American Agricultural Economics Association for his research on state trading organizations.

Ching-Cheng Chang, Associate Research Fellow, Institute of Economics, Academia Sinica; also Associate Professor, Department of Agricultural Economics, National Taiwan University, Taipei, Taiwan, ROC. Dr Chang received her BA and MA in Agricultural Economics from National Taiwan University and PhD in Agricultural Economics from Pennsylvania State University. Her primary research interests are in economic analysis of domestic and trade policies concerning agricultural income, prices, environment, and food security. Current activities include applications of an agricultural sector model for Taiwan on global warming and El Niño, development of a world rice trade model, as well as applications of DEA to the efficiency of the rural financial sector.

Yu-Hui Chen, Associate Professor, Department of Agricultural Economics, National Taiwan University, Taipei, Taiwan. Professor Chen received her BS in Agricultural Economics from the National Taiwan University, Taiwan; both an MA and a PhD in Agricultural Economics from the University of Wisconsin, Madison. Her primary research interests are in agricultural policy, applied econometrics, and agricultural marketing; other fields of specialization include international trade and agribusiness.

Wen S. Chern, Professor, Department of Agricultural, Environmental, and Development Economics, The Ohio State University, Columbus, Ohio, USA. Professor Chern received his BSc in Agricultural Economics from National Chung-Hsing University, Taiwan; an MSc in Agricultural Economics from the University of Florida; and both an MA in Statistics and a PhD in Agricultural Economics from the University of California, Berkeley. His primary research interests are in food consumption behaviour, nutrition and health, food security in Pacific Rim countries, and applied econometrics; other areas of specialization include consumption economics, energy, and health economics.

Tsu-Tan Fu, Research Fellow at the Institute of Economics, Academia Sinica; also Professor, Department of Agricultural Economics, National Taiwan University, Taipei, Taiwan. Dr Fu received his BA and MS in Agricultural Economics from National Taiwan University and PhD in Agricultural Economics from the University of Georgia, USA in 1987. His primary research interests are in agricultural and food policy issues, efficiency and productivity measurement, and consumer behaviour analysis.

Yujiro Hayami, Professor of International Economics, School of International Politics, Economics and Business, Aoyama-Gakuin University, Tokyo, Japan. Professor Hayami received his BA in Liberal Arts from University of Tokyo, Japan; and PhD in Agricultural Economics from Iowa State University, USA. His primary interest is in agricultural development in developing economies.

Mahabub Hossain is currently the Acting Deputy Director General for Research of the International Rice Research Institute, Manila, Philippines. He began his career as a Staff Economist in the Bangladesh Institute of Development Studies in 1970 and rose through the ranks to serve as the Director General of this development policy research institute during 1989–92. He also served the International Food Policy Research Institute, Washington, DC as a visiting scientist during 1985–87, when he published the highly acclaimed IFPRI Research Reports on the Grameen Bank Credit Program, and the Development Impact of Rural Infrastructures. At IRRI, he has been leading the project on 'socioeconomic study, technology impact and policy analysis', and providing support to Management in planning and prioritization of rice research issues. Dr Hossain earned his PhD in economics in 1977 from the University of Cambridge, England. He is a fellow of the Economic Development Institute of the World Bank. He was awarded the first gold medal by the Bangladesh Association of Agricultural Economists for his outstanding contribution to the understanding of the rural economy of Bangladesh.

Chung L. Huang, Professor, Department of Agricultural and Applied Economics, The University of Georgia, Athens, Georgia, USA. He was born in Taiwan and earned his BA degree in Economics from Tunghai University in 1967. Professor Huang received his MA degree in Economics from Central Missouri State University in 1972 and his PhD degree in Agricultural Economics from Virginia Polytechnic Institute and State University in 1976. Much of his research is focused on the economics of food demand and consumption behaviour including topics related to consumer perceptions and attitudes toward food quality and safety.

Deng-Shing Huang, Research Fellow, Institute of Economics, Academia Sinica, Taiwan, ROC. Dr Huang received his BA from National Taiwan Oceanic University, MA in Economics from National Taiwan University and PhD in Economics from University of Rochester. His primary research interests are in international trade, economic integration, and East Asian studies. His current research includes Taiwanese business group and trade patterns, trade and development in East Asian countries, FDI, and labour imports of Taiwanese manufacturing firms.

Tsorng-Chyi Hwang, Professor, Department of Agricultural Economics, National Chung-Hsing University, Taichung, Taiwan. Professor Hwang received his BSc in Agricultural Economics from National Chung-Hsing University, Taiwan; and both his MA and PhD in Agricultural Economics from The Ohio State University. His primary research interests are in agricultural trade, marketing, finance, policy, and applied econometrics.

Toshiyuki Kako, Professor, Department of Food and Environmental Economics, Kobe University, Kobe, Japan. Professor Kako received his BSc in Agricultural Science from Gifu University, Japan; an MSc in Agricultural Economics from Kyoto University; and both an MA in Economics and a PhD in Agricultural Economics from the University of California, Davis. His primary research interests are in technological change in rice production, and food security in Northeast Asian countries; other areas of specialization include agricultural policy and agricultural development economics.

Kamhon Kan, Associate Research Fellow at the Institute of Economics, Academia Sinica, Taipei, Taiwan. Dr Kan received his BSc majoring in Economics from Hong Kong University and his PhD in Economics from Virginia Polytechnic Institute and State University. He has been Research Fellow at the Center for Operations Research and Econometrics, Université de Louvain, Belgium; and Financial Economist at the Bank of England, London. His research specialization is in applied microeconometrics.

Gwo-Jiun Mike Leu, Associate Professor, Division of Applied Economics, School of Accountancy and Business, Nanyang Technological University, Singapore. Dr Leu obtained his first degree from the National Taiwan University in Agricultural Economics. He was also awarded his MSc from the University of Nebraska at Lincoln, MA and PhD from the University of California at Berkeley. Prior to joining the School of Accountancy and Business, he was formerly a Principal Research Officer with the Australian Bureau of Agricultural and Resource Economics. His professional interests are in international trade and finance in Pacific Rim countries, commodity price and policy analysis, applied econometrics and statistics. He has also conducted many training programmes for Chinese and Vietnamese executive officers.

Mad Nasir Shamsudin is Associate Professor and Head, Department of Agribusiness and Information Systems, University of Putra, Malaysia. He received his BSc in Agricultural Economics from Louisiana State University, and PhD in Agricultural Economics from Mississippi State University. His primary research interests are in agricultural trade policy analysis and forecasting. Currently he is conducting research in the area of trade liberalization and its impact on·food industry.

Shun-Yi Shei, Research Fellow at the Institute of Economics, Academia Sinica, Taipei, Taiwan. Shei obtained his BSc degree in agricultural Economics from National Taiwan University; both MSc and PhD in agricultural Economics from Purdue University. He joined the Institute of Economics in 1978 and became a research fellow in 1982. His main research interests are in exchange rate and agricultural trade barriers, food security, and food self-sufficiency issues.

Mercedita A. Sombilla is currently an Affiliate Scientist of the Social Sciences Division and an Acting Head of the Liaison, Coordination and Planning Unit of the International Rice Research Institute, Manila, Philippines. Prior to her joining IRRI in 1995, she worked as a Research

Analyst at the International Food Policy Research Institute (IFRI) in Washington, DC, USA in 1991, and was later promoted to a Post Doctoral Fellow in 1993. At IFPRI, she was one of the key persons that developed the global food supply and demand model which underpinned the Institute's highly successful 2020 Vision project. She continued this modelling work when she joined IRRI, thereby enabling her to strengthen knowledge of the long-term global markets and demand and supply prospects for rice and other commodities. In addition to the modelling work, Dr Sombilla's research focus is also on the identification and analysis of factors (biophysical, socioeconomic, policy and institutional factors) that account for yield differentials in rice using farm-level data collected from farmers in Bangladesh. As Acting Head of the Liaison, Coordination and Planning Unit, she works with IRRI scientists to develop proposals, formulate and implement strategies to mobilize donor support, prepare project completion report, and maintain liaison with donors. Dr Sombilla earned her PhD in Agricultural Economics in 1991 from the University of Minnesota where her field of study was on international rice trade.

Alan J. Webb is currently an agricultural marketing consultant based in Taipei where he is engaged in analysis of Asian commodity markets. Prior to coming to Taipei in January 1999 he was a Professor of Economics at the University of Putra, Malaysia where he taught international trade and agribusiness courses and worked on a number of agricultural development and policy analysis projects. He also served as a Senior Economist with the Economic Research Service, USDA where he worked for 15 years prior to going to Malaysia in 1994. Alan Webb holds a BA degree in International Relations from American University, an MA in Economics from the University of Arkansas and a PhD in Agricultural Economics from Oklahoma State University.

Chia-Hsun Wu, PhD student, and formerly research assistant, in the Department of Agricultural Economics, National Taiwan University, Taipei, Taiwan, ROC. Ms. Wu received her BA and MA in Agricultural Economics from National Taiwan University. Her primary research interests include agricultural trade and development.

Min-Hsien Yang, Professor, Department of International Trade, Feng-Chia University, Taiwan. Professor Yang received his BSc in Agricultural Marketing from the National Chung-Hsing University, Taiwan; an MSc and a PhD in Agricultural Economics from the National Taiwan University. His primary research interests are focused on agricultural policy, agricultural marketing and commodity pricing, international trade, and welfare economics; other areas of specialization include cross-strait agricultural cooperation and endogenous economic growth.

Acknowledgements

The Institute of Economics, Academia Sinica and the Council of Agriculture, Executive Yuan, jointly sponsored the Taipei International Conference on East Asian Food Security Issues in the 21st Century. We would like to thank Dr Sheng-Cheng Hu, Director and Dr Tsu-Tan Fu, Deputy Director of the Institute of Economics for their support for this book project.

Almost all of the papers went through a double-blind review. We are grateful for the following reviewers for their time and effort in providing many constructive comments on the papers:

Neal Blue, *The Ohio State University*
Howdy Bouis, *International Food Policy Research Institute*
Jeffery Hopkins, *Economic Research Service, USDA*
Jordan Lin, *Economic Research Service, USDA*
Won Koo, *North Dakota State University*
David Price, *Washington State University*
Eric J. Wailes, *University of Arkansas*

We would also like to thank Judy Petticord for her able assistance in editing and reformatting many chapters.

The Institute of Economics provides the support for preparing the camera-ready copy of the manuscripts. We are grateful for the excellent assistance of Min-Hui Hsu and the staff of the Institute of Economics for their efficient logistic support.

1. Introduction

Wen S. Chern, Colin A. Carter and Shun-Yi Shei

1. INTRODUCTION

This book contains the selected papers presented at the Taipei International Conference on 'East Asian Food Security Issues in the 21st Century' held in Taipei, Taiwan 16–17 April 1998. The conference was organized and hosted by the Institute of Economics, Academia Sinica and it was also co-sponsored by the Council of Agriculture, Executive Yuan. The conference attracted many scholars who came together to address the important and timely issue of food security among Asian countries including China, Indonesia, Japan, Malaysia, Singapore, South Korea, Taiwan, Thailand, the Philippines, and Vietnam. Although all in East Asia, these countries are fairly diverse in their stages of economic development and natural resource endowment, and, thus, the views on food security were very divergent as may be expected. This is, of course, one of the reasons why such a conference is worthwhile in providing a forum for discussion and debate. Note that not all country reports are included in this volume. This book includes mostly the papers with quantitative models dealing with various aspects of demand, supply, and trade of key agricultural products affecting food security in Asia.

The divergence of views on food security is best illustrated by the keynote address delivered by Yujiro Hayami (chapter 2). He argues that food security is a real problem only for low-income countries, and it is a fallacy to use 'food security' as a justification for agricultural protection in countries such as Japan and Taiwan. He points out that the occurrence of a food crisis due to war, natural calamities, political conflicts, or food embargoes, has a very low probability. Such a crisis, if it occurs, can be effectively dealt with by proper food management measures, such as rationing, food storage, trade and diversification of food supply sources. Mike Leu's paper (chapter 10) echoes this optimistic view in his analysis of the success in achieving food security in Singapore. Singapore and

Hong Kong with very limited land resources have no other choice but to become highly dependent on food imports. In such a situation, agricultural trade is indeed indispensable for their food security.

It is important to define food security more clearly for the purpose of discussion and debate in relation to East Asia. There are several concepts of food security being used by the authors in this book. First, food security is not the same as 'self-sufficiency in food'. Many papers cite the declining rates of self-sufficiency in food as a food security concern. However, no one seems to argue that self-sufficiency in food is a must for food security. Most, if not all, participants in the conference agree that no country can, or should attempt to, achieve 100 per cent self-sufficiency in all foods under any circumstances. On the other hand, many agree that the food and agricultural sector is relatively unique in our economic system, and that it may deserve special treatment. Food is not just a necessity for subsistence, but can also be a luxury in achieving a high quality of life. Domestic agriculture not only produces food, but also contributes to the psychological well-being of people, an ecological balance, and resource preservation. The issue is not simply economic efficiency and comparative advantage.

Consider the case of Taiwan, where the contribution of domestic agricultural production to GDP has been declining as the agricultural share of GDP declined from 32.2 per cent in 1952 to merely 2.7 per cent in 1997. It is highly unlikely that any significant cutback in Taiwan's agriculture will hurt its economy in any tangible way. However, Taiwan has been trying to protect its domestic production of rice and meats in the bilateral negotiations for its accession to the World Trade Organization (WTO). The underlying reason is 'food security', and it is not defined purely on economic efficiency grounds. Under this situation what is the correct definition of 'food security'? One possible definition may be that 'psychologically domestic residents feel comfortable with regard to food availability'! These non-economic factors often contribute to the complexity of any discussion of food security issues (see, for example, Min-HseinYang and Yu-Hui Chen, chapter 8). Even though the papers contained in this volume all conduct economic analyses, the motivation for doing such analyses may be sometimes based on other non-economic dimensions of food security concerns.

The second important concept of 'food security' is based on the perceived relative importance of staple versus non-staple foods. It is often perceived that it is acceptable to import non-staple foods or feeds, but staple foods must be produced domestically. Many agricultural policies in East Asia are based on this concept of food security. Rice is the most important staple food in East Asia, and this is the reason why rice is the subject of study of several chapters in this book. Rice is one of the most contested agricultural commodities in trade negotiations with Japan, South Korea, and Taiwan.

The third concept of 'food security' discussed in this book relates to food quality. In many high-income countries, food security is defined as having a high-quality food supply to maintain the existing high standard of living. This concept is analogous to the concept of poverty. The level of poverty is typically defined with respect to a country's standard of living. Thus, the subsistence level varies from country to country, depending on the country's stage of economic development. As household incomes increase, the demand for high-quality and safer food will increase. Consumers are paying increasing attention to the safety and quality attributes of food supply. The chapter by Tsu-Tan Fu, Chung Huang, and Kamhon Kan (chapter 11) addresses this concept of food security and the quality aspect of food insecurity in Taiwan. The current debate on genetically modified organisms (GMO) in Japan and other Asian countries, though not addressed in the 1998 conference, will surely add another dimension to the already complex food security issues in East Asia.

Most, if not all, of the papers included in this volume conduct statistical analyses, some highly technical and involving complex modelling while others are more descriptive. As a whole, the book presents many estimates of food supply and demand functions. Several papers also provide food supply and demand forecasts. Since each study is based on a unique database and a specific model, the modelling results are all conditional on the choices of data and models. Likewise, the estimates of food demand and supply elasticities are also conditional on model specification and data. Thus, there are differences in econometric results as can be expected. For example, Toshiyuki Kako (chapter 7) found rice to be an inferior good in Japan while Wen Chern (chapter 6) showed a positive income elasticity of rice demand in the same country. It is important to recognize that there is information generated by these differences since they contribute to our further understanding of the complexity of food security issues and market uncertainties. The remainder of this chapter summarizes each chapter included in this book.

As noted earlier Yujiro Hayami (chapter 2) argues that high-income economies, such as Japan and Taiwan, do not have a food security problem. With respect to contingent crisis, such as war, his prescribed policy measure is to enlarge domestic stockpiles. If a cyclical crisis, such as a bad crop on a large scale occurs, the low-income countries will be devastated because of the lack of foreign currency reserves to import food. For high-income countries, however, the best approach to deal with this type of crisis is to promote trade liberalization. Hayami also dismisses the possibility of a food embargo imposed against Taiwan or Japan by food exporters. Finally he suggests that in order to cope with the Malthusian type of crisis, Japan and Taiwan need to maintain their potential productive capacity to produce food. Furthermore, agricultural research and development (R&D) must be promoted. Despite his insightful analysis, the main question remains, namely: 'To what extent should Taiwan, Japan and South Korea protect rice, the main staple?'. It is important to learn what other analysts have to say in the following chapters.

In chapter 3, Colin Carter discusses some long-run issues associated with China, the world's largest producer and consumer of food. For the past 50 years, China's central government has placed a large weight on the economic well-being of urban residents, and has overemphasized the importance of keeping food prices low, to the detriment of its farmers. China has been essentially self-sufficient in food, but with a high associated economic cost. Carter stresses the point that continued economic growth in the agricultural sector and integration of the rural–urban economies is critical for ensuring China's transition away from that of a lower-middle-income country. In China, policy has stressed both regional and national self-sufficiency with regard to food production. Assuming that this strategy cannot continue for much longer, Carter discusses the implications of expanded intra-provincial and international agricultural trade liberalization. This strategy would allow farmers in each region to produce according to their comparative advantage and would lead to income gains. Carter shows that, as a result of current policy, the gap between urban and rural incomes has widened since the early 1980s. In most rural regions China has abundant labour that is immobile due to policy and local institutions. In some cases farmers are forced to grow grain to ensure regional and national self-sufficiency. The number of farmers has increased and the marginal productivity of farm labour is low in grain production. When and how the income gap problem is solved will have important implications for the global food market, as discussed in Carter's chapter.

Chapter 4 by Mercedita Sombilla and Mahabub Hossain provides an excellent overview of the rice economy in Asia. Rice is such an important staple for most Asians that many urban poor and rural landless people in Asia spend 50–70 per cent of their income on rice. Sombilla and Hossain analyse various factors affecting the emerging trends in rice supply and demand, and how these will affect Asia's self-sufficiency in rice. As may be expected rice demand will critically depend upon income growth, urbanization, and population growth. On the other hand, the rice supply cannot be easily expanded as urbanization and industrialization have increased the scarcity of land resources for rice production, and growth in rice yields has stagnated in recent years. The IMPACT model developed at the International Food Policy Research Institute (IFPRI) jointly with the International Rice Research Institute (IRRI) was used by the authors to forecast rice production and demand for 11 individual Asian countries. These countries include India, Pakistan, China, Japan, Indonesia, Malaysia, the Philippines, and the rice-exporting countries of Thailand and Vietnam. Under their baseline scenario, Asia will continue to dominate the world rice market. Regional production will increase by 22 per cent from 327 million metric tons (mmt) in 1993 to 400 mmt in 2010, · while rice demand will increase from 318 mmt in 1993 to 395 mmt in 2010. Some countries, such as Japan and China, will have excess demand while Thailand, Vietnam, and Myanmar will continue to export rice. According to this projection, a lower economic growth scenario will result in a much smaller volume of net exports of rice from Asia and this will adversely affect food security in this region. Sombilla and Hossain conclude that rice is critically important for alleviating poverty and promoting food security in Asia. While trade can help countries achieve food security, many rice-producing countries are faced with the challenges of improving yield, while at the same time preserving natural resources and protecting the environment.

In chapter 5, Ching-Cheng Chang, Deng-Shing Huang, and Chia-Hsun Wu estimate the ramifications of an ASEAN 'free trade area' on agricultural trade between Taiwan and the ASEAN region (that is, Indonesia, Malaysia, the Philippines, Thailand, and Singapore). Their chapter begins by explaining how Taiwan and the ASEAN region have become increasingly integrated into the world economy, and they outline the factors that could lead to closer ties in agricultural trade within the ASEAN region. The authors employ a 'revealed comparative advantage index' and a 'trade intensity index' to estimate where comparative advantage lies and to study whether existing trade patterns are consistent with comparative advantage. They use the GTAP database to estimate these two indices. They find that the ASEAN region's comparative advantage has shifted towards fishery products and Taiwan's comparative advantage has shifted away from livestock and fishery products. Regarding the free trade area, Chang, Huang, and Wu find there is potential for increasing the level of agricultural trade, and they estimate that there would be associated welfare gains. This bodes well for food security in the region.

Wen Chern in chapter 6 argues that demand-side factors play a key role in determining the future food balance. He uses econometric models of food demand in China and Japan to illustrate the uncertainties in projecting food demand in these countries. He estimates both original and linear approximate versions of the almost ideal demand systems (AIDS) of food demand for urban and rural China, as well as for Japan. His results show that in both countries, rice and grain are still normal goods. Higher per household income will induce higher per household demand for food grain in these countries. But other demographic factors, such as urbanization in China and westernization in Japan, will play a key role in shaping the future demand for food in general and grain or rice in particular. His study also provides useful estimates of the income and cross-price elasticities of meat products. These elasticities need to be incorporated into any projection of the future demand for meats, which will translate into the demand for feedstuff. Although feed demand is an important component of the overall food supply and demand balance, it is generally not considered as critically important as staple foods, such as rice, when assessing food security. His econometric results also provide important insights into the problems associated with the use of the linear approximate of AIDS in food-demand analysis.

Toshiyuki Kako (chapter 7) compares the changes in dietary patterns in Japan and Korea. He focuses on daily calorie supply and the protein, fat, and carbohydrates (PFC) to calorie ratios and their relationships to economic development in these two countries. He also projects supply and demand of rice up to the year 2010 and discusses their implications. Specifically, Kako identifies several interesting similarities and differences in food production and consumption patterns between the two countries. He attempts to explain why, in these two countries, food imports have increased and self-sufficiency in food has declined. According to his projection under the WTO's minimum access, Japan will increase its rice imports from 380 000 metric tons (mt) in 1995 to 1.52 mmt in 2010. Similarly, Korea's rice imports will increase from a mere 30 000 mt in 1995 to 310 000 mt in 2010. These projections are based on his estimates of negative income elasticities of rice in both countries. Rice imports could be higher than his projection if rice is not an inferior good. In his analysis, Japan will have to enhance its rice diversion program in order to reduce its excess stocks of rice. In Korea, he predicts a rice shortage in the future because the decrease in rice acreage is predicted to be higher than the increase in rice yields. With respect to beef trade liberalization, its impact on the Japanese domestic market has been very moderate. Specifically, only the low-quality beef, such as dairy beef, has suffered from competition from imported beef. The recent declines in Wagyu beef production were attributed to the instability of farm incomes. The aging Japanese work force in beef production may be a more significant threat to the future of the Japanese domestic beef industry than imported beef. Kako also points out that food security concerns are a psychological matter in Japan. A public opinion poll carried out in 1996 showed that the majority of people in Japan were anxious about the future supply of food. In order to alleviate these fears, he suggests that the governments in Japan and Korea should establish appropriate food security policies based on projected domestic production, reserved stocks, and imports.

Min-Hsein Yang and Yu-Hui Chen (chapter 8) attempted to quantify the impacts of the two rice import policies for Taiwan, namely tariffication versus limited access. Their study is based on a public choice model in which trade policy may be derived either from the self-interest or social-concerns approach. For their empirical analysis, they construct a seven-equation model of the rice economy in Taiwan. The model is then used to conduct a long-term and a short-run multiplier analysis of the two rice policy alternatives. These multiplier analyses yield comparative statics results on rice production, consumption, and price under the two policy regimes. The estimated net changes in social welfare are then computed from the relative changes in consumer and producer surplus. Their welfare analysis shows that both policies result in a net increase in social welfare. Furthermore, the policy option based on tariffication yields a larger increase in net social welfare. But the policy based on limited access is estimated to be less harmful to rice farmers in Taiwan. Finally, the political preference function is combined with the social welfare effect to calculate the change in political support ratings for different import policy scenarios. These results show that the political support rating declines no matter what policy is followed by the government. The study highlights the precise difficulties facing the policy makers in dealing with the rice market liberalization issues in many Asian countries.

In chapter 9, Tsorng-Chyi Hwang analyses the factors affecting import demand for rice in Hong Kong and Singapore. Hong Kong and Singapore have over the years diversified their sources of rice imports. The author intends to use the experience of Hong Kong and Singapore as a basis for formulating a rice import policy for Taiwan. Hwang estimates a linear approximate AIDS model for rice import allocation in these two countries. In Hong Kong, the six largest import sources include Thailand, Australia, rest of the world (ROW), China, Vietnam, and the US. Singapore has imported most of its rice from Thailand, ROW, India, the US, Australia, and Vietnam. The results indicate that various sources of rice import supplies are very price elastic, an indication of a very competitive market faced by Hong Kong and Singapore. Furthermore, some sources are complementary while others are competitive. The results show that the supply of US rice is very price elastic in the Singapore market, but very price inelastic in the Hong Kong market. Thus, US rice appears to have a comparative advantage over other sources of rice supply in Hong Kong. Hwang indicates that the potential rice import structure in Taiwan would be different from Hong Kong and Singapore because of strong consumer preference for Japonica rice. US rice, with its high quality and high price, is likely to dominate the Taiwanese rice import market, after Taiwan's accession to the WTO.

Mike Leu in chapter 10 presents a case study for Singapore in achieving food security through trade. As a small city-state, Singapore cannot produce enough food to feed its people. By 1996, Singapore's self-sufficiency rates were 1 per cent for meats, 10 per cent for fish, 3 per cent for vegetables, and 36 per cent for eggs. Leu reviews the series of government policies to ensure an adequate and safe food supply from 1966 to present. His welfare analysis shows that Singapore is able to import more and better food by specializing in industrial goods production and exchanging these goods for food at a favourable price. Leu rightly points out that food security is often confused with food self-sufficiency. He argues that Singapore has achieved food security with only a 10 per cent overall self-sufficiency rate. This case study documents a successful approach to ensure a diverse supply of food from the best sources in the world at low prices. One must remember, however, that Singapore has a very unique situation in that it does not have to deal with the livelihood of many farmers and has few land resources to allocate and to preserve. Whether or not the success story of Singapore in achieving food security is applicable to other countries like Taiwan, Japan, and South Korea is debatable.

In chapter 11, Tsu-Tan Fu, Chung L. Huang, and Kamhon Kan investigate the demand for hydroponically grown vegetables (HGV) in Taiwan. The HGV are free of pesticides and thus are considered to be safer than conventionally produced vegetables. The study is based on a household survey on the willingness to pay (WTP) for these products. The authors estimate a joint probit and ordinal probit model, using data from 400 female homemakers in Taipei, Taiwan. The ranking of the respondents' WTP, as the dependent variable, is expressed as a function of age, education, income, price, perception of risk, attitude toward the use of pesticides, and other variables. Their econometric results show that there are many factors that would affect the consumer's WTP for safer vegetables. Among them are income, education, perceived pesticide risks, presence of small children in the family, and health status. Taiwan is among the heaviest users of pesticides (per ha) in the world. The safety of vegetables and fruits has been a real concern to the consumer in Taiwan. As household incomes increase, there will be increasing demand for higher-quality and safer foods. Safer foods contribute to the consumer's well-being and standard of living as measured by utility. The widely publicized debate on the genetically modified (GM) foods may alter Taiwan's food demand and supply balance in the future. It is important that we take into account these important quality attributes when debating food security issues in East Asia.

Oilseeds are important crops because they not only provide vegetable oils for human consumption and the food processing sector, but they also supply an important source of protein meal for poultry and livestock. In chapter 12, Alan Webb and Mad Nasir Shamsudin analyse changing trends in the demand for vegetable oils including palm oil and meals in Asia. Since oilseeds are usually crushed into oil and meal, they are closely related to the food and feed markets. Four major oilseeds studied in this chapter include soybeans, rapeseed, sunflower, and palm oil. In order to assess the demand for oilseeds, Webb and Shamsudin estimate income and price elasticities of demand for beef, pork, and poultry for eight Asian countries. They point out that income growth and the global production mix of oilseeds will shape the supply–demand balance of vegetable oil and protein meal markets in Asia for the next decade. Their projections show that all regions in Asia will face a growing deficit in protein meal in the next century. If East Asia's aggregate income growth begins to exceed 5 per cent, it will put pressure on the world's ability to supply protein meal to the region. Interestingly, the regional balance for vegetable oils is the reverse of protein meal at low levels of income growth. With this imbalance between meal and oil, Asian countries must decide on whether they should import meal and/or oil directly, or build crushing capacity to crush imported seeds to meet the demands for meal and oil. The large and growing exports of palm oil from Southeast Asia has sharpened Asia's oilseed balance. Import of high oil content seeds, such as rapeseed and sunflower seeds for domestic crushing, may end up contributing to the region's vegetable oil surplus. This suggests that the region may need to either import protein meal, or import and crush soybeans with high meal content. As a final note, Webb and Shamsudin indicate that the Asian food security issue related to oilseeds is closely tied to economic growth. Rising incomes will shift consumers away from traditional staples like rice and put pressure on local agriculture to produce more income-sensitive commodities, like livestock, and feed sources, such as oilseeds. Additional oilseed production will adversely affect the security of a staple food supply in many Asian countries in the future.

2. Food security: fallacy or reality?*

Yujiro Hayami

1. INTRODUCTION

I am puzzled why agricultural economists in Taiwan chose 'food security' as the theme of this conference at this particular juncture of history. My puzzle is based on the conviction that food insecurity is a real problem to low-income economies but not to Taiwan, which has now entered a high-income stage comparable to those of OECD members.

I am aware, however, that the food security concern has been raised in Japan also, since it reached a similar stage of economic development in the 1970s. It has been loudly voiced as a major justification to ward off agricultural trade liberalization and to increase subsidies to agriculture. Underlying such an argument is the assumption that it is indispensable to promote self-sufficiency for achieving greater food security. This assumption is highly questionable, however,

Confusion seems to have stemmed from the lack of clear understanding on the natures of different types of food crises, which different policies are required to deal with. In this regard it is useful to classify food crises into: (1) contingent crisis, (2) cyclical crisis, (3) political crisis, and (4) Malthusian crisis. The first is the crisis created by the sudden disruption of food imports as a result of war or some other catastrophe. The second represents the case of diminishing food supplies and escalating prices as a result of worldwide poor harvests along the cycle of weather. The third is the embargo from food exporters for reasons of world politics. The fourth is a secular decline in food supply relative to population, which may culminate in famine on a world scale.

I will try to examine how real or fallacious these potential crises are to high-income economies, such as Japan and Taiwan, as compared with low-income economies. I will also try to identify effective policies to counteract these different crises.

*This paper draws mainly on Hayami (1986, pp. 227—39; 1988, pp. 121—23).

11

2.   CONTINGENT CRISIS

Of the crises of the first type, neither Japan nor Taiwan has ever experienced the serious local conflicts or natural calamities that cut off critical transportation routes, resulting in a significant halt of food imports such as during and in the aftermath of World War II. Such contingencies, if they occur, are unlikely to culminate in a crisis, because it is not difficult for economies like Japan and Taiwan, equipped with various transportation means and routes, to compensate for the cut-off of supply via one route by supply from other sources. For example, the longshoremen's strike in the US west coast in 1971, which is said to have been the worst in history, lasted as long as 134 days and resulted in a major decrease of wheat exports from the United States to Japan by as much as 680 000 tons. However, the total wheat imports to Japan in that year did not decline but increased from the previous year by 190 000 tons, through effective shifts in the source of supply to other wheat exporters.

Thus, the cut-off of a transportation route, if it remains a local phenomenon, can easily be coped with in advanced economies by means of shifts in the supply source and, therefore, needs no special preparation beyond market adjustments; this is especially so to Japan and Taiwan, which have easy access to various parts of the world through various sea lanes. However, it can pose a serious problem for low-income economies which have few alternative sources within their possible reach. Especially, in some land-locked economies, such as in Sub-Saharan Africa, the closure of one railroad or one highway due to local warfare or natural calamity can trigger a major famine.

Next consider global warfare that results in the total closure of sea lanes. The memory of the food shortages during World War II is still fresh in the memory of many Japanese people. However, what will be the probability of such a contingency emerging in the forseeable future, especially since the demise of the Cold War? Still, one could argue that preparations must be made for this contingency, since the disaster could be extremely large, however small its probability may be. For such a crisis, the maintenance of food self-sufficiency as in peacetime is not at all effective. In Japan and Taiwan, for example, farm production depends heavily on machines run by oil. Once a global crisis has occurred on such a scale as to cut off all the sea lanes, not only food but also oil imports will be disrupted so that mechanized farm production cannot be maintained. Thus, peacetime food self-sufficiency is no guarantee to food security in a crisis.

The foremost means of preparing for such a crisis would be to enlarge domestic stockpiles. Expanded livestock farming would also be a very effective contingency step, in that livestock can be slaughtered for meat in times of shortage and the operational stock of feed grains can itself be used for food. In this regard the liberalization of grain imports has the effect of enhancing food security, as it reduces feed prices in support of domestic livestock production.

It is essential that the policies designed to survive such a crisis be implemented before the crisis hits. Seeds, materials, and manpower mobilization plans must be ready so that food rationing can be instituted, and parks, golf courses and other areas organized for cultivation as soon as the crisis strikes. The fact that virtually no effort has been made to prepare such contingency plans in Japan seems to be prima facie evidence in support of the hypothesis that neither government nor agricultural pressure groups in Japan has ever thought of such a crisis as having any significant probability. I wonder if the situation is similar in Taiwan.

3. CYCLICAL CRISIS

It is important to recognize that major hikes on food prices on international markets due to bad crops on a global scale, as experienced in the 'World Food Crisis' of 1973–74, are not a crisis for high-income economies that have the financial capacity to pay the high prices. Indeed, prices on the world food market skyrocketed owing to the large-scale imports by the Soviet Union to compensate for the poor domestic harvest in 1972. Within a year of 1973 the prices of cereals and soybean were two or three times higher. Nevertheless, imports to Japan did not decrease but increased from 1972 to 1973 – from 4 020 000 to 4 070 000 tons for wheat, 6 050 000 to 7 770 000 tons for corn, and 3 400 000 to 3 640 000 tons for soybean (this increase occurred despite the US embargo on soybean exports). In fact, the rates of increase in Japanese imports of corn and soybean for 1972–73 were higher than those for 1971–72.

The World Food Crisis of 1973–74 was an abnormal phenomenon compounded by various *ad hoc* factors other than poor harvest. The year 1972 was a bad crop year, but total grain output for the world that year decreased from the previous year by only about 3 per cent. Moreover, world grain output increased by about 8 per cent from 1972 to 1973. Why did a rather modest decline in 1972 result in two to three fold increases in grain prices in the international market? It was because: (1) world demand for agricultural products increased due to simultaneous economic booms in the EC, Japan, and the United States in 1972; (2) grain stocks had been reduced by 1972 to a low level as the result of strong production controls by the USA and Canada as a counter measure to the depressed grain market in the late 1960s; (3) sudden grain purchases on the international market by the Soviet Union to compensate for its domestic production shortfall; hitherto the policy adopted to reduce domestic grain consumption was to slaughter animals in the years of poor grain harvest; and (4) panic purchase of primary commodities in general under the first oil crisis of 1973–74.

Considering so many *ad hoc* factors compounded the 1973–74 crisis, the probability of another crisis of the same magnitude does not seem high. However, a similar situation could emerge any moment today. For the past decade and a half the world has experienced depressed food prices. Depressed international food markets since the early 1980s have been the result of a major acceleration of investments in agriculture, not only private but also public investments, such as irrigation and agricultural research, that were induced by sharply increasing food prices in the 1970s. As those investments were translated into high agricultural productivity in the next decade, the growth in food production outpaced the growth in the population, resulting in low food prices. The situation has been reversed since the 1980s: low food prices have depressed investments in agriculture, resulting in a deceleration in the growth of the world food supply. Under such a situation, a natural hazard, such as the severe drought in Indonesia in the 1997/98-crop season, could trigger a crisis.

Even if such a crisis did occur, there would be no difficulty for Japan and Taiwan to secure purchases of necessary foodstuffs, with their much larger foreign currency reserves today than in the 1970s. However, it can create a real crisis for low-income economies with no such financial capacity. International collaborative schemes are called for to prevent the crisis from hitting the low-income economies.

Holding of large-scale international grain reserves, such as proposed in the UN World Food Conference in 1974, has proved infeasible, because of the extremely high costs as well as the insurmountable difficulties of resolving conflicts between exporters and importers. An international agreement of some practicality at present is the IMF's Food Cereal Import Facility, by which special credits will be advanced to finance cereal imports to low-income economies to maintain consumption at a tolerable level.

While this IMF facility is a scheme designed to cope with cyclical crises, the contingent crises, such as local famine, in low-income economies, as a result of war or natural hazards, need other types of programs, such as early warning systems of crop failure and local emergency food reserves. It must be the duty of the food-secure economies to contribute to the programs that alleviate food insecurity in low-income economies.

However, a more basic contribution to the stability of the world food market and, hence, to food security could be for us to refrain our consumption and, hence, imports at the time of a world food shortage. The most effective means to do this is to promote trade liberalization so that food price increases on the international market will be transmitted to price increases in our domestic market with the effect of reducing our consumption, as elucidated by Johnson (1973). Is it not appropriate for us to accept some increases in food prices and, correspondingly, save a piece of meat or an egg for the sake of preventing poor people in low-income economies from suffering famines in the years of global poor harvest?

4. POLITICAL CRISIS

Some have expressed concern that high dependence on food imports may subject the importing nation's autonomy to the risk of political leverage by exporters. A frequently cited example is the embargo of grains to the Soviet Union organized by USA as a sanction against the Soviet's invasion of Afghanistan. This embargo was exercised from 1980 January to April 1981. Its effect, however, was highly questionable.

Despite the embargo, the Soviet Union was able to secure the necessary imports from other exporters, such as Argentina and Brazil, who did not participate in this sanction, as well as through transfers via the third countries, especially those in Eastern Europe. The embargo resulted in a significant loss to the Soviet Union to the extent that shifts in supply sources and transfers through the third countries raised the costs of food imports. However, the damage was equally large or even larger to the USA who lost a major export market. As a result, the USA was forced to lift the embargo without obtaining any concession from the Soviet Union on the Afghanistan issue.

The experience of the US grain embargo casts doubt on the effectiveness of the political clout of food exporters on importers. Indeed, the USA is in a position to exercise its political clout on Japan, not so much because it is a major exporter of foods to Japan, but because it is a major import market for automobiles and other industrial products from Japan. It is unlikely that Japan and Taiwan will become a target of grain embargoes so long as we observe international orders (unlike Saddam Hussein). In this respect, it would be counterproductive to the enhancement of food security if a country continued to adhere to strong agricultural protectionism in violation of international agreements, such as the agreements of the GATT Uruguay Round.

5. MALTHUSIAN CRISIS

World population, though its growth is expected to decelerate significantly, will likely reach 10 billion from the present 6 billion during the twenty-first century. Much of this growth will occur in low-income economies within the next three decades. It is a legitimate concern if the earth is to continue to feed this rapidly growing population and a concern that has been expressed repeatedly since Thomas Robert Mathus (1798).

To cope with this crisis we must make major efforts to maintain and enhance domestic agricultural production capabilities. However, the need is for the development of potential productive capacity and not for the continued production of products with which we are at a comparative disadvantage. So long as irrigation facilities and other land improvements are kept up, the land used for forage crops now can be easily converted to grain production later, should the situation demand. Agricultural research and development must be promoted from the long-term point of view. Although domestic production of barley, soybeans, and other staple food crops may be inefficient at present, this situation could change if the global supply and demand balance deteriorated sharply in the future. Thus our long-term security needs demand that research into agricultural technology be steadily promoted in preparation for such a crisis. Above all, the best policy for high-income economies, such as Japan and Taiwan, to cope with such a Mathusian crisis is to cooperate with agricultural development in developing countries, thereby forestalling the crisis. Agricultural research and development are the most effective means for such cooperation.

6. FOOD SECURITY OR NATIONAL SECURITY?

Ensuring food security is one of the government's most important responsibilities, and food policies must be forcefully promoted to this end. However, to tie food security to short-term improvements in domestic self-sufficiency not only impedes preparations for an open trade system but also carries the very considerable risk of diverting attention from the programs that need to be undertaken for true security.

It is most important to recognize that the security of any nation today cannot be maintained without international cooperation. Food is no exception to this rule. If food self-sufficiency is promoted at the cost of international cooperation, it has only a negative effect. How ineffective the promotion of food self-sufficiency is, when disregarding international harmony, was evident from Japan's experience during and in the aftermath of the Second World War. Before the war, the Japanese Empire, including Korea and Taiwan, boasted self-sufficiency of food staples. How insecure that food security was is alive in the memory of all the Japanese who experienced hunger during the war. The following criticism of late Professor Seiichi Tobata, the founder of agricultural economics in Japan, on the food security argument before the war is directly applicable today:

> But it was not duly explained why food alone is considered so important in crisis. The crisis in the modern world can hardly be coped with by such low economic power as to secure food alone... It was surprising that a disproportionately large weight was attached to food in the design of total war. *A country is in danger not because food becomes short of supply. Rather, when the country is in danger, food becomes short of supply...* It was a farce to observe that those who voiced loudly for food self-sufficiency were wearing clothes made in wool and cotton imported from abroad. (Tobata, 1956, p. 597, italic by this author)

REFERENCES

Hayami, Y. (1986), *Nogyo Keizairon* (Agricultural Economics), Tokyo: Iwanami Shoten.

Hayami, Y. (1988), *Japanese Agriculture under Siege: The Political Economy of Agricultural Policies*, London: Macmillan.

Johnson, D. G. (1973), *World Agriculture in Disarray*, London: Macmillan; New York: St. Martin's Press.

Malthus, T. R. (1926; original publication 1798), *An Essay on the Principle of Population, as it Affects the Future Improvement of Society, with remarks on the Speculation of Mr. Godwin, Mr. Condorcet and other writers*, reproduced for the Royal Economic Society, London: Macmillan.

Tobata, S. (1956), 'Nihon Nogyo no Ninaite' (Carriers of Japanese Agriculture), *Nihon Nogyo Hattatsu Shi* (History of Japanese Agricultural Development), Vol. IX, Tokyo: Chuokoronsha, 561–604.

3. The urban–rural income gap in China: implications for global food markets

Colin A. Carter

1. INTRODUCTION

With the exceptions of the agricultural and financial sectors, China has essentially become a market economy and indications are that it will enjoy a sustained period of high economic growth well into the next century (Naughton, 1996). However, growth in China's agriculture has slowed since 1984 (Wen, 1993; Crook, 1996) and this seems to be related to a policy bias against agriculture. From 1978 to 1984 agriculture grew at 7.6 per cent but this slowed to 4 per cent from 1985 to 1994 (Crook, 1996). Agriculture remains underdeveloped in China largely because the government still purchases (at fixed prices) more than 50 per cent of the grain sold off the farm. The government forces some farmers to produce grain and supports this policy by discouraging integration between the rural and urban economies.[1] As a result, rural product and factor markets are distorted. Nowhere is this more evident than in the labour market (Banister, 1996; Carter, Zhong, and Cai, 1996; Cook, 1997; Knight and Song, 1995; Riskin, 1996; Taylor, 1993; Yang and Zhou, 1996). Despite large increases in rural non-agricultural employment since 1978, the absorption has not kept up with population growth and the job of shifting labour out of agriculture is far from complete.

As of 1995, there were approximately 50 million more farmers in China than at the beginning of economic reforms in 1978 (see table 3.1), cultivating a slightly smaller land base.[2] China's Minister of Agriculture has recently stated that 'one-third of the 438 million rural workers is in surplus' (Liu, 1994). It is unclear what is meant by this statement or how this issue will be resolved, but whatever course of action the government takes to raise returns to labour in agriculture will have important implications for world food markets. The theme of this chapter is the link between China's rural labour migration policy and its grain policy, and the long-run implications for world food markets.[3]

Table 3.1 China's labour force (millions): 1978–95

Year	Total	Urban	Rural	Rural Agriculture
1978	401	95	306	283
1982	453	114	339	301
1986	513	133	380	312
1990	567	147	420	341
1995	624	173	450	330

Source: Statistical Yearbook of China (SSB, various years).

It is understating the case to say that the domestic balance of long-term supply and demand for grains in China is an important global issue. By the year 2030 China's population will reach about 1.6 billion (a 400 million increase), per capita incomes could be approaching those of other East Asian nations, and total domestic grain demand will be an estimated 640 million metric tons (mmt). Various grain balance forecasts for China have been surveyed by Huang, Rozelle, and Rosegrant (1997), and by Fan (1997). They found that some observers believe China is facing an agricultural crisis in grains. At one extreme of the range of the supply–demand estimates it has been calculated that China may need to import about 216 to 378 mmt of grain by the year 2030 (Brown, Flavin, French and Starke, 1995), which is an amount greater than total world trade in grains today. Others argue that China will not experience a major grain problem and will continue to be able to feed itself with little or no net imports.

Of course, policy uncertainty makes these types of long-run supply–demand forecasts very difficult. Most of the grain balance forecasts for China assume the current policy framework is sustained, which is doubtful. On the supply side, the forecasts have not adequately accounted for any policy correction to the ongoing problem of immobile labour and government interference in the grain market. In particular they have not paid appropriate attention to the urban–rural income gap, the goal of self-sufficiency,[4] labour market imperfections, and the resulting problem of low labour productivity in agriculture (especially in grain production). Furthermore, they have ignored the fact that China's agriculture has a comparative advantage in labour-intensive crops, not grain. Policy has tilted China's agricultural production away from its comparative advantage which lies in non-grain activities.

As long as China's government forces some farmers to produce grain and supports this policy by also discouraging labour movement out of agriculture, agricultural output growth will be held back and agricultural incomes will lag further behind non-agricultural incomes. In addition to the economic cost, this issue has potential social unrest implications. According to some analysts, China's inability to integrate these poor inland regions into the rapidly industrializing economy in other parts of the country poses the threat of rural rebellion, provincial defiance, and national instability (Goldstone, 1995). If current policy persists, China will probably import less grain than it otherwise would and thereby place less upward pressure on world grain prices. However, at the same time, it will fail to further diversify its own agriculture, leading to fewer exports of other food products.

2. POLICY BIAS AGAINST AGRICULTURE

In the early 1950s, China's communist government chose a strategy of giving top priority to the development of heavy industry. Urban labour costs were reduced by a 'cheap food' policy and urban housing subsidies (Lin, Cai, and Li, 1996). To maintain this urban-biased regime, the government introduced a household registration system (hukou) that treated the urban and rural population separately, so that the number of subsidized urban residents was limited. Peasants could not change their occupation or residence. Even though most urban food subsidies were eliminated by the mid 1990s, the hukou system remains as a barrier to migration (Mallee, 1995; Wu, 1994; K. Zhou, 1996).[5]

In China, there remains an important division between the rural and urban economies and overall economic growth has been very unequal (Yang and Zhou, 1996). Indeed, the gap in China's urban–rural living standards is wider than anywhere else in Asia (Lardy, 1994, p. 24) and it is reflective of the policy bias against agriculture (see figure 3.1 for evidence of the urban–rural income gap).[6] The government continues to extract agricultural surplus through the procurement system, and relies on political and administrative measures to ensure supply of grain (Carter and Rozelle, 1996; Crook, 1997). In agriculture, China's pursuit of market efficiency has been gradual, because stability is viewed by the Chinese leadership as being more important than growth (McMillan and Naughton, 1991).

This is not to suggest that significant progress has not been made in food market development as a result of agricultural reform from 1979, because it has. Reform not only led to rapid rural economic growth and improved production incentives, but food markets have also developed quite rapidly (Carter and Rozelle, 1996). However, the point is that at present grain farmers are not fully free to make production decisions and the government remains unwilling to let market forces prevail.[7]

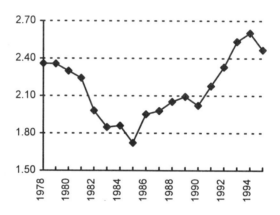

Figure 3.1 Ratio of urban to rural per capita incomes in China: 1978 to 1995

Source: *Statistical Yearbook of China* (SSB, various years).

The policy response to the 1993–94 bout of inflation is indicative of the fact that the government is willing to rely on administrative measures in order to control prices of basic goods like grain. The grain price increase in late 1993 and the decline of grain production in 1994 were viewed by the government as a signal that more administrative control was necessary. It was announced at the end of 1994 that non-governmental agencies were not allowed to buy grain directly from farmers, especially when quotas had not yet been filled, and that government agencies should prevail in the grain market. A blockade on rice and corn exports was imposed in late 1994.

The goal of regional self-sufficiency was reiterated at the 1995 session of the People's Congress, where it was announced that provincial governors were responsible for the grain supply in each province.

Regardless of whether or not it has a comparative advantage in grain production, each province must continue to maintain its grain supply under this policy – the *governors grain bag responsibility system*. Crook (1997) argues that the *grain bag responsibility system* was effective for the central government in that it raised the sown area to grain in both grain self-sufficient and deficit provinces, boosted production, and lowered imports. Crook's assessment was based on 1995 and 1996 data. Preliminary data for 1997 also support his conclusion. In 1997, grain market prices fell significantly from 1996 levels but acreage remained about the same under the *grain bag responsibility system*.

The experience of China over the past 20 years clearly indicates that market-oriented reform is the major force driving economic and agricultural growth. However, the government seems reluctant to give up on the long-term development strategy of pursuing industrialization at the cost of agriculture. A low-cost yet adequate supply of domestic grain is at the core of this strategy.

3.   CHINA'S ABUNDANT AGRICULTURAL LABOUR

China's rural population and number of agricultural workers are enormous. With a total population exceeding 1.2 billion, China's rural population accounts for roughly three-fourths of this number and about three-fourths of the employed population is rural (but estimates of these ratios vary). The *Statistical Yearbook of China 1996* (State Statistical Bureau), reports that approximately 330 million workers remain in China's agriculture, which represents over 70 per cent of the rural work force (450 million in total). However, according to the 1990 National Population Census (conducted on 1 July 1990 and published by the Population Census Office), the rural labour force and agricultural labour force is underreported in the SSB *Statistical Yearbook*. The Census data suggest there could be an additional 80 to 100 million employed in agriculture.[8]

Based on the official per capita income figures (shown in table 3.2), it could be argued that the percentage of China's labour force in agriculture is consistent with other low-income economies. However, China's population and employment structure is inconsistent with others if, instead, we accept that, based on purchasing power parity, China's real per capita income level is three times the official level (Lardy, 1994). This would classify China as a lower-middle-income economy instead of a low-income economy. Furthermore, China's 1990 census data showed that agriculture employs over 70 per cent of the economy's total employed

Food security in Asia

population, rather than the SSB's 59 per cent estimate reported in table 3.2.

Table 3.2 International comparison of employment in agriculture: 1993

International economies	Per capita GNP ($US)	Rural population (% of total)	Employment in agriculture (% of total)
China	490	74	58.6
Low-income economies (excluding China and India)	300	72	52.6
Lower-middle-income economies	1 590	46	44.5
Middle-income economies	2 480	38	31.0
Upper-middle-income economies	4 370	27	19.5
High-income economies	23 090	23	4.5
World average:	4 420	49	22.9

Source: Carter, Zhong and Cai.

Another important feature of China's rural labour force is that, owing to unbalanced regional economic development, agriculture's share of the labour force differs widely across regions. While the percentage of the province's work force in agriculture has declined dramatically in the eastern developed regions (to about 48 per cent, on average), that in the western underdeveloped areas has remained at a very high level (about 68 per cent, on average).

In China, because of policy constraints, many individuals have little choice but to stay on their family farm and share work with other family members (K. Zhou). The fact that labour is stuck in agriculture is indeed a large problem in China (Banister, 1996; Carter, Zhong and Cai, 1996; Cook, 1997; Prosterman, Hanstad, and Ping, 1994; Riskin, 1996; Sabin, 1995; Taylor, 1993). Taylor provides a survey of academic articles on rural labour that were published in China. He finds evidence that 30–40 per cent of China's rural workers are redundant. Taylor explains: 'The primary reason why rural surplus labour has continued to exist in China is that tight restrictions on rural-to-urban migration and the existence of fixed land resources in rural areas have simply forced more peasants to make a living from tilling the soil than is necessary' (Taylor, 1993, p. 282). Estimates of *surplus labour* (Taylor) generally calculate the number of working days required to produce the current agricultural output mix, then subtract this estimate from the total number of labour days available, adjusting for peak seasonal labour requirements.

The term *surplus labour* means different things to different people. The notion that developing countries can be characterized as having 'surplus' rural labour (or disguised unemployment) is attributed to Lewis (1954, 1958). Fei and Ranis (1964) found evidence in support of the idea that disguised unemployment exists, as have a number of other researchers (see Oshima, 1958). However, the Lewis postulate is controversial; some economists argue that, theoretically, surplus labour cannot exist, and they have criticized the Lewis model for its implication that the marginal productivity of labour may be zero in agriculture (see Schultz, 1964; Jorgenson, 1970).

Lewis argued that it is irrelevant whether the marginal productivity of farm labour is zero or just less than the wage rate. Johnston suggests that Lewis has been misinterpreted by some scholars. Johnston points out that Lewis did not subscribe to the naive view that a large percentage of the labour force could be removed from agriculture, leaving the level of agriculture output unchanged, without substitution of some other inputs or substitution of additional labour from those remaining in farming. In fact, Lewis argued that workers remaining in agriculture could maintain output by their willingness and ability to work harder. Similarly, Johnston and Mellor suggested that the remaining stock of labour would be utilized more intensively.

With regard to pre-reform China, Jorgenson draws on the earlier work of Oshima, and notes that China did not have a problem of surplus labour in the 1950s: 'The situation in south-eastern Europe, Egypt, China, and Southeast Asia appears to be one of labor shortage rather than labor surplus' (Jorgenson, 1970, p. 340). Jorgenson also writes: 'To date, there is little reliable empirical evidence to support the existence of more than token – 5 per cent – disguised unemployment in underdeveloped countries' (p. 342). Alternatively, Lin explains that in China in the 1950s, 'The main rationale for collectivization was rooted in the notion that mobilizing rural *surplus labour* would increase rural capital formation and, hence, increase production' (Lin, 1995, p. 7, italics added).

Under the commune system (after collectivization), there was a lack of monitoring of labour and lack of incentives to work, so it was common for people to go to work but do nothing. During this pre-reform period, underemployment existed but the problem was not very conspicuous. After implementation of the household responsibility system (HRS), individual incentives were improved and, as a result, effective labour input increased sharply (Lin, 1992; McMillan, Whalley, and Zhu, 1989). Thus the abundance of rural labour became more and more obvious following the introduction of the HRS.

Although a large number of agricultural workers have shifted out of the agricultural sector, the growth rate of the agricultural labour force is still quite high relative to the limited cultivated land. From 1978 to 1995, land under cultivation decreased by 4.4 per cent, while the number of agricultural workers increased by 16.6 per cent.

Carter, Zhong, and Cai (1996) calculated the rural labour supply and demand in each province and estimated that the industrial-to-farm labour productivity gap will not close significantly until 139 to 170 million workers permanently shift out of agriculture. This is similar to the estimate provided by Sabin who came up with a figure of 162 million, 38 per cent of the rural labour force. This figure is not inconsistent with related estimates of a total 'floating population' of 50 to 100 million alone,[9] which is a subset of the agricultural work force.

Using household survey data from Shandong province, Cook found evidence that labour appears to be constrained from freely moving out of agriculture. According to Cook's estimate, the daily agricultural shadow wage is only 1 yuan, compared to the shadow wage of 7 yuan in off-farm activities. Cook also found that, for those households engaged in off-farm work, a large gap remains for farm versus non-farm wages. This is consistent with the Yang and Zhou result that labour productivity in urban/state enterprises is substantially higher than in agriculture and rural industries.

Rozelle *et al.* (1997) have studied rural migrant labour with data from an extensive survey of about 200 villages. In total, these survey data indicated there were about 153 million village residents engaged in off-farm work in either self-employed activities (55 million), migrants (41 million), local wage earners (19 million), or commuters (37 million). Rozelle *et al.* write 'In 1995, the authors' survey estimates that 34 per cent of the rural labour force found employment off the farm' (1997, p. 5). This estimate is surprisingly low because the SSB data indicate that 28 per cent (129 out of 450 million) of the rural labour force was employed in township and village enterprises (TVE) alone (SSB, 1996, p.87).

From 1978 to 1995, the average annual increase in TVE employees was around 9 per cent. Because labour migration to the cities is controlled by the government, the TVEs have been very instrumental in absorbing surplus labour from agriculture. In light of the rapid growth rate of the TVEs, one might expect that they will continue to play an important role in absorbing agricultural labour. However, about 80 per cent of TVE output is in the coastal regions, and the exit of labour from agriculture is thus regionalized. In addition, the TVEs are becoming more and more capital intensive. The capital–labour ratio, in terms of the original value of fixed assets per worker, was 1930 yuan in 1993, compared to 1104 in 1984, which represents an increase of 75 per cent in nine years, in real terms.

The TVE capital intensity has increased due to rising labour costs in the coastal provinces, a large inflow of international investment capital, and increasing competition from state-owned enterprises and from foreign firms. In response to greater competition, the TVEs are attempting to move to enter new markets for higher quality products that are not as conducive to labour-intensive production lines. If the TVEs could readily employ low-wage workers from outside the coastal areas there would be less substitution away from labour. Overall, the increase in capital intensity of the TVEs has lessened their ability to absorb labour from agriculture.

4. POLICY OPTIONS AND IMPLICATIONS FOR GRAIN MARKETS

Relaxation of China's grain or labour migration policies will have long-run differing implications for world grain markets. In other words, if there are significant policy changes the eventual market impact will vary, depending on whether the policies are changed independently or simultaneously. For example, if the government allows greater migration out of agriculture without changing grain policy, grain production will fall, but perhaps not by much given the abundance of rural labour. The question is whether the remaining labour is willing to work harder if grain prices remain set by government and procurement quotas remain unchanged. If outmigration leads to a lower labour–land ratio, and if incomes are based partly on average rather than marginal labour returns, there should be additional incentives for the remaining workers to work harder. So, by shifting labour out of agriculture and leaving grain policy unchanged, China produces somewhat less grain and fails to fully diversify its agriculture. At the same time, farm incomes will rise but the extent of any increase would be constrained by mandatory grain procurement at fixed prices.

If instead, China eliminates its grain self-sufficiency policy, but does not change labour migration policy, then the composition of agricultural output will shift away from grains towards more labour-intensive agricultural commodities. China's agriculture diversifies, labour productivity and farm incomes rise, inter-provincial trade in grain expands, and China's grain imports increase more quickly. However, imports are less than if out-migration were simultaneously permitted.

Generally speaking, with scarce arable land and abundant labour, China has a comparative advantage in those cash crops produced by using relatively little land and plentiful labour. However, China is so vast that there are different resource endowments among regions, and a comparative advantage in grains may remain in some provinces. According to a Ministry of Agriculture survey on production costs conducted in 1991, among grain crops, it cost 12.3 working day (WD) units to produce wheat on one mu (1/15 ha), 18.2 to produce rice, and 13.8 to produce corn; among cash crops, it cost 38.4 working days for the production of cotton, 40.4 for sugar cane, and 235.6 for tea.

In this discussion, perhaps the migration and grain policies cannot and should not be treated separately. Restrictions on labour mobility are used primarily to retard urbanization but they also keep agricultural labour in place and, in combination with the grain policy, ensure low returns to labour. If labour market restrictions are lifted then the grain self-sufficiency policy would be much more difficult for the government to enforce as a stand-alone policy. Alternatively, if grain self-sufficiency is abandoned, then the labour market restrictions are much less of a problem for farmers as diversification out of grain would raise labour productivity. The existing labour market restrictions clearly help the government enforce its grain policy.

Economic theory suggests the optimal approach would be to relax both sets of policies, abolishing mandatory quotas and allowing farmers greater freedom to produce what they want, while also allowing labour to migrate. In this case China would become more dependent on international grain markets. However, the freeing up of labour market restrictions would likely be complemented by significant rural investment which would partially counteract the tendency for domestic grain output to fall.

One further policy option for China is to copy Japan, South Korea, or Taiwan, and shift from taxation to subsidization of agriculture once it becomes a small share of the economy. However, this outcome is doubtful given the unique situation in China where over 70 per cent of the total population lives in rural areas and over 70 per cent of the rural workforce remains engaged in agriculture. The combination of the political clout of urban consumers and the budgetary constraints on subsidizing agriculture would likely prevent this from happening.[10]

It goes without saying that following Japan and raising the price of farm produce above world levels will raise returns to the specific factor of production – namely land. In a land-scarce–labour-abundant economy like that of China, the supply elasticity of labour is very high, while that for agricultural land is very low. Hence, the effect of raising the price of farm products may just result in raising the return to land and discouraging out-migration of labour (Johnson, 1991). But this approach would raise rural incomes and in an equitable way, since land is distributed evenly across households.

5. SUMMARY

China's central government is preoccupied with supplying cheap domestic grain to urban residents and it strives for both regional and national self-sufficiency in grain. As long as the government forces farmers to produce grain and restricts labour mobility, farm incomes will be kept low. Labour is an abundant resource in rural China and it suffers from low marginal productivity and from being underpriced. Low labour productivity in agriculture has become a significant problem in China. The current task faced by China's government is to adopt a practical agricultural development policy based on the existence of abundant farm labour.

Since the economic reforms in 1978, some policies affecting labour mobility have gradually been abolished or have been loosened up. For instance, a market-based housing system has appeared in some regions, and the official distribution channel is no longer the only feasible way to obtain housing in the larger cities of China. An urban household registration (that is, an urban *hukou*) can now be purchased by rural residents. Because of the obstacles to permanent rural out-migration, recent urbanization has been characterized by increases in the temporary 'floating' population in the cities. However, the labour market reforms are not complete.

In China, grain production is relatively land intensive compared to many other agricultural products (for example, cotton, sugar, fruits, tobacco, and vegetables), which are more labour intensive. Hence, the comparative advantage of grain production in China is questionable, but production is distorted towards grain through current policy. For many countries, during the process of economic growth, the nation's comparative advantage in agriculture declines, and this is expected to happen in China (Anderson, 1990). In the long run China will most likely develop an increasing grain deficit due to the combined factors of rising domestic incomes, a growing population, and a declining sown acreage. This chapter has argued that the size of the long-run deficit will also depend on policy developments related to labour markets and mandatory grain procurement.

Food security in Asia

NOTES

Reprinted with permission from the *American Journal of Agricultural Economics*, Vol. 79, No. 5, 1997.

[1]   Crook (1997) explains how current policy interferes with grain markets. The basic feature of current policy is mandatory government grain purchases at fixed prices, below market prices (as of 1996). Crook's argument that farmers are underpaid for government procured grain is supported by other results, such as those in Croll and Ping. They surveyed eight villages in four different provinces (in 1994/95) and found that farmers in every village viewed agriculture as an unprofitable and unattractive activity.

[2]   Growth in the absolute size of the agricultural labour force is not unusual for a developing economy. Tomich, Kilby, and Johnston discuss patterns of structural transformation in countries like China, with abundant rural labour. They point out that in most countries it takes several decades before the absolute size of the agricultural labour force peaks and begins to decline, even with rapid growth of the non-agricultural labour force.

[3]   Rural land policy is also intertwined with grain policy and labour policy. However, land policy is not specifically addressed in this paper.

[4]   The self-sufficiency goal is operational at both the national and regional level. Its inclusion as a policy goal in this paper is not meant to be interpreted to literally mean that China does not or will not import grain in some years. China has been an important wheat importer in recent years but imports have been a small share of consumption and domestic stocks remain large. The point is that China strives to be self-sufficient in grain and recently has been a net grain exporter on a regular basis.

[5]   From 1986 it has become permissible for a farmer to change from a rural to a non-rural *hukou*. However, in recent years, the cost of buying an urban *hukou* is thought to be several thousand dollars (Zhou, 1996, chapter 6).

[6]   The urban–rural income gap shown in figure 3.1 is narrower than the gap between urban and farm incomes. However, farm income data are not readily available. Farmers make up about 70 per cent of rural income earners and the other 30 per cent non-farm rural income earners work mainly in township and village enterprises, and typically earn wages above farm levels.

[7]   There is some debate over the extent to which China's grain markets are efficient, as measured by spatial integration. Using monthly 1992 to 1995 data from rice markets in 35 cities, Zhou, Wan, and Chen found a lack of integration among markets. They attributed their findings to government intervention in the grain market and transport difficulties. Alternatively, Rozelle, *et al.* (1996) came to the opposite conclusion. Rozelle *et al.* tested market integration using provincial prices for rice, wheat, and maize between 1988 and 1995. The frequency of their data was every ten days. Rozelle *et al.* found that marketing

and price reforms in the early 1990s have led to a striking increase in the integration of markets. While not perfectly integrated, they found most rice and maize markets have become increasingly integrated after the liberalization policies of the early 1990s and this integration continued through the mid 1990s.

[8] This large discrepancy in the official labour statistics is not widely discussed, with the exception of Banister and Harbaugh. The discrepancy is due to alternative definitions of labour force ages, different sampling procedures, and timing of the sampling.

[9] The *Wall Street Journal* (12 December 1995) reported that China's 'floating population' totals at least 70 million.

[10] China has applied for WTO membership. The terms of accession to the World Trading Organization may also preclude China from shifting from taxation of agriculture to subsidization.

REFERENCES

Anderson, K. (1990), *Changing Comparative Advantages in China*, Paris: Organisation for Economic Co-operation and Development (OECD).

Banister, J. (1996), 'China: Population Dynamics and Economic Implications', in Joint Economic Committee, Congress of the United States (ed), *China's Economic Future: Challenges to US Policy*, Washington, DC: Government Printing Office, August.

Banister, J. and C. W. Harbaugh (1992), 'Rural Labor Force Trends in China', *China: Situation and Outlook Series*, 59–68. Technical Report no. RS-92-3, US Department of Agriculture, Washington, DC, July.

Brown, L. R., C. Flavin, H. French, and L. Starke (1995), *State of the World: 1995*, New York: W.W. Norton.

Carter, C. and S. Rozelle (1996), 'How Far Along is China in Developing its Food Markets?', in Joint Economic Committee, Congress of the United States (ed), *China's Economic Future: Challenges to US Policy*, Washington, DC: Government Printing Office, August.

Carter, C., F. Zhong, and F. Cai (1996), *China's Ongoing Agricultural Reform*, San Francisco: 1990 Institute. Distributed by University of Michigan Press.

Cook, S. (1997), 'Surplus Labour and Productivity in Chinese Agriculture: Evidence from Household Survey Data', Working Paper, Institute of Development Studies, University of Sussex, Brighton.

Crook, F. (1996), 'An Assessment of China's Agricultural Economy: 1980–2005', in Joint Economic Committee, Congress of the United States (ed), *China's Economic Future: Challenges to US Policy*,

Washington, DC: Government Printing Office, August.

Crook, F. (1997), 'Current Agricultural Policies Highlight Concerns About Food Security', in China Situation and Outlook Series, WRS-97–3, Economic Research Service, Washington, DC, June.

Croll, E. J. and H. Ping (1997), 'Migration For and Against Agriculture in Eight Chinese Villages', *China Quarterly*, (March): 128–46.

Fan, S. (1997), 'Why Do Projections On China's Future Food Supply and Demand Differ?', Washington, DC: International Food Policy Research Institute, EPT Division, EPTD Discussion Paper No. 22, March.

Fei, J. C. H. and G. Ranis (1964), *Development of the Labor Surplus Economy*, Homewood, IL: Irwin.

Goldstone, J. A. (1995), 'The Coming Collapse of China', *Foreign Policy*, 99 (Summer): 35–52.

Huang, J., S. Rozelle, and M. W. Rosegrant (1997), 'China's Food Economy to the Twenty-First Century: Supply, Demand, and Trade', Washington, DC: International Food Policy Research Institute, Discussion Paper No. 19, January.

Johnson, D. G. (1991), 'Agriculture in the Liberalization Process', in L. Klause and K. Kihwan (eds), *Liberalization in the Process of Economic Development*, Berkeley, CA: University of California Press, 283–331.

Johnston, B. F. (1970), 'Sectoral Independence, Structural Transformation, and Agricultural Growth: A Comment', in C. R. Wharton, Jr. (ed.), *Subsistence Agriculture and Economic Development*, Chicago: Aldine Publishing.

Johnston, B. F. and J. Mellor (1960), 'The Nature of Agriculture's Contributions to Economic Development', *Food Research Institute Studies*, 1(3) (November): 335–56.

Jorgenson, D. W. (1970), 'The Role of Agriculture in Economic Development: Classical versus Neoclassical Models of Growth', in C. R. Wharton, Jr. (ed), *Subsistence Agriculture and Economic Development*, Chicago: Aldine Publishing, Chapter 11.

Knight, J. and L. Song (1995), 'Towards a Labour Market in China', *Oxford Review of Economic Policy*, 11(4) (Winter): 97–117.

Lardy, N. R. (1994), *China in the World Economy*, Washington, DC: Institute for International Economics.

Lewis, W. A. (1954), 'Economic Development with Unlimited Supplies of Labour', *Manchester School of Economics and Social Studies*, 22 (May): 139–91.

Lewis, W. A. (1958), 'Unlimited Labour: Further Notes', *Manchester School of Economics and Social Studies*, 26 (January): 1–32.

Lin, J. Y. (1992), 'Rural Reforms and Agricultural Growth in China', *The American Economic Review*, 82: 34–51.

Lin, J. Y. (1995), 'Dynamics of Change and Productivity Effects of Agricultural Liberalization on China's Agriculture', Staff Paper, China Center for Economic Research, Peking University.

Lin, J. Y., F. Cai, and Z. Li (1996), *The China Miracle: Development Strategy and Economic Reform*, Hong Kong: The Chinese University of Hong Kong.

Liu, Jiang (Minister of Agriculture) (1994), 'Some Problems in Rural Reform and Development', Opening address to the International Conference on China's Rural Reform and Development in the 1990s, Beijing, China, 3–6 December 1993. *Foreign Scholars View Rural China*, Miao Jianping (ed), Beijing: Huaxia Press, p. 10.

Mallee, H. (1995), 'China's Household Registration System under Reform', *Development and Change*, 26: 1–29.

McMillan, J. and B. Naughton (1991), 'How to Reform a Planned Economy: Lessons from China', *Oxford Review of Economic Policy*, 8(1): 130–44.

McMillan, John, John Whalley, and Lijing Zhu (1989), 'The Impact of China's Economic Reforms on Agricultural Productivity Growth', *Journal of Political Economy*, 97: 781–807.

Naughton, B. (1996), 'The Pattern and Logic of China's Economic Reform', in Joint Economic Committee, Congress of the United States (ed.), *China's Economic Future: Challenges to US Policy*, Washington, DC: Government Printing Office, August.

Oshima, H. (1958), 'Underemployment in Backward Economies: An Empirical Comment', *Journal of Political Economy*, 66(3)(June): 259–63.

Prosterman, R., T. Hanstad, and L. Ping (1994), 'Reforming China's Rural Land System: A Field Report', RDI Report No. 85, Research Development Center, University of Washington, Seattle, November.

Riskin, C. (1996), 'Social Development, Quality of Life and the Environment', in Joint Economic Committee, Congress of the United States (ed), *China's Economic Future: Challenges to US Policy*, Washington, DC: Government Printing Office, August.

Rozelle, S., L. Guo, M. Shen, J. Giles, and T. Low (1997), 'Poverty, Networks, Institutions, or Education: Testing Among Competing Hypotheses on the Determination of Migration in China', paper presented at the 1997 annual meeting of the Association for Asian Studies, Chicago, 13–16 March.

Rozelle, S., A. Park, J. Huang, and H. Jin (1996), 'Dilemmas in Reforming State–Market Relations in China's Agricultural Sector',

Working Paper, Food Research Institute, Stanford University, Stanford, CA.

Sabin, L. (1995), 'The Development of Urban Labor Markets in Contemporary China', unpublished Ph.D. dissertation, Harvard University.

Schultz, T. W. (1964), *Transforming Traditional Agriculture*, New Haven, CT: Yale University Press.

State Statistical Bureau (SSB) (1985–96), *Zhongguo Tongji Nianjian* (*Statistical Yearbook of China*), Beijing: Statistical Publishing House.

Taylor, J. R. (1993), 'Rural Employment Trends and the Legacy of Surplus Labor, 1978–1989', in Y. Y. Kueh and R. F. Ash, (eds), *Economic Trends in Chinese Agriculture: The Impact of Post-Mao Reforms*, New York: Oxford University Press.

Tomich, T., P. Kilby, and B. F. Johnston (1995), *Transforming Agrarian Economies: Opportunities Seized, Opportunities Missed*, Ithaca and London: Cornell University Press.

Wen, G. J. (1993), 'Total Factor Productivity Change in China's Farming Sector: 1952–1989', *Economic Development and Cultural Change*, 42(1) (October): 1–41.

Wu, Harry Xiaoying (1994), 'Rural-to-Urban Migration in the People's Republic of China', *China Quarterly*, 139 (September): 669–98.

Yang, D. T. and H. Zhou (1996), 'Rural–Urban Disparity and Sectoral Labor Allocation in China', Working Paper, Durham, NC: Duke University, August.

Zhou, K. X. (1996), *How the Farmers Changed China*, Boulder, CO: Westview Press.

Zhou, Zhang-Yue, Guang-Hua Wan, and Liang-Biao Chen (1996), 'Integration of Rice Markets: The Case of Northern China', paper presented at the Second Asian Conference of Agricultural Economists, Bali, Indonesia, 6–9 August.

4. Rice and food security in Asia: a long-term outlook

Mercedita A. Sombilla and Mahabub Hossain

1. INTRODUCTION

Asia has made considerable progress in improving food security since the advent of the green revolution. Sustained increases in food availability came from impressive growth in rice production and from rapid economic growth that enabled food-deficit countries to meet shortages through commercial imports. Yet, despite improvements in food availability, the region is still home to more than half a billion chronically undernourished people. A major concern is whether this incidence of undernutrition in the region will decline in the coming decades. Many factors adversely affect the region's food security position. These include food production performance, population growth, income growth and distribution, and availability of foreign exchange to enable food importation. Emerging trends indicate that many countries will remain vulnerable to food insecurity. Failure to do the right thing now will further exacerbate the precarious food security situation especially in many low-income countries.

The chapter reviews recent events that have significantly influenced food security and discusses key emerging issues in food supply and demand that will affect food security in the coming years. The analysis is focused on rice because of its importance not only as a source of energy in Asian diets but also as a source of income especially among the rural people. The next section highlights the role of rice in the Asian economy and culture. This is followed by an analysis of the factors that influence emerging trends in demand and supply as well as of future food balances particularly that of rice. A section is devoted to a brief discussion on the political considerations for either pursuing a self-sufficiency policy in domestic production or achieving self-reliance through trade to sustain food security. The final section presents the policy and research implications.

35

2. RICE AND THE ASIAN ECONOMY

In Asia, rice occupies a position of overwhelming importance in the regional food system. The bulk of Asian diet is primarily rice (table 4.1). Being the principal staple food, it accounts for about 40 per cent of total per capita calorie intake in the region (figure 4.1). But such percentage share goes up to more than 65 per cent in low-income countries such as Bangladesh, Myanmar, Cambodia, Vietnam, and several states in Eastern and Southern India. The urban poor and the rural landless, the most vulnerable groups with regard to food security, spend 50–70 per cent of their incomes on rice.

Table 4.1 Level of food consumption (kg capita per year) in selected Asian countries, 1996

Country	Rice (milled)	Wheat	Maize	Cereals	Roots/ tubers	Vegetable	Fruits	Fish	Meat
Bangladesh	155.2	20.6	0.0	176.3	13.4	11.3	11.4	9.4	3.5
India	78.7	56.8	7.5	166.0	22.0	53.0	35.1	3.8	4.5
Indonesia	146.4	20.3	40.2	206.9	74.6	26.5	43.0	15.2	10.4
Thailand	110.9	11.5	0.3	122.8	7.2	30.8	99.8	25.9	23.1
Malaysia	85.0	25.5	3.9	129.8	25.2	38.5	50.5	53.5	49.8
Philippines	95.9	13.8	9.9	119.7	38.3	68.7	112.7	32.6	26.6
Vietnam	163.8	4.9	16.0	184.7	45.1	51.5	48.0	12.6	19.3
Myanmar	213.7	2.2	2.4	221.3	5.3	47.8	21.6	15.5	7.9
China	92.4	84.3	11.0	192.7	63.4	146.2	54.1	19.0	41.2
South Korea	93.9	49.4	17.7	167.1	18.0	186.3	86.4	50.3	37.0
Japan	62.2	45.3	22.8	132.0	34.6	108.9	55.8	71.0	44.7

Source: FAO (1998).

Equally important is its role in providing livelihood to the Asian population. Rice farming is the single most important source of employment and income for the rural people. Nearly 150 million households in Asia depend on rice cultivation for their livelihood (Box 1, IRRI 1997c). In countries with per capita income of US$500 or less, rice accounts for 20–33 per cent of the gross domestic product (GDP), and 33 –50 per cent of the agriculture value added (Hossain and Fischer, 1995). A number of in-depth village studies conducted by the International Rice

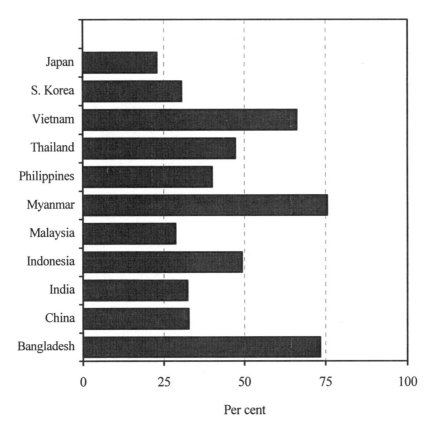

Figure 4.1 Percentage of rice to total per capita calorie intake, 1996

Research Institute in collaboration with policy research institutions in national systems (country studies in David and Otsuka, 1994) found that farm household incomes are at an average level of about US\$1 000 yr^{-1}, of which 40–60 per cent came from rice cultivation (table 4.2).

Rice is also inextricably woven in to the region's social and cultural milieu. It is mentioned in the scriptures of the ancient Asian civilization (Huggan, 1995). Its cultivation was considered as the basis of the social order, playing a major role in Asia's religions and customs. In Japan, the emperor is considered the direct descendant of the rice prince. In Thailand, rice is considered to be the gift of the fruitful womb of the goddess Mae Phosop. In China and Bangladesh, a polite way of greeting a visitor is 'Have you eaten your rice today?'. Until today, rice remains a symbol of

Table 4.2 Average farm household income (US$ yr^{-1}) in selected Asian countries, by source

Countries	Total household income (US$)	Sources of income (%)		
		Rice	Non-rice	Non-farm
Bangladesh	977	38	30	32
China	871	43	30	27
Tamil Nadu, India	1010	52	36	12
Lampung, Indonesia	721	36	44	20
Nepal	1105	43	46	11
Philippines	1072	57	18	25
Thailand	1763	49	20	31

Sources: Compiled from unpublished data collected from household surveys under the collaborative IRRI/NARS project, 'Differential Impact of Modern Rice Technology in Favorable and Unfavorable Production Environments'. For country case studies, see David and Otsuka (1994).

success in the modern world of the Japanese automobile industry. The word Toyota means 'beautiful rice field' and Honda means 'main rice field'. The aesthetic contribution of the rice landscape is also of great value. Fields are terraced on to steep mountainsides, flow with contours of valleys, and slice their own lines across flat lands. The geometry of rice farms is just awesome. But to hundreds of species—some hidden in the soil, others buzzing through the air—these are home.

Playing such a major role in the lives of producers, consumers, and the cultural heritage of the Asian society, rice has become a strategically and politically important commodity. It has been used as an intervention point for promoting growth and food security. Economic development and industrial growth are closely linked to a sustainable supply of rice at low and stable prices. The first sign of civil unrest is often traced to rising rice prices, which aggravates the food insecurity of the growing rank of urban workers and the rural landless.

3.   EMERGING TRENDS IN RICE DEMAND

Economic growth in Asia has led to two contrasting trends in per capita rice demand. While some countries such as Japan and South Korea have shown gradual decline in per capita rice consumption over the past two decades, others continue to exhibit rising trends. Economic growth, more rapid rate of urbanization, and changes in occupational structure tend to depress demand increases. However, population growth, which remains high in many countries, and the objective to alleviate poverty will continue to boost rice demand.

3.1 Per Capita Income Growth and Grain Consumption

Economic theory says that, as per capita income increases, the proportion of income spent for staple foods tends to decrease. Asia has been no exception to this rule. In fact, the absolute consumption of rice per head of population has been declining in Japan and South Korea since the early 1960s and late 1970s, respectively. It is now being experienced in the newly industrialized countries of Thailand and Malaysia. Rapid economic growth in Thailand has influenced the gradual decline in per capita demand for rice in recent years. Per capita rice demand in Malaysia is still rising slightly, but is also on the verge of reversing direction with continued prosperity. Countries that belong to the low-income group, however, still show a relatively strong and positive demand response to a rise in incomes. In the Philippines and Indonesia, continued economic growth will further increase the demand for rice as the fight against poverty strengthens. In other countries, such as those in South Asia, where diets are still heavily based on maize, sorghum, barley, and millet, a further rise in per capita income will shift demand towards rice. Estimates show that, even at the highest rate of economic growth, it will still take several years before many of these countries will start substituting rice for other commodities.

3.2 Rapid Urbanization and Changes in Occupational Structure

Rapid urbanization accompanied by economic growth hastens the diversification of diets, shifts demand from the staples to food with less energy and which is easier to prepare, and increases the frequency of eating away from home. All of these will reduce the demand for rice in the urban sector, but not if the urban poor continue to proliferate. Estimates show that 63 per cent of the urban poor in the developing world, or about 83 million people, are found in the metropolitan areas of Asia (Pinstrup-Andersen and Pandya-Lorch, 1995). Many of these people are engaged in heavy, manual activities that require diets with high energy. The extent of undernutrition in the urban areas is relatively high. When compared with the standard nutrition yardstick of 1.4 times the basal metabolic rate (BMR), about 32 per cent of Thailand's urban population are categorized as undernourished (Hussein and Lunven, 1997). Similar conditions exist in other Asian countries where the proportion of undernourished in their urban sectors is high compared with their rural sectors.

Urbanization also promotes demand for high-quality food and processed products. For rice, this means a shift in demand from the low- to the high-quality variety. A typical example is the pattern of demand for rice in Japan. Figure 4.2 shows the increase in per capita demand for high-quality non-glutinous rice among non-farm households over the past years in place of the standard quality as Japanese incomes rose. The same pattern is now observed in China with the growing demand for the better -quality japonica rice, replacing the low-quality hybrid variety. Demand for rice-based processed products, such as noodles, rice cakes, and the like has also increased, especially among the working-class population who are always on the go and have little time to prepare food.

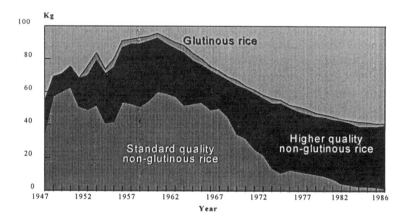

Figure 4.2 Changes in rice consumption in Japanese non-farm households (per capita annual data)

Source: Comprehensive Time Series Report on the Family Income and Expenditure Survey 1947
    −1986.

3.3 Rapid Population Growth

The major boost to rice demand increases will still come from population growth, however. Table 4.3 shows that Asia's population will grow at

1.08 per cent per annum over the next 25 years, increasing by about 31 per cent from 3.1 billion in 1995 to 4.1 billion in 2020. This projected growth rate is much slower than in the past three decades but, because of the current population base, the absolute size of the increase will be huge. China and India, where the projected annual population growth rates are 0.7 and 1.3 per cent respectively, will contribute an additional 572 million people by 2020. As can be noted from the table, the largest population increases will come from the low-income, poverty-stricken countries like Bangladesh, Myanmar, India, Vietnam, and the Philippines, where per capita rice consumption is still expected to be on the rise.

Table 4.3 Projections of population (millions) in Asia, 1995−2020

Country	1995	2010	2020	% change 1995−2020	Annual growth (%) rate (1995−2020)
China	1220	1344	1449	19	0.69
India	929	1158	1272	37	1.26
Indonesia	197	240	264	34	1.17
Bangladesh	118	153	171	45	1.50
Vietnam	73	93	104	41	1.39
Thailand	58	65	68	16	0.61
Myanmar	45	59	64	16	0.61
Japan	125	127	124	−1.0	−0.04
Philippines	68	87	100	47	1.56
South Korea	45	50	52	16	0.58
Asia	3147	3754	4121	31	1.08

Note: Asia includes countries in South, Southeast, and East Asia.

Source: UN (1997).

4. EMERGING TRENDS IN RICE SUPPLY

Prior to the 1960s, growth in rice production was slow and came mostly from expansion of cultivated lands. With the introduction of IR8 in the mid-1960s and the succeeding high-yielding varieties (HYVs) thereafter, dramatic changes in rice production took place. Yields increased up to three times higher than those realized from traditional cultivars (Khush, 1995) and accounted for almost all of the production increment. Production, however, has slowed down in recent years. The annual growth rate in rice between 1985 and 1997 was estimated only at 1.8 per cent. This is a drastic reduction from the 2.9 per cent growth during 1975–85 and the 3.3 per cent growth a decade earlier (FAO, 1998), raising concerns regarding the ability of the region to produce the rice needed to meet future demand.

4.1 Growing Scarcity of Production Resources

The dominant inputs to rice production are land, water, and labour. Economic prosperity in Asia has brought about competing demand for these resources, affecting their relative scarcities and prices and in turn the relative profitability of rice farming.

Rapid industrialization and growth of the urban population have put tremendous pressure (and will continue to do so) on the need to divert agricultural land to meet the demand for housing, factories, and roads. Arable land per capita has been declining over the years in many countries (table 4.4). The irrigated farm areas are prone to such conversion because of their relative accessibility. Compounding the problem is the economic pressure to release some areas under rice cultivation to accommodate the greater production of high-value crops like vegetables, fruits, and livestock products, the demand for which has grown stronger with urbanization and the associated change in food habits. Rice area harvested has started to decline even in the low- and middle-income economies. In China, rice area harvested declined from 37 million ha in 1976 to about 31 million ha in 1997. In Java, Indonesia, nearly 50 000 ha of land is taken out of rice cultivation every year.

The development of irrigation facilities has been the key factor towards impressive rice production increases in Asia. Water, which was once regarded as an abundant resource in the region, is now becoming scarce. Large areas of irrigated land are being abandoned because waterlogging and salinization have rendered them sterile. For many countries, growth in irrigated area has significantly slowed down in the last decade compared with the early years of the green revolution. Construction of new irrigation facilities is no longer an easy option because of the high capital investment cost. Public and private investments for irrigation development as well as for their maintenance have declined and are no longer easy to avail of (Rosegrant and Svendsen, 1993). There are also rising concerns on the health (for example, spread of water-related

Table 4.4 Resource availability in selected Asian countries

	Per capita arable land[a] (ha)		Cultivated rice area per capita[a] (ha)		Expansion of irrigated area[a] (%)		Agricultural wages[b] (US$)	
	1965	1995	1965	1995	1965–80	1980–98	1961	1993
Bangladesh	0.15	0.07	0.16	0.08	6.96	5.93	0.29	1.45
India	0.32	0.18	0.07	0.05	2.57	2.65	–	–
Indonesia	0.17	0.09	0.07	0.06	0.65	0.42	–	–
Thailand	0.37	0.29	0.20	0.15	3.62	3.44	0.36	2.51
Malaysia	0.09	0.09	0.06	0.03	2.05	0.40		
Philippines	0.14	0.08	0.10	0.06	3.48	1.74	0.80	2.56
Vietnam	0.14	0.07	0.13	0.09	3.07	1.75		
Myanmar	0.41	0.21	0.20	0.14	1.90	4.47	0.26[1]	8.00
China	0.14	0.08	0.04	0.03	2.04	0.62	–	–
South Korea	0.08	0.04	0.04	0.02	0.58	−0.70	0.70	37.80
Japan	0.05	0.03	0.03	0.02	0.25	−0.76	1.35	51.93

Note: [1] 1979.

Sources: [a] FAO (1998).
[b] Wages are in real terms. IRRI (1997a).

diseases, such as malaria, river blindness, and schistosomiasis) and environmental (waterlogging, salinity, fish production, and quality of groundwater) effects of irrigation, which hamper further expansion of these facilities. While the percentage of water withdrawal for agriculture in Asia is currently the largest at 86 per cent, we expect that this will be significantly reduced with rapid urbanization and industrialization. Per capita water availability has already declined from 40 per cent to 60 per cent between 1955 and 1990 in most Asian countries. This is expected to go down further over the next 30 years due to population growth.

The surplus-labour phenomenon in the rural areas in the early 1960s no longer applies in many countries. With opportunities for more remunerative employment rising elsewhere, rural workers have moved out of agriculture to the manufacturing and service sectors. The growing scarcity of labour is reflected in the wage rates. Agricultural wage rates in real terms have risen by hundreds of folds in many Asian countries between 1961 and 1993. These increases are still relatively low when compared with those in high-income countries, like Japan and South Korea.

4.2   Gradual Approach to the Technological Frontier

Stagnation of yield growth has been observed in many countries of Asia. In Japan and South Korea, rice yield has long remained at around 6.5 t/ha after reaching that level in the late 1960s and the late 1970s, respectively (figure 4.3).[1] Countries in South and Southeast Asia are starting to show the same pattern of yield stagnation although at levels lower than their East Asian neighbours. These areas belong to the humid and sub-humid tropics, where attainable yields will be less because of less sunshine hours and high incidence of pests (Hossain, 1997). Recent studies explain that this trend comes from the fact that the best farmers' yields are now approaching the levels that scientists are able to attain in their experimental fields with today's knowledge (Pingali, Hossain, and Gerpacio, 1997).

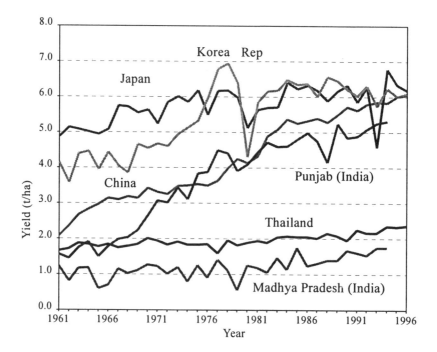

Figure 4.3 Trends in rice yield, selected Asian countries, 1961–96.

Source: IRRI (1997a).

It should be noted that the impressive performance of current technology was made possible by the combined effect of irrigated land expansion, the adoption of modern rice varieties, and the application of fertilizers. The gradual exhaustion of these frontiers in the last three decades has led to the general slowdown of productivity growth. Most rice farms are now irrigated and planted to modern rice varieties and, in most of the irrigated areas, fertilizer use is already optimal (David and Otsuka, 1994). All these allowed the intensive monoculture of rice in irrigated lands, the long-run effect of which led to rapid soil and water quality deterioration, making it difficult for farmers to sustain high yields (Cassman and Pingali, 1995; Pingali, Hossain, and Gerpacio, 1997).

5.   RICE SUPPLY AND DEMAND IN 2010

Will Asia be able to sustain rice productivity growth to ensure enough supply to meet the growth in demand? This question looms on the horizon as we approach the next millennium. Recent projection studies show that as long as economic, social, and political conditions (especially prior to the Asian financial crisis) continue, the global food balance situation will be optimistic, with prices of most commodities falling and food security of many countries improving. The section that follows presents the International Model for Policy Analysis of Agricultural Commodities and Trade (IMPACT) model's projection results on rice in 2010.

5.1   The Structure of IMPACT[2]

IMPACT is a global trade model developed at the International Food Policy Research Institute (IFPRI) in collaboration with the International Rice Research Institute (IRRI), primarily as a tool for analysing the effects of changes in the economic and social structures of countries on commodity market performances. It is built upon existing global trade models and then substantially modified to allow for the long-term projection of prices, supply, demand, and trade. In its present structure, IMPACT is (i) a partial equilibrium model with its focus on the agriculture sector; (ii) global, covering 37 countries/regions and 17 commodities; (iii) non-spatial (and hence cannot be used to analyse bilateral trade patterns); and (iv) synthetic, because of its use of demand and supply parameters (income and price elasticities) derived from other studies.

IMPACT is specified as a set of country or regional submodels, each with a particular structure within which supply, demand, and prices for some categories of agricultural commodities are determined. The 37 country and regional agricultural submodels are linked through trade, a specification that highlights the interdependence of countries and commodities in the world agricultural economy.

The model uses a system of supply and demand elasticities, incorporated into a series of linear and non-linear equations, to approximate the underlying production and demand functions. Domestic production of crops and livestock is determined by area and yield, each of which is expressed as a function primarily of prices and some exogenous variables that represent the impact of research and infrastructure development. Domestic demand of a commodity is the sum of its demand for food, feed, and other industrial uses. Food demand is a function of prices, income, and population. Feed demand, on the other hand, is a derived demand determined by changes in livestock production, feed ration, and prices. Demand for other uses is just a proportion of the previous year's demand, based on food and feed demand changes. The country/regional submodels are linked to each other through trade. Commodity trade by country is the difference between domestic production and demand. Countries with positive trade are net exporters, while those with negative values are net importers. This specification does not permit a separate identification of countries that are both importers and exporters of a particular commodity. Stocks are not explicitly modelled because markets are assumed to be in equilibrium over the intermediate and longer time horizon.

Commodity prices are determined when the market clears, that is, when the sum of net trade across countries is equal to zero. The world price (PW) of a commodity is the equilibrating mechanism such that, when an exogenous shock is introduced in the model, PW will adjust and each adjustment is passed back to the effective producer and to consumer prices. Changes in domestic prices subsequently affect commodity supply and demand, necessitating their iterative readjustments until world supply and demand achieve a balance, and world net trade is again equal to zero. Domestic prices consist of world prices, expressed in terms of the producer subsidy equivalent (PSE) and consumer subsidy equivalent (CSE), and the marketing margin (MI), which reflect other factors, such as transport costs or product quality differences. These primarily account for the wedge between domestic and world prices. Other policy instruments that explicitly shift demand and supply relationships or limit trade are also modelled. The US acreage reduction program, for example, is reflected in the model as a production control mechanism by limiting the area of production.

5.2   Intersectoral Linkages

Despite its focus on the agricultural commodities, relationships have been incorporated into IMPACT to link income growth in the agricultural and non-agricultural sectors via sectoral growth multipliers. These relationships, despite their being rudimentary, provide the model with a mechanism to translate the impact of developmental growth in one sector to the other. Growth in the non-agricultural sector, for example, is translated back to agriculture through its effect on production from improved delivery of necessary inputs, more rapid technology development, and increased investment in agriculture (Hazell *et al.*, 1991, McGuirck and Mundlak, 1991). As non-agricultural income increases, agricultural production responds directly to higher prices from the strengthened demand and indirectly from the effects of investments in capital, and research and development. On the other hand, agricultural income growth creates a feedback effect on the non-agricultural sector, through increased demand for non-agricultural products and services (Bautista, 1991; Badiane, 1991).

5.3   Baseline Assumptions

Baseline projections usually describe the best assessment of future developments in the world food situation based on the continuation of current conditions, including price and market policies.[3] In IMPACT, the baseline assumptions include those on population changes, growth in incomes, rate of urbanization, and non-price changes in area and yield. Rate of population increases are based on the medium-variant projections of the United Nations (UN, 1997). Gross Domestic Product (GDP) growth assumptions, on the other hand, come primarily from the IMF, *Economic Outlook* reports (IMF, various issues). Closely related to population and income growth changes is the rate of urbanization. This has a significant effect on demand structures as it accelerates dietary transition from the basic staples to high-value products, like fruits, vegetables, processed foods, and meat and dairy products. Urbanization is not explicitly incorporated into IMPACT, however. Its effect is reflected in the assumptions on income and price elasticities that are adjusted in accordance with income growth.[4] The income elasticities are shown in table 4.5. Those of prices are not shown but they are relatively small.

Another fundamental assumption of the baseline projection is that the rates of public investments in agricultural research and infrastructure will continue at the prevailing level in the late 1980s and early 1990s. Based on this, Evenson and Rosegrant (1995) developed an accounting structure

Food security in Asia

incorporating sources of growth for area and yield that are independent of price effects. The sources of growth considered in the analysis include the contribution of public agricultural research, management research, conventional plant breeding, wide-crossing/hybridization breeding, biotechnology (transgenic) breeding, private sector agricultural research and development, agricultural extension markets, infrastructure, and irrigation.[5] Projected growth in yield and area is derived from an analysis

Table 4.5 Income elasticities for food: IMPACT baseline assumptions

Food item	Developed Region	Latin America	Sub-Saharan Africa	WANA	Asia
Beef	−0.10–0.22	0.19–0.43	0.55–0.62	0.35–0.55	0.35–0.70
Pig meat	−0.18–0.04	0.32–0.53	0.48–0.70	0.45–0.53	0.40–0.70
Sheep meat	0.10–0.20	0.20–0.53	0.20–0.50	0.38–0.40	0.48–0.75
Poultry meat	0.10–0.20	0.30–0.52	0.48–0.68	0.55–065	0.42–0.80
Wheat	0.05–0.16	−0.10–0.18	0.18–0.32	0.13–0.20	0.00–0.30
Maize	−0.40– −0.05	−0.40–0.03	−0.02–0.25	−0.15	−0.25–0.10
O. grains	−0.30–0.00	−0.30– −0.10	−0.05–0.25	−0.35– −0.15	−0.45–0.30
Rice	−0.10–0.20	0.09–0.25	0.18–0.28	0.09	−0.20–0.28
Root tubers	−0.05–0.20	0.02–0.17	0.04–0.12	− 0.22	−0.12–0.20

of recent past trends, examination of future yield potential for crops and livestock, and in-depth assessment of future sources of growth, including public investment in research, extension, and infrastructure and future patterns of growth in these investments. The general pattern projected is for a small additional decline in the rates of growth of crop yields compared with the already low rates experienced in the past decade. However, if investment rates in agricultural research are maintained, this decline should not accelerate. Projected growth rates in area are dampened to reflect the lagged effects of declining investments in irrigation.

Policy effects in IMPACT incorporate the pre-Uruguay Round trade regime. Proposed policy changes under the General Agreement on Tariffs and Trade (GATT) were not readily available for inclusion in a form applicable to the model. The baseline analysis does include, however, policy changes for some countries and commodities, whose magnitude and direction of impact were clear and are expected to have great influence on future food markets.[6]

5.4 The Asian Rice Market under the Baseline Scenario

Asia will continue to dominate world rice production and consumption. Regional production under the baseline will increase by about 22 per cent from the 1993 level of 327 million tons (milled rice equivalent) to about 400 million tons in 2010. Percentage rise in demand will be slightly higher at 24 per cent from 318 million tons in 1993 to 395 million tons in 2010 (table 4.6). The projected trend comes mainly from population growth that will remain rapid until 2005 in many Asian developing countries where per capita demand for rice will continue to be strong.

The baseline scenario also projects some changes in the relative distribution of total production and consumption among the different subregions in Asia. Southeast Asia will maintain its almost a quarter share of the region's total production and consumption. Total rice demand in this subregion will increase by about 29 per cent, a large portion of which will be accounted for by the Philippines. South Asia will increase its respective share to both regional production and consumption by about 3 percentage points from 32 per cent in the early 1990s to 35 per cent in 2010. India is projected to increase by 33 per cent, Bangladesh by 35 per cent, and the rest of South Asia by about 60 per cent. East Asia's contribution to the total production and demand of the region will be reduced. The gradual fall of rice demand in Japan will be partly offset by relatively strong growth in other East Asian countries like North Korea. The projected patterns of growth in both production and consumption of rice in the different subregions are primarily influenced by the expected shifts in demand for better quality staples (from coarse grains and tubers) in South Asia and to high-value products (low energy source) in East Asia as rapid income growth and urbanization continue.

5.5 Trade Performance by Country

Thailand will continue to have huge rice surpluses for export, primarily more from the rapid decline in demand growth rather than from production growth. Myanmar's net rice exports, on the other hand, will increase significantly as rice area planted to HYVs expand further, thereby enabling the country to continue reaping the benefits of the green revolution technology that was delayed because of the country's inability to import chemical fertilizers due to scarcity of foreign exchange. Vietnam's export surpluses will be maintained at around 2 million tons

Table 4.6 Baseline and slow economic growth projections for rice in Asia (milled equivalent)

Countries/ regions	Base year, 1993			Baseline, 2010			Slow economic growth, 2010		
	Production	Demand	Net trade	Production	Demand	Net trade	Production	Demand	Net trade
South Asia	103 300	101 686	1614	137 832	137 193	639	136 457	135 891	566
India	78 122	77 402	720	103 475	102 576	899	102 132	101 670	462
Pakistan	3616	2334	1282	5155	3755	1400	5 138	3729	1409
Bangladesh	17 827	17 921	-94	23 687	24 388	-702	23 651	24 139	-488
Other S. Asia	3735	4029	-294	5516	6475	-959	5 536	6353	-817
Southeast Asia	80 080	73 595	6519	102 830	94 947	7884	100 234	92 771	7463
Indonesia	32 428	32 786	-359	39 879	41 654	-1775	38 117	40 060	-1944
Thailand	13 134	7645	5489	15 352	8400	6953	14 846	8499	6347
Malaysia	1310	1945	-635	1623	2661	-1038	1623	2614	-991
Philippines	6388	6545	-157	9122	9267	-145	8618	8862	-244
Vietnam	14 724	12 796	1928	19 177	16 993	2185	19 237	16 893	2344
Myanmar	9774	9411	398	14 072	12 391	1681	14 157	12 305	1853
Other SE Asia	2322	2467	-145	3604	3580	23	3637	3538	99
East Asia	143 286	143 177	109	158 657	163 050	-4392	156 922	161 920	-4999
China	125 866	124 968	898	142 788	143 690	-902	141 096	142 453	-1357
Japan	9243	9596	-352	7090	9801	-2711	7041	9857	-2816
Other E. Asia	8177	8613	-437	8778	9557	-779	8785	9610	-825
Asia	326 666	318 458	8242	399 320	395 189	4129	393 613	390 582	3031

Notes: Area in 000 hectares.
Yield in kgs per hectare.
Production, demand and net trade in 000 tons.

50

over the projection period (1993–2010), as resources that fuelled rapid growth in the past decade become exhausted. Malaysia's imports, on the other hand, will increase by about 65 per cent while Indonesia's will more than quadruple. In the Philippines, the demand will increase by more than 40 per cent, owing to the high growth of the population, but it will manage to maintain low import levels with projected production growth almost matching the growth in demand.

China will continue to play a marginal role in the rice trade as it tries to adhere to its policy of self-sufficiency. It will continue to constantly shift from a minimal net importer to a net exporter or vice versa, depending on world market supply and prices. This behaviour strongly reflects the ability of China to increase or decrease production, primarily through area manipulation, to ensure availability of the commodity that remains its primary staple food. The Japanese rice import market will double from 359 000 tons in 1993 to 779 000 tons in 2010 as production declines faster than demand. Further expansion is expected as the government complies with the new trade regime that prescribes for a more open market policy. This will also be the case in the other East Asian countries of South Korea and Taiwan that are included in the Other East Asian group. Rice imports in North Korea will further increase as production performance remains poor and rice demand strengthens.

India's strong production performance in 1995 and 1996 and Pakistan's maintenance of past rice export levels enabled South Asia to be a significant net exporter in the early 1990s. But it was a short-term phenomenon in response to the scarcity in the world rice market. The baseline projection shows that the present favourable export situation will not exist for long, as India moves back to continue a more normal trend in production growth, and stronger internal demand with economic prosperity and alleviation of poverty. At the projected growth rate of 1.7 per cent, the country will increase its exports but only marginally from the level of about 720 000 tons to close to 900 000 tons in 2010. This will partly fill the import needs of other South Asian countries (primarily Bangladesh and Sri Lanka), which are projected to widen their supply and demand gap, from the combined effect of slower production growth as production resources become exhausted, while demand for the commodity will remain strong because of rapid increases in population and further rises in per capita rice demand. Pakistan's rice exports will continue to rise but only marginally as resource constraints will also hamper more rapid increases in production expansion. The subregion's net exports will therefore be gradually reduced from the more than 1.6 million tons in 1993 to 639 000 tons in 2010.

5.6   Rice and Food Security

Baseline scenario results show that total calorie intake per capita in the
region will increase from the average level of 2553 kcal per day in 1993
to 2794 kcal in 2010 (table 4.7). The country variation will be large in
Bangladesh and other Southeast Asian countries where per capita calorie
intake will rise from about 2000 kcal in 1993 to about 2200 kcal in 2010.
In the more advanced Asian economies (like Malaysia, China, and Other
East Asian), per capita calorie intake will increase to levels of more than
3000 kcal. The relatively large calorie increase in some countries partly
comes from increased per capita demand in other commodities that is
made possible by price and income effects. As cereal prices continue to
fall, consumers are more able to purchase other food commodities while
maintaining almost the same levels of demand for their rice. The regional
average contribution of rice to total calorie intake in 2010 remains high at
35 per cent. The share of rice to total calorie intake in poorer economies,
such as Bangladesh, Vietnam, Myanmar, and the Philippines, will actually
rise slightly. But even in Thailand and Indonesia where marked declines
in per capita rice demand are projected, its contribution to total calorie
intake will still be close to about 50 per cent.

The 10 per cent improvement in the region's total per capita calorie
intake, however, will only lead to a small dent in terms of the reduction of
malnourished children in the region. In 2010, about 133 million children
between the ages nought and five will still be considered malnourished,
only about 5 per cent less than the number in 1993. Except for India, the
rest of South Asia will barely witness any improvements in their
nutritional status.

5.7   The Effect of Slow Economic Growth on the Rice Economy

The baseline results assume that economic growth prior to 1993 will be
sustained through the projection period. The current financial crisis in
Asia, however, seems to cast some doubts on the validity of this
assumption. In view of this, an alternative scenario depicting slower
economic growth in some Asian countries is simulated. In this scenario,
the baseline income growth assumptions for Indonesia, Thailand,
Malaysia, Philippines, South Korea, and Japan are reduced by an average
of 50 per cent in the Philippines to about 80 per cent in Thailand, starting
from 1997. The slower growth affects the agricultural sector through
reduced investment allocation, which would hinder further expansion in
irrigated areas and slow down research and extension activities, all of
which would have a direct effect on productivity growth. The effect of

changes on relative prices on the domestic market for tradable and non-tradable commodities and of inputs due to massive currency devaluation could not however be captured by the model.

Asia's projected demand for milled rice in 2010 under this scenario will be relatively smaller (391 million tons) compared with the projected level under the baseline (395 million tons). This is because of slightly higher prices with lower excess supply in the world market from the large production cut, especially in countries affected by the current economic turmoil, which are mostly the major rice producers.

Asia will have much lower net exports under this scenario compared with the baseline results (table 4.6). Exports from Thailand will only be about 6.3 million tons compared with the almost 7 million tons projected under the baseline for the same period. The reduction will come from production growth slowdown, most of which will be captured by the local market. The same trend is projected for Indonesia and the Philippines. As a result, imports for these countries will slightly increase. Malaysia's projected imports will be lower as production growth will be maintained while demand growth will slow down. Vietnam and Myanmar will take advantage of the situation and will fill the subregion's excess demand for rice. South Asia's net trade position will barely be affected. India's lower exports will be balanced by lower imports from Bangladesh and other South Asian countries. East Asia's imports will remain the highest as Japan, South Korea, and other East Asian countries experience further reductions in production, combined with strong demand growth in the latter group of countries. The rise in prices that results from a tighter market does not seem to stimulate a strong positive response from China. Under this scenario, China is projected to have larger imports in 2010.

The more serious consequence of this scenario, however, will be food security, particularly in the Southeast Asian countries affected by the economic turmoil. As table 4.7 shows, the slow economic growth scenario will lead to lower per capita calorie intake in developing Asia and the developing region as a whole compared with the baseline levels. This reduction is estimated to result in about 169 million malnourished children in 2010 in the developing world; this is about 1.7 million more than the number projected in the baseline. For developing Asia, the figures are 115 million and 2 million, respectively.

6. SUSTAINING FOOD SECURITY THROUGH TRADE

National food security can be achieved not only through self-sufficiency in the domestic production of staple grains but also through some reliance on trade. There are some conditions essential for countries to achieve food self-reliance and ensure longer-term food security. One is the assurance of the existence of a more stable market for grains. A fundamental reality of the global grain economy is that some regions are able to produce grains efficiently in amounts exceeding their own needs, while others must access adequate and secure supplies from abroad. Unless grain importers have access to commercially available world food supplies, claims in these countries of the need for self-sufficiency will be difficult to resist. These claims come even from countries highly dependent on external trade. Historically, this condition has not been fulfilled because the international rice market that has remained thin with

Table 4.7 Projected per capita calorie intake and number of malnourished children (nought to 5-year-old)

Country	Per capita calorie intake (kcal)			Malnourished children (millions)		
	1993	2010		1993	2010	
		Baseline	Slow economic growth		Baseline	Slow economic growth
India	2397	2634	2626	75 996	59 667	60 034
Pakistan	2399	2551	2549	9942	10 848	10 860
Bangladesh	2021	2201	2185	11 397	10 611	10 757
Other South Asia	2256	2428	2414	2425	2819	2851
Indonesia	2610	2827	2600	3815	2872	3325
Thailand	2366	2657	2374	752	491	608
Malaysia	2781	3008	2765	692	525	607
Philippines	2370	2579	2417	3042	2564	2879
Vietnam	2302	2561	2553	4784	3145	3166
Myanmar	2621	2721	2707	2054	1879	1895
Other Southeast Asia	1958	2043	2026	941	1031	1046
China	2758	3078	3075	24 408	16 825	16 860
Other East Asia	2791	2986	2815	–	–	
Developing Asia	2553	2794	2758	140 248	113 277	114 888
Developing region	2568	2748	2724	185 345	167 349	169 034

trade volume at only 4—5 per cent of total world production. Variable national conditions, such as floods, droughts, and typhoons, cause shortages and surpluses to occur from year to year, producing wide fluctuations in marketable surplus and making the world rice market highly volatile. The current size of the international market is 17 per cent of the rice needs in China and 19 per cent of the combined consumption of India and Indonesia. If these countries decided to meet even 10 per cent of their rice needs through imports, the additional demand would swamp the world market.

The other condition pertains to the ability of countries to access the world market for their additional food needs. Countries should achieve favourable economic growth to obtain sufficient foreign exchange for the purchase of food imports. At the same time, households should have productive employment and adequate incomes to allow them to acquire the food needed from the market. Countries in East and Southeast Asia are fortunate in this respect, especially those that have not been very much affected by the recent financial crisis. Depending on how fast they recover, the Philippines and Indonesia may have to strive to increase rice production domestically to save the use of foreign exchange for some other import needs.

Provided there is free trade in rice, it is not difficult for high-income food-deficit countries and affluent consumers to access rice from the market, even when there is scarcity. The market will distribute the scarce supply in favour of the affluent who can pay higher prices. It is the poor consumers in low-income countries who will suffer when there is scarcity of the staple food. A surge in food prices will not only accentuate the precarious poverty situation now prevailing in the low-income countries but will also have far-reaching effects on their domestic economies. Since rice is a major component of their food basket, the increase in prices will contribute significantly to inflation and will put upward pressure on industrial wages as organized labour bargains for sustaining growth in real incomes. Industrial profits will shrink and the competitive strength of the economy in the production of labour-intensive manufactures will erode. Considering this political cost, many Asian countries may opt to maintain a safe capacity of domestic production of the staple food, despite the additional economic cost of pursuing this activity.

7. IMPLICATIONS FOR RESEARCH AND POLICY

The role of rice in alleviating poverty and promoting food security improvements in Asia is critical. Sustaining past impressive growth in rice production, made possible by the green revolution technology will be more difficult, however, with the gradual exhaustion of what used to be abundant production resources and with rice yields approaching the maximum that scientists are able to attain with today's knowledge. Moreover, with the implementation of new trade rules, prescribed by the recently concluded GATT negotiations, the protection of the domestic market that provided incentives to rice producers in the past will gradually be removed. Many Asian countries, particularly those in the middle- and high-income groups, will find it difficult to compete with low-income economies, where wage rates and opportunity cost of family labour are still low, or with large land-surplus countries in the developed world who reap economies of scale because of large-size farms (Pingali, 1995).

Rice research – which in the past had as its primary objective increasing yields and land productivity – must take the additional challenge of how to simultaneously increase productivity of labour, water, and chemical fertilizers, while preserving natural resources and protecting the environment. The move to a *green* (growth in grain production), *green* (in a manner that protects the soil and water quality and preserves biodiversity) *revolution* should now be vigorously pursued. Several technologies are now in the pipeline which are geared toward the development of high-productivity and environmentally sustainable production systems. Continued public and private support for these activities and other development endeavours has to be ensured if we are to attain the much needed increases in food supply in the future.

As profit maximization will become the force that motivates rice production in the coming years, especially amidst more global market integration and rapid urbanization, the once subsistence farms will gradually become much more commercially oriented. The scenario will be one where tiny landholdings will be consolidated into medium- and large-scale farms to gain competitive strength in the international market. Rice science must also address the needs of the next generation of commercial farmers who may wish to use information-intensive precision farming, as currently practiced in developed countries.

Major changes have to take place in both internal and external political and policy commitments to support overall economic growth. Trade liberalization is already a major and complicated step toward further improvement of the food markets and promotion of economic efficiency. Trade liberalization alone will not solve the problem. Along with this is the need for governments to rethink the fundamental approach to policy adjustments, including greater support to the maintenance and development of research and to irrigation infrastructure. Formulation of a strategy for mutual collaboration among Asian countries is needed toward better management of risks resulting from sudden changes in the economic and political environment that are detrimental to food security.

NOTES

1   Yield levels for Japan and South Korea could increase by about 20 per cent more from improved farm management. Proper plant care is not regularly provided primarily because of rising labour and other input costs.

2   For more detailed description of the model, including the specification of equations, refer to Rosegrant, Agcaoili-Sombilla, and Perez (1995). IMPACT has undergone several extensions and modifications from its original version. These are described in Rosegrant *et al.* 1997.

3   In the current version of IMPACT, price and market policies are primarily those that prevail prior to the completion of the GATT negotiations. Likewise, with 1993 for its base year, the baseline assumptions reflect conditions prior to the Asian financial crisis that started only in the middle of 1997. Updating of the base year from 1993 to 1997/98 is underway. Such updating will also include some revisions in the model parameter, such as the growth rate and elasticity parameters.

4   This is unlike the original version of IMPACT, where income and price elasticities of demand are fixed. In the updated version, the demand parameters are adjusted for income growth.

5   In the updated version of IMPACT, the effect of irrigation is incorporated into the area function, through potential increases in cropping intensities and in the yield function, through the addition of a yield differential (between irrigated and non-irrigated crops) that represents the improvement that could be realized with the conversion of farm areas into irrigated ecosystems. The non-price exogenous growth rate assumptions for area and yield as shown in table 4.9 are smaller than those in the original IMPACT version (Rosegrant, Agcaoili-Sombilla, and Perez, 1995 and Rosegrant *et al.,* 1997).

6   For example, the partial opening up of the Japanese market to world trade is incorporated as well as the elimination of subsidies to Eastern Europe and the former Soviet Union. The effect of the exchange rate policy is not included in the current version of the model. This should be considered in future modifications.

REFERENCES

ADB (Asian Development Bank) (1995), 'Key Indicators of Asian and

Pacific Countries', Manila, Philippines.

Badiane, O. (1991), 'Regional Agricultural Market and Development Strategies in West Africa', *Quarterly Journal of International Agriculture*, 30 (1): 37–50.

Bautista, R. (1991), 'Agricultural Growth and Food Imports in Developing Countries: A Reexamination', S. Naya and A. Takayama (eds), *Economic Development in East and Southeast Asia: Essays in Honor of Professor Shinichi Ichimura*, ISAS and East–West Center.

Cassman, K. G. and P. L. Pingali (1995), 'Intensification of Irrigated Rice Systems: Learning from the Past to Meet Future Challenges', *Geojournal*, 35: 299–306.

David, C. C. and K. Otsuka (1994), *Modern Rice Technology and Income Distribution in Asia*, Boulder and London: Lynne Rienner Publishers.

Evenson, R. E. and M. W. Rosegrant (1995), 'Developing Productivity (non-price and area) Projections for Commodity Market Modeling', Paper presented at the final workshop on the Projections and Policy Implications of Medium and Long-term Rice Supply and Demand, 23–26 April Beijing, China.

FAO (Food and Agriculture Organization) (1998), FAO Stat Database, Rome.

Hazell, P. B. and S. Haggblade (1990), 'Rural–urban Growth Linkages in India', Policy, Research and External Affairs Working Papers, World Bank, Washington, DC.

Hossain, M. (1997), 'Rice Supply and Demand in Asia: A Socio-economic and Biophysical Analysis', P. S. Teng *et al.* (eds), *Application of Systems Approaches at the Farm and Regional Levels*, 263–79.

Hossain, M. (1995), 'Rice Production for Sustaining Food Security: Achievements and Emerging Trends for Asia and Bangladesh', Paper presented at a seminar in Dhaka University, July , Bangladesh.

Hossain M. and K. S. Fischer (1995), 'Rice Research for Food Security and Sustainable Agricultural Development in Asia: Achievements and Future Challenges', *GeoJournal*, 35: 286–98.

Huggan, R. (1995), 'Co-evolution of Rice and Humans', *GeoJournal*, 35: 262–65.

Hussain, M. A. and P. Lunven (1997), 'Urbanization and Hunger in the Cities', *Food Nutrition Bulletin*. 9: 50–61.

IMF (International Monetary Fund) (various issues), *World Economic Outlook*, Washington, DC.

IRRI (International Rice Research Institute) (1997a), 'World Rice Statistics, 1993–1994', PO Box 933, Manila, Philippines.

IRRI (International Rice Research Institute) (1997b), 'Rice Almanac',

2nd edn, PO Box 933, Manila, Philippines.

IRRI (International Rice Research Institute) (1997c), 'Sustaining Food Security beyond the Year 2000: A Global Partnership for Rice Research', in Medium-term Plan, 1998–2000, PO Box 933, Manila, Philippines.

Khush, G. S. (1995), 'Modern Varieties – Their Real Contribution to Food Supply and Equity', *GeoJournal*, 35: 275–84.

McGuirk, A. and Y. Mundlak (1991), 'Incentives and Constraints in the Punjab Agriculture', IFPRI Research Report, Washington, DC.

Pingali, P. L., M. Hossain, and R. V. Gerpacio (1997), 'Asian Rice Bowls: The Returning Crisis?', CAB International, Wallingford, Oxon, United Kingdom.

Pingali, P. (1995), 'GATT and Rice: Do We have our Priorities Right?', in 'Fragile Lives in Fragile Ecosystems', Proceedings of the International Rice Conference, 13–17 February, PO Box 933, Manila, Philippines.

Pinstrup-Andersen, P. and R. Pandya-Lorch (1995), 'Intensifying Agriculture and Effectively Managing Natural Resource', Food, Agriculture and Environment Discussion Paper. International Food Policy Research Institute, Washington, DC.

Rosegrant, M. W., M. Agcaoili-Sombilla, R. Gerpacio, and C. Ringer (1997), 'Global Food Markets and US Exports in the 21st Century', Paper presented at the Illinois World Food and Sustainable Agriculture Program Conference on Meeting the Demand for Food in the 21st Century: Challenges and Opportunities for Illinois Agriculture, 28 May, Urbana-Champaign, Illinois.

Rosegrant, M. W., M. C. Agcaoili-Sombilla, and N. Perez (1995), 'Global Food Projections to 2020: Implications for Investment', International Food Policy Research Institute, Washington, DC.

Rosegrant M. W. and M. Svendsen (1993), 'Asian Food Production in the 1990s: Irrigation Investment and Management Policy', *Food Policy*, 20: 203–23.

UN (United Nations) (1997), *World Population Prospects*, 1996 Revision. New York.

World Bank (1997), *World Development Report*, Oxford: Oxford University Press.

5. The implications of the ASEAN free trade area on agricultural trade between Taiwan and the ASEAN

Ching-Cheng Chang, Deng-Shing Huang and Chia-Hsun Wu

1. INTRODUCTION

The Association of Southeast Asian Nations (ASEAN) was established on August 1967 when five countries, Indonesia, Malaysia, the Philippines, Thailand, and Singapore, signed the Bangkok Declaration. Brunei became the sixth member in 1984, followed by Vietnam in 1995, and Cambodia and Laos in 1997.[1] ASEAN has shown outstanding economic performance over the past two decades. Before the currency crisis of July 1997, it was recognized as the fastest-growing region in the world, aside from China and the East Asian newly industrialized economies (NIEs). The ASEAN region is also one of the most important agricultural regions in the world. For many agricultural export commodities, the ASEAN countries have a large share in the world market. With a population of more than 300 million people and high income and population growth, ASEAN also offers a large and growing import market for agricultural products.

During the same period, the economic development of Taiwan has gained high international recognition due to rapid trade expansion in spite of rather unfavourable development in terms of trade. In response to the trade liberalization requests from the US and other major trading countries Taiwan's government has taken several effective actions, such as lowering the tariff rate and removing trade barriers for the importation of foreign agricultural products. If Taiwan is admitted into the World Trade Organization, the nominal tariff rate for agricultural products would be dropped from the base period (1992) level of 20.6 per cent to 12 per cent within the scheduled implementation period. Domestic support would also be reduced by 20 per cent.

The growing interdependence of the world market has made the agricultural sectors in Taiwan and ASEAN increasingly integrated into the world economy. During the 'Uruguay Round' of the GATT (General Agreement of Tariffs and Trade) which was concluded in December 1993, agricultural trade liberalization was one of the key issues. In contrast to former GATT negotiations, developing countries, like ASEAN, played a more active role owing to the fact that their economies still relied to a certain extent on the agricultural sector. As a result, the agricultural policy in Taiwan as well as in the ASEAN countries has entered a phase where more fundamental reforms of market and income support policies are necessary.

One consequence of the Uruguay Round negotiations is that uncertainties surrounding the world trading system multiply. Regionalism achieved renewed support, partly as a bargaining device in the negotiation process and partly as a protectionist counter to progress in the Round (Robertson, 1997). Thus, the treatment of agriculture in a world of trading blocs is very likely to become an important issue.

During the fourth ASEAN summit in Singapore in 1992, the ASEAN Free Trade Area (AFTA) was established, which called for the reduction of tariffs on all manufacturing goods (including processed agricultural products) over a 15-year period under a common effective preferential tariff (CEPT) scheme. Primary agricultural products were excluded owing to food security concerns and the fear of negative distribution effects. Nevertheless, there are also several factors that could lead to closer ties in agricultural trade within the ASEAN region. First, the growing population and per capita income are creating a more diversified demand pattern for agricultural products. On the supply side, rapid economic development will result in major structural changes, paving the way to more specialization in agricultural production in the ASEAN region. Therefore, despite the various obstacles, it is likely that more agricultural products will be included in the future free trade scheme.

Given the importance of agriculture to national output and employment, it is appropriate to examine the implications of regional trade arrangements for the agricultural sector. The purpose of this chapter is to provide the *ex-ante* estimates of the static trade effects of incorporating primary agricultural products into the AFTA among the ASEAN countries and on the exports of Taiwan's agricultural products.

The remainder of this chapter is organized as follows. It will start with an overview of some general characteristics of agricultural trade in Taiwan and the ASEAN countries. Section 3 presents the comparative advantage and intensity in the export markets. Then a description of the quantitative assessment of the prospects for trade effects will follow, and section 5 addresses policy implications.

2. THE ROLE OF AGRICULTURAL TRADE IN TAIWAN AND ASEAN

Unlike Taiwan, agriculture is still a central sector of the ASEAN economies though its importance has been declining in recent years owing to very rapid industrial development. Table 5.1 illustrates the role of agriculture in the economy in terms of its contribution to GDP, trade and the labour force. Here, Brunei is excluded since it has a very limited agricultural basis. For the same reason, Singapore is also relatively unimportant in our discussion. In 1980, with the exception of Singapore, agriculture in ASEAN still had a share of about 20 per cent of total GDP.

Table 5.1 The role of agriculture in ASEAN and Taiwan, 1980—96

		Indonesia	Malaysia	Philippines	Thailand	Singapore	ASEAN total	Taiwan
Share of ag. in GDP (%, at market price)	1980	24.8	22.9^e	25.1	23.2	1.3	20.0	7.7
	1990	19.4	19.0^e	21.9	12.6	0.3	12.0	4.2
	1996	16.3	12.2^e	21.5	10.4	0.2	9.0	3.3
Ag. GDP growth (%,annual, at constant price)^a	1981—90	3.3^d	3.7	0.9	3.5	−6.3	3.5^b	1.8
	1991—96	2.9	2.1	1.8	2.9	4.4$^{(f)}$	2.9^b	0.1
Share of ag. in exports^c (%)	1980	6.8	14.8	34.7	45.8	7.9	31.5	8.6
	1990	11.1	11.5	18.4	28.6	5.1	17.7	4.0
	1996	11.2	8.7	9.9	19.8	3.6	12.6	3.1
Share of ag. in imports^c (%)	1980	12.3	11.5	7.8	4.6	8.2	9.2	8.6
	1990	4.3	6.4	10.2	4.7	5.9	6.2	5.3
	1996	9.9	5.0	15.6	3.6	4.4	6.9	5.2
Share of ag. in labour force (%)	1980	55.0	35.1	48.8	70.1	1.5	57.7	19.3
	1990	54.5	24.7	41.5	62.1	0.4	54.0	12.6
	1996	40.8^e	16.4	38.6	38.1	0.2	39.3	9.9
Growth of ag. labour force (%,annual)^a	1981—90	1.7	−0.3	1.5	1.3	−8.2	1.5^b	−1.8
	1991—96	−3.8	−3.9	1.9	−8.3	−8.2	−3.6^b	−3.4

Notes: ^{a} Geometric mean is used in calculating the average annual growth rate.

^{b} Weighted average with 1990 and 1996 data as weights, respectively.

^{c} Agriculture includes food, live animals, beverage, tobacco, animals, vegetable oil and fats.

^{d} Arithmetic mean is used and the growth rates for 1982—83 and 1987—88 are excluded due to an inconsistent price basis.

^{e} At constant price.

^{f} Geometric average of 1992—1996.

Source: Asian Development Bank, *Key Indicators of Developing Asian and Pacific Countries, 1997* and own calculations.

The decline of its GDP share over the past decades has been very pronounced, in particular in Indonesia, Malaysia, and Thailand. Only the Philippines shows a very modest decrease. Contrary to the Philippines, all the other ASEAN countries have undergone deep structural changes, with the manufacturing sector evolving as the key growth sector. By 1990 the manufacturing sector had replaced agriculture as the leading sector in the economies of all ASEAN countries. However, from the real agricultural GDP growth rates, Indonesia, Malaysia, and Thailand show that the agricultural sector still has considerable growth momentum, even when the decline in agricultural prices accelerated.

Similar to the GDP development, the share of agricultural trade in total trade has been declining during the past two decades. In 1980, agriculture was the major export earner of the ASEAN countries and the share of agriculture in total exports exceeded the corresponding GDP share. Nevertheless, in 1996 agricultural exports still accounted for more than 10 per cent of total exports for Thailand and Indonesia, with Taiwan and Singapore holding a share of 3 per cent. Thailand is the only country where the contribution of agriculture to exports still exceeds the corresponding GDP share. The low agricultural export share of Indonesia over the past decade can be attributed to the dominating role of petroleum exports. Singapore, which has a negligible agricultural production base, derives its rather significant export share from its role as an important part of transshipment.

On the import side, the share of agriculture is less significant and exceeds 10 per cent only in the Philippines. Indonesia and the Philippines are the only two countries where the shares have been increasing in the 1990s. In Indonesia, the import share of agriculture, which is the lowest among the ASEAN countries in the 1960s, went up considerably in the 1980s, a time when Indonesia had to import a large amount of food products. This trend is reversed as a result of the enormous efforts to achieve self-sufficiency in rice and other major food products.

The most significant role of agriculture is certainly its importance in employment and income generation. In Taiwan, the share of the agricultural labour force has dropped from 19.3 per cent in 1980 to below 10 per cent in 1996. However, for ASEAN as a whole, slow but positive growth is observed in the 1980s with more than half of its labour force still working in agriculture in the early 1990s, but this share has been dropping dramatically since then. In Thailand the agricultural labour force even dropped from 62 per cent to 38 per cent with an 8.4 per cent reduction annually during the period 1990–96. A similar situation occurs in Indonesia. Clearly, these shares have been declining in line with the rapid developments observed for GDP and trade in the region.

Table 5.2 summarizes some basic agricultural trade indicators. The absolute value of agricultural trade has been rising in the 1980s and 1990s for both exports and imports, in spite of the declining relative importance of agricultural trade. Again, the only two exceptions occur in the early 1990s, when the Philippines has shown a decrease in agricultural exports and Indonesia in imports in absolute terms. Thailand stands out on the agricultural export side by doubling their agricultural exports in the 1980s. Moving into the 1990s, the upward trend in exports remains in both ASEAN and Taiwan, but import growth has begun to accelerate significantly.

From the agricultural balance of trade, both Taiwan and Singapore are net importers while all other ASEAN countries are net exporters of agricultural products in the 1990s. The Philippines also became a net

Table 5.2 Major agricultural trade indicators of Taiwan and ASEAN [a], 1980—96

		Indonesia	Malaysia	Philippines	Thailand	Singapore	ASEAN Total	Taiwan
Ag. exports (mUS$) [b]	1980	1637 (16.3)	1917 (19.0)	2009 (20.2)	2976 (29.6)	1523 (15.1)	10 062 (100.0)	1708
	1990	2845 (16.7)	3389 (19.9)	1508 (8.9)	6595 (38.7)	2694 (15.8)	17 031 (100.0)	2711
	1996	5573 (18.6)	6768 (22.6)	2032 (6.8)	11050 (36.9)	4499 (15.1)	29 922 (100.0)	3627
Ag. imports (mUS$) [b]	1980	1336 (24.9)	992 (18.6)	644 (12.0)	427 (8.0)	1958 (36.5)	5357 (100.0)	1352
	1990	931 (10.0)	1871 (20.2)	1330 (14.4)	1551 (16.7)	3585 (38.7)	9266 (100.0)	2931
	1996	4253 (22.2)	3915 (20.4)	2702 (14.2)	2589 (13.4)	5723 (29.8)	19 182 (100.0)	5314
Balance of ag. trade (mUS$)	1980	301	925	1288	2549	−435	4705	356
	1990	1914	1518	178	5044	−889	7765	−220
	1996	1320	2853	−670	8461	−1224	10 740	−1687
Overall degree of openness [c]	1980	48.0	57.4	43.4	48.6	369.8	70.3	95.5
	1990	41.5	110.4	47.9	65.6	302.8	88.6	76.0
	1996	41.1	159.6	66.1	69.6	272.5	100.5	79.9
Degree of openness of Ag. trade [d]	1980	16.7	62.5	32.6	106.9	2320.7	40.1	96.2
	1990	17.0	77.7	29.2	75.9	6473.2	53.1	84.2
	1996	26.7	141.9	26.4	71.0	5578.3	60.1	99.6

Notes: [a] Agriculture includes food, live animals, beverage, tobacco, animals, vegetable oil, and fats.
[b] Figures in brackets refers to the share in ASEAN total.
[c] Percentage share of total exports and imports in GDP (in current prices).
[d] Percentage share of agricultural exports and agricultural imports in agricultural GDP (in current prices).

Source: Asian Development Bank, *Key Indicators of Developing Asian and Pacific Countries, 1997* and own calculations.

importer in 1996. In table 5.2, though the degree of openness in ASEAN as a whole is much lower than for the overall economy during the 1980s and 1990s, it is rather high for Singapore, Malaysia, and Thailand in 1996. In Taiwan, the degree of openness in agricultural trade went down during the 1980s, but it jumped back up rapidly in the 1990s. It is much higher than that of overall trade in 1996.

The importance of intra-ASEAN trade within the region and on world agricultural markets can be seen from table 5.3. From the last three columns, the intra-ASEAN trade is 14 per cent of total ASEAN exports to the world during the 1980s and remains at a similar level in the early 1990s. Among ASEAN members, the intra-regional exports for the Philippines and Thailand is not as important as it is for Indonesia, Malaysia and Singapore. Table 5.3 also shows that Taiwan's exports to ASEAN is 9 per cent of its total exports to the world in the 1980s, but rises to 21 per cent in the 1990s. Therefore, the ASEAN region has become increasingly integrated with Taiwan's agricultural export market.

On the import side, the last three rows of table 5.3 suggest that the share of intra-ASEAN trade to total imports has dropped dramatically from 43 per cent to 29 per cent. While Malaysia and Singapore depend heavily on intra-ASAN imports, their relative shares have declined from 52 to 39 per cent and from 67 to 58 per cent, respectively. Indonesia, the Philippines, and Thailand import very limited proportions from their member countries. The share of Taiwan's imports from ASEAN to total imports has also declined from 22 per cent to 16 per cent. Therefore, the dependence on foreign imports is increasing not only for ASEAN but also for Taiwan. This trend is expected to continue following the current import liberalization process.

3.   COMPARATIVE ADVANTAGE AND INTENSITY OF AGRICULTURAL EXPORTS

Before proceeding any further, it will be helpful to explore the feature of agricultural trade between AFTA and Taiwan with less aggregated data. More specifically, we would like to address the following three questions. First, which products within Taiwan's agriculture sector are most likely to be affected by AFTA? Next, are there any export markets that are common to both AFTA and Taiwan? If so, to what extent will the export market be affected?

For the first question, we need to identify the products that can substitute or compete with each other in the export market between Taiwan and ASEAN members. Theoretically, among Taiwan's exports the

Table 5.3 Trade Flow of ASEAN, Taiwan, and Rest of the World: Primary Agricultural Commodities, 1981–83 and 1991–93 Average

Unit: 1000 US dollars; %

From \ To	Indonesia	Malaysia	Philippines	Thailand	Singapore	Taiwan	ASEAN	ROW	Taiwan[b]	ASEAN[b]	ROW[b]
1981–83 Average											
Indonesia	0	17 377	869	9647	327 539	101 054	355 432	2 069 637	4.00%	14.07%	81.93%
Malaysia	1518	0	2728	20 640	460 895	197 224	485 781	2 296 739	6.62%	16.30%	77.08%
Philippines	383	4646	0	314	11 381	21 007	16 725	531 202	3.69%	2.94%	93.37%
Thailand	23 985	111 034	17 599	0	135 241	41 138	287 858	1 794 374	1.94%	13.56%	84.51%
Singapore	7575	180 002	12 288	8956	0	59 286	208 821	1 240 977	3.93%	13.84%	82.23%
Taiwan	5674	17 873	555	2431	48 368	0	74 900	755 860	0.00%	9.02%	90.98%
ASEAN	33 462	313 059	33 483	39 557	935 056	419 710	1 354 617	7 932 930	4.32%	13.95%	81.72%
ROW	595 993	265 533	262 324	198 455	422 713	1 501 521	1 745 019	97 809 556	1.49%	1.73%	96.79%
Taiwan[a]	0.89%	3.00%	0.19%	1.01%	3.44%	0.00%	2.36%	0.71%			
ASEAN[a]	5.27%	52.49%	11.30%	16.45%	66.50%	21.85%	42.67%	7.45%			
ROW[a]	93.84%	44.52%	88.51%	82.54%	30.06%	78.15%	54.97%	91.84%			
1991–93 Average											
Indonesia	0	81 492	6 863	93 813	451 046	53 607	633 215	2 850 497	1.52%	17.90%	80.58%
Malaysia	7 962	0	29 465	67 601	596 762	224 599	701 789	2 507 789	6.54%	20.44%	73.02%
Philippines	2 416	7 548	0	2 424	10 501	13 149	22 888	933 738	1.36%	2.36%	96.28%
Thailand	18 715	137 656	5 865	0	191 514	116 319	353 750	4 077 097	2.56%	7.78%	89.66%
Singapore	5 878	197 618	16 847	32 963	0	86 737	253 307	1 039 479	6.29%	18.36%	75.35%
Taiwan	9 132	20 544	10 219	187 332	203 472	0	430 699	1 587 738	0.00%	21.34%	78.66%
ASEAN	34 970	424 314	59 040	196 801	1 249 823	494 411	1 964 948	11 408 600	3.57%	14.17%	82.27%
ROW	1 112 815	641 970	486 032	1458 774	697 571	2 606 739	4 397 161	124 674 865	1.98%	3.34%	94.68%
Taiwan[a]	0.79%	1.89%	1.84%	10.17%	9.46%	0.00%	6.34%	1.15%			
ASEAN[a]	3.02%	39.04%	10.63%	10.68%	58.11%	15.94%	28.93%	8.29%			
ROW[a]	96.19%	59.07%	87.53%	79.16%	32.43%	84.06%	64.73%	90.56%			

Notes: [a] This row contains percentages of imports from Taiwan, ASEAN members, rest of the world in total world imports.
[b] This column contains percentage of exports to Taiwan, ASEAN members, rest of the world in total world exports.

Source: Calculations based on GTAP 3 Data Base (McDougall, 1997).

Food security in Asia

most likely affected products should be confined to those for which
ASEAN also has a comparative advantage on the world market. In other
words, the AFTA-affected products for Taiwan should be featured in
having a comparative advantage on the world market not only to Taiwan
but also to ASEAN members. It follows immediately with the question:
how to pin down the products for which both Taiwan and ASEAN
members would have a comparative advantage?

In the literature, post-trade observations are often used in an attempt to
approximate comparative advantage, so-called *revealed comparative
advantage* (*RCA*).[2] Beginning with Liesner (1958), there are 'many
varieties of measures of comparative advantage, as addressed in Vollrath
(1991) and Webster (1991). However, according to Ballance, Forstner,
and Murray (1987), these measures do not provide consistent results. In
this chapter, we choose Balassa's (1965) RCA index which is defined as

$$RCA_i^k = (X_i^k / X_i) / (X_w^k / X_w)$$ (5.1)

where X is the value of exports; the superscript K denotes the commodity
group; the two subscripts i and w are, respectively, the exporting country
and the world. The theoretical underpinning of this index can be
understood from writing the formula in alternative form as below

$$RCA_i^k = (X_i^k / X_i) / (X_w^k / X_w)$$
$$= X_i^k /[X_i \cdot (X_w^k / X_w)]$$
$$= X_i^k / E(X_i^k)$$

in which $E(X_i^k)= X_I \cdot (X_w^k / X_w)$ represents country $i's$ expected exports of
good k, in a hypothetical world in which there is no geographical
specialization of international trade. Thus, the index is actually equivalent
to the ratio of actual to expected trade, as defined in Kunimoto (1977).
Thus, a value greater than unity indicates a stronger comparative
advantage for the country in the export of a given commodity.

As for the second question, we will use the trade intensity index to pin
down which goods and which market (for example, the US and/or Japan
to which both AFTA and Taiwan export intensively) indicate the position
of competition. The trade intensity indices of ASEAN as a whole and
Taiwan is calculated according to the following equation (Aggarwal and
Pandey, 1992; Kim and Weston, 1993):

$$I_{ij} = (X_{ij} / X_i) / [M_j / (M_w - M_i)] ,$$ (5.2)

where the country code is denoted by the subscripts. Term I_{ij} denotes the export intensity of country i with country j; X_{ij} is exports of country i to country j; X_i is total exports of country i; M_i is total imports of country i; M_j is total imports of country j; and M_w is total world imports. The trade intensity index can be used to measure the extent to which the share of one country's exports to the other is smaller or larger in relation to the receiving country's share in world imports. An index above unity indicates a greater intensity of trade than expected.

In this and the following sections, the Global Trade Analysis Project (GTAP) Database Version 3 (McDougall, 1997) is used to calculate the revealed comparative advantage and trade intensity indices for exports of primary agricultural commodities. In the GTAP database, primary agricultural commodities are aggregated into eight groups: paddy rice, wheat, other grain products, non-grain crops, wool, other livestock, forestry products, and fishery products. Although the data set is highly aggregated, it provides complete trade flow statistics over the period 1964 −93.[3] It also provides elasticity estimates for our later calculations.

The calculated RCA indices for the exports of each agricultural commodity group for three consecutive periods of 1964−73, 1974−83, and 1984−93 are listed in table 5.4 for the ASEAN country and Taiwan.[4] The results indicate that Taiwan has comparative advantages in exporting rice and fishery products during the 1960s and 1970s, but for rice the magnitude of these advantages is decreasing rapidly over time. In the 1990s, other livestock (pork mainly) has gained advantages over the others and has become one of the main export products beside fishery products.[5] In comparison, most of the ASEAN countries possess comparative advantages in exporting forestry, fishery products and non-grain crops, but the trends are different among these commodity groups. ASEAN has experienced growing comparative advantages in exporting fishery products in the 1990s; while a slightly decreasing but stable trend is observed for the non-grain crops. It appears that the cause of the low level of intra-regional trade may be the presence of a low degree of complementarity in trade and production structures in the region. Nevertheless, some discrepancies exist for individual countries. For example, Thailand's comparative advantage in exporting rice increases sharply during the late 1980s and early 1990s. Indonesia and the Philippines lose their comparative advantages in exporting their forestry products during the 1980s, while Malaysia's advantage in exporting forestry products remains high and persistent well into the 1990s.

Tables 5.5 and 5.6 present, respectively, the calculated results of the trade intensity indices for ASEAN as a whole and for Taiwan during 1991 −93. The relatively higher frequency of more than unity value indicates the stronger trade linkages between the exporting and receiving countries.

Food security in Asia

Table 5.4 The revealed comparative advantage indices of ASEAN and Taiwan for primary agricultural exports, 1973—93 [a]

		Paddy rice	Wheat	Other grains	Non-grain crop	Wool	Other livestock	Forestry	Fishery
Taiwan	1964—73	4.050	0.003	0.015	1.314	0.027	0.536	0.949	3.302
	1974—83	1.062	0.016	0.040	0.698	0.289	1.191	0.635	7.267
	1984—93	0.195	–	0.042	0.462	0.504	1.307	0.093	4.475
Indonesia	1964—73	0.006	–	0.104	1.517	0.003	0.200	1.881	0.299
	1974—83	0.069	–	0.027	1.034	0.003	0.159	5.583	0.809
	1984—93	0.751	–	0.037	1.517	0.001	0.205	0.433	1.300
Malaysia	1964—73	0.035	0.001	0.002	1.323	0.001	0.057	3.755	0.666
	1974—83	0.004	0.006	0.014	1.205	0.013	0.068	5.122	0.498
	1984—93	0.004	0.003	0.002	1.066	0.052	0.429	6.839	0.235
Philippines	1964—73	0.132	–	0.006	0.894	–	0.044	7.670	0.158
	1974—83	0.060	0.031	0.002	1.356	0.001	0.148	3.060	1.218
	1984—93	0.010	0.052	0.016	1.383	0.002	0.133	0.862	1.695
Singapore	1964—73	0.163	0.036	0.043	1.753	0.007	0.415	0.033	0.375
	1974—83	0.058	0.028	0.306	1.766	0.012	0.336	0.146	0.656
	1984—93	0.016	0.014	0.256	1.509	0.015	0.403	0.235	1.158
Thailand	1964—73	3.072	0.002	2.582	1.249	0.003	0.279	0.223	1.152
	1974—83	1.808	0.001	1.579	1.342	0.001	0.204	0.087	1.484
	1984—93	4.334	0.007	0.783	1.250	0.001	0.188	0.073	1.770

Note: [a]Arithmetic means are used in calculating the ten-year average RCA indices.
– No exports.

Source: Calculated from GTAP Database (McDougall, 1997).

For ASEAN as a whole (table 5.5) the values of the export intensity index for almost all agricultural commodity groups are significantly higher in the case of Australia and other Asian countries. The intensities are also rather high for exporting rice to non-EU12 countries and exporting non-grain crops to North and South America. For forestry products the export market is concentrated in Asia, in particular China. The export market for fishery products is more concentrated in India and Australia than it is in the Asian market.

For Taiwan, the results in table 5.6 suggest that the frequency of more than unity is much lower and mainly concentrated in the case of Asian countries in non-grain crops, livestock, and forestry products. In order to identify the possible overlap in export markets in terms of its intensity, the results in tables 5.5 and 5.6 are compared in table 5.7. In table 5.7, the overlap of the export market is not very significant. In the case of fishery products in which both ASEAN and Taiwan possess high comparative advantages, no overlap is suggested. Even though non-grain crops appear to have greater potential for market overlaps, it is not likely to be serious given the large variety of products within this group. These results seem to imply that possible trade diversion caused by AFTA would be limited. Further analysis, such as calculating the export similarity index using less aggregated data, may provide more detailed information.

Table 5.5 The export intensity index of ASEAN, 1991−93 average [a]

	Paddy rice	Wheat	Other grains	Non-grain crop	Wool	Other livestock	Forestry	Fishery
Australia	1.66	18.30	11.32	2.20	8.60	1.56	2.16	3.02
New Zealand	1.30	0	1.42	0.90	0	1.58	2.88	1.56
Japan	0	0	0.04	1.64	0.54	1.30	0.84	0.90
Korea	140.62	1.48	1.28	2.18	4.04	0.46	0.68	0.66
China	0.66	0.02	0.06	3.64	1.54	5.78	4.16	1.58
Taiwan	0	3.02	0.28	1.14	0.02	1.94	2.16	2.02
India	0	1.48	6.70	1.22	1.40	0.84	1.18	4.36
RAS	0.64	0.02	375.28	1.42	0.64	1.42	7.50	1.18
United States	0.52	0	0.04	0.46	0	0.64	0.84	0.80
Argentina	0	0	0	1.64	0	0.08	0	0.02
Brazil	0	0	0	1.38	0	0.08	0	0
Chile	0	0	0	1.38	0	0	0	0.04
RSM	0.04	0.06	0.12	1.04	0	0	0	0.04
EU12	0.84	4.72	0.22	0.68	0.32	0.50	0.58	0.48
EU3	7.28	0	0.04	0.16	0	0.10	0.02	0.32
EFT	2.14	0	0.06	0.10	0.04	0.04	0.86	0.26
CEA	0.54	0	0.02	0.38	0	0.02	0.02	0.08
FSU	0	0	0	0.64	0	0.04	0.04	0.02
MEA	0.70	0.02	0.26	1.00	4.06	0.04	2.40	0.62
SSA	0.90	0.04	0.34	0.90	0	0.62	1.20	0.16

Notes: [a] The regional abbreviations used in this table are as follows:
RAS: Rest of South Asia
CAM: Central America and the Caribbean
RSM: Rest of South America
EU12: European Union 12
EU3: Austria, Finland and Sweden
EFT: Iceland, Norway, Switzerland (EFTA)
CEA: Central European Association
FSU: Former Soviet Union
MEA: Middle East and North Africa
SSA: Sub-Saharan Africa

Source: calculated from GTAP Database (McDougall, 1997).

Food security in Asia

Table 5.6 The export intensity index of Taiwan, 1991–93 average [a]

	Paddy rice	Wheat	Other grains	Non-grain crop	Wool	Other livestock	Forestry	Fishery
Australia	0	0	53.7	0.4	0	1.2	0.5	0.5
New Zealand	0	0	0.4	0.3	0	0.2	0	0.1
Japan	0	0	0	4.5	0.8	5.6	1.5	1.5
Korea	0	0	23.2	1.3	10.8	0.8	0.5	0.4
China	2480.8	0	0.2	6.7	1.7	1.4	5.1	0.8
India	0	0	0	2.4	0.3	13.9	0.1	0
RAS	0	0	0	0.2	0	0.2	1.4	0.3
United States	0.1	0	0.1	0.4	0	0.3	1.4	0.6
CAM	0.1	0	0.1	0.5	0	0.1	0.3	0
RSM	0	0	0	0.4	0	0.5	0	0
EU12	1.2	0	0.1	0.1	0.1	0.2	0	0.1
MEA	1.8	0	0	0	0	0	0.1	0.2

Note: [a] The region abbreviations used in this table are as follow:
   RAS: Rest of South Asia
   CAM: Central America and the Caribbean
   ASM: Rest of South America
   EU12: European Union 12;
   MEA: Middle East and North Africa

Source: calculated from GTAP Database (McDougall, 1997).

*Table 5.7 Overlap of trade intensity indices between ASEAN and Taiwan,
   1991–93 average*

	Paddy rice	Wheat	Other grains	Non-grain crop	Wool	Other livestock	Forestry	Fishery
Australia			**			*		
Japan				*		*		
Korea			*	*	*			
China				*	*	*	*	
India				*				
Rest of S. Asia							*	

Note: * The indices of ASEAN and Taiwan are both between 1.0 and 2.0.
      ** The indices of ASEAN and Taiwan are both greater than 2.0.

Source: Based on the calculated results in table 5.3 and table 5.4.

4. IMPACTS OF AFTA AND ITS MEASUREMENT PROBLEMS

A commonly asked question about regional economic integration, including a free trade area, customs union, economic union, etc., is how the member and non-member countries are affected. Studies on the effects of economic integration can be dated back to Viner (1950) in his classic article 'The Customs Union Issue'. As is well documented in the literature, the impacts can be grouped into two categories: static effects and dynamic effects. The dynamic effects as addressed by Krenin (1964) refer to the long-term impacts of growth and are subject to unsolvable difficulties of measurement as discussed in Mayes (1988). Thus, we focus on the static effects, initially raised by Viner (1950), including trade creation (TC) and trade diversion (TD).

There are two approaches to measuring TC and TD, namely the partial equilibrium approach and general equilibrium approach. In the literature, estimating static effects usually proceeds, first, by using pre-integration data to estimate the price elasticity of imports and then calculating the changes in relative prices, arising from a decline in trade barrier, to estimate the direct price effect of integration of TC and TD. For example, Houthakker and Magee (1969) estimate the following logarithmic import function in prices and incomes

$$\ln M_t = a + b\ln RP_t + c\ln Y_t + e_t,$$

where M_t denotes imports in period t, and RP_t denotes the relative price of imports to domestic products and Y_t denotes a measure of income; a, b, and c are parameters and e is an unobservable residual. The direct price effect of integration can then be estimated by multiplying the estimated price elasticity of b by the estimated price change owing to integration (Krenin, 1973; Mayes, 1978).[6]

Another frequently adopted approach includes the computable general equilibrium model and other large models. However, these models (for example, Deppler and Ripley, 1978; Llewellyn, Potter, and Samuelson, 1985, or the COMET model of Barten, D'alcantra, and Cairn, 1976), as discussed in Mayes (1988, p. 45), usually face the problems of (a) the size of the model required and (b) the constancy of parameters over time. Because of the limitation of data sources, we adopt the partial equilibrium approach as in Verdoorn (1960) and Verdoorn and Schwartz (1972). Although this approach does not provide a complete analysis of TC and TD, it does provide some indication of the welfare effects of AFTA and a closer look at product groups, where each is likely to be significant.

In this chapter, the *ex-ante* effect is calculated basically following Verdoorn's (1960) partial equilibrium approach, which requires an import demand elasticity and an elasticity of substitution between member and non-member countries for each commodity group. There are several assumptions behind the approach: (1) imports from a member country are imperfect substitutes for imports from other non-member countries; (2) imports from both member and non-member countries are imperfect substitutes for domestic production; (3) the trade effects of tariff reductions do not have any repercussions on income and exchange rates; and (4) the exports have an infinite elastic supply, such that the whole effect of any tariff change has been passed on to prices.

Assume that there are n import varieties of the product X under consideration. Each variety corresponds to one trade partner. Consider a constant elasticity of substitution (CES) type of utility function as follows

$$U = \left(\sum_{j=1}^{n} X_{j}^{\alpha} \right)^{\frac{1}{\alpha}}, \qquad (5.3)$$

where U denotes the utility function; X_j is the consumption of the product imported from country j; and α is a parameter, $0 < \alpha < 1$, reflecting a positive and decreasing marginal utility of each variety imported. The elasticity of substitution (ε) between any two imported varieties is a constant and

$$\varepsilon = \frac{1}{(1-\alpha)} \qquad (5.4)$$

Thus, the corresponding import demand can be derived from the following utility maximization framework

$$\underset{(X_j)}{Max} \left(\sum_{j=1}^{n} X_{j}^{\alpha} \right)^{\frac{1}{\alpha}} \qquad (5.5)$$

$$s.\, t.\ \sum_{i}^{n} P_{j} X_{j} = E \qquad (5.6)$$

where P_j is the domestic price of variety j and E is the total expenditure on the product imported. Taking the natural logarithm and using the Lagrangian method, the import demand for the jth variety, X_j, can be derived as follows

$$X_j = \frac{E \cdot P_j^{-\varepsilon}}{\displaystyle\sum_j^n P_j^{1-\varepsilon}} \qquad (5.7)$$

Assuming the changes in tariffs are fully reflected in the import prices, the trade creation effect (TC_a) is

$$TC_a = \left[\varepsilon + (1-\varepsilon)Sa\right]M_a\left[\frac{\Delta ta}{1+ta}\right], \qquad (5.8)$$

where subscript a denotes the importing country; t_a is the initial level of tariff in the importing country; Δta is the reduction in tariff by preferential trading agreement; and $Sa = Pa^{1-\varepsilon} / \sum P_i^{1-\varepsilon}$. Equation $Pa^{1-\varepsilon} / P_i^{1-\varepsilon}$, which by equation (5.7) equals $PaXa/E$, is the share of imports from country a.

As shown in equation (5.8), trade creation (TC_a) is derived by multiplying the total imports from member countries (M_a) with the product of a share-adjusted substitution elasticity term and the percentage change in price induced by the tariff changes owing to regional integration.

The trade diversion effect (TD_a) is presented in equation (5.9) as follows

$$TDa = \left[(\varepsilon - 1)Sa\right] \cdot Mo \cdot \left[-\frac{\Delta ta}{1+ta}\right] \qquad (5.9)$$

It is calculated by multiplying the total non-member imports (M_o) with a share-adjusted elasticity of substitution term and the percentage change in price induced by the tariff changes.

The trade effects are estimated using the 1993 data in the GTAP Database. The elasticity of substitution between domestic and imported products for rice, wheat, other grain, non-grain crops and wool is 2.2. It is 2.8 for other livestock, forestry, and fishery products.[7] The initial level of the tariff for each commodity is calculated by dividing the differences

Food security in Asia

between the world price and domestic market price with the domestic market price. Since the estimates of the tariff equivalent quota and other non-tariff barriers are not available for the ASEAN countries, it is assumed that the prevalence of all non-tariff barriers would also be removed to the extent that permits tariff-induced trade expansion to take place.

The calculated results of the *ex-ante* trade effects of the AFTA with the 100 per cent tariff cut for primary agricultural commodities are summarized in table 5.8. For ASEAN as a whole, the free trade agreement

Table 5.8 Trade effects of AFTA on primary agricultural commodities

(unit: 1000 US dollars)

	Indonesia	Malaysia	Philippines	Thailand	ASEAN-4 total	Singapore	ASEAN-5 total
I. Trade creation							
Paddy rice	4	–	–	–	4	369	373
Wheat	–	42	–	361	403	661	1064
Other grains	1650	14 097	23	285	16 055	2246	18 301
Non-grain crop	17 060	172 643	20 666	15 640	226 009	383 191	609 200
Wool	–	2	–	91	93	3	96
Other livestock	275	6805	242	2512	9834	162 386	172 220
Forestry	19	380	375	3798	4572	731	5303
Fishery	344	16 586	881	9585	27 396	59 465	86 861
Total [a]	19 352 (58%)	210 555 (43%)	22 187 (39%)	32 272 (18%)	284 366	609 052 (50%)	893 418
II. Trade Diversion							
Paddy rice	−395	–	–	–	−395	−7	−402
Wheat	–	−111 823	–	−7824	−119 647	−560	−120 207
Other grains	−8	−1110	−215	−4	−1337	−166	−1503
Non-grain crop	−2813	−2231	−2306	−1537	−8887	−5961	−14 848
Wool	−139	−241	–	−4392	−4771	−23	−4795
Other livestock	−1028	−34	−3348	−709	−5119	−639	−5758
Forestry	−5	−0	−31	−419	−455	−1	−456
Fishery	−24	−513	−267	−64	−868	−2132	−3000
Total [b]	−4412 (0%)	−115 952 (16%)	−6167 (1%)	−14 949 (1%)	−141 480	−9489 (1%)	−150 969
TOTAL	14 940	94 603	16 020	17 323	142 886	599 563	742 449

Notes: [a] Numbers in parentheses are percentages in total imports from member countries.
   [b] Numbers in parentheses are percentages in total imports from non-member countries.
   − no trade.

Source: calculated from GTAP Database (McDougall, 1997).

is estimated to yield trade creation amounting to US$893 million and trade diversion amounting to US$151 million. These results indicate that adding primary agricultural products to AFTA would lead to positive net trade creation for all the ASEAN countries, since the trade creation effects outweigh the trade diversion effects. The corresponding US$742 net trade gains in primary agricultural commodities range from US$15 million for Indonesia, Philippines, and Thailand to nearly US$600 million for Singapore. Because of superior port facilities and the free trade policy regime, much of the trade of Singapore with other ASEAN countries is of an entrepôt nature. Therefore, adding trade with Singapore may significantly overestimate the value of intra-ASEAN trade. In table 5.8, when Singapore is excluded, the trade creation of the ASEAN-4 falls to US$284 million, while net trade creation drops to US$143 million. Despite limited trade among ASEAN members, the AFTA is likely to be a welfare-improving arrangement for the agricultural sector through increasing trade flows between its member countries.

For producers in different commodity groups, the implications of AFTA vary. While the free trade agreement generates positive trade effects for non-grain crops and fishery products, products like rice and wheat suffer a negative impact. Nevertheless, the substantial consumer surplus resulting from a tariff cut in agricultural commodities provides many implications for the policy makers. It is likely that consumers in this region would benefit from a decline in food prices, which may help to increase food consumption and reduce poverty in rural areas.

5. CONCLUDING REMARKS

This chapter discussed the current trade situation in the ASEAN region and the potential trade benefits arising out of a free trade agreement on primary agricultural commodities. Using the GTAP database, the export intensity and comparative advantage for ASEAN as well as Taiwan are compared. The results suggest that the ASEAN countries have experienced growing comparative advantages in exporting fishery products in the 1990s; while a slightly decreasing but stable trend is observed for non-grain crops. Taiwan's comparative advantages in exporting livestock and fishery products are decreasing rapidly. The results on the export intensity index indicate that ASEAN's export market is concentrated in Asia and Australia. The overlap of export markets between Taiwan and ASEAN is not very significant.

Using a partial equilibrium static trade model, the *ex-ante* estimates of the potential impacts of AFTA on agricultural trade are computed. The estimates provide the magnitudes of trade creation and trade diversion effects for each of the ASEAN countries and for each commodity group. The results suggest that a free trade scheme could create a net trade creation effect, that is, increases in trade flows between ASEAN countries on agricultural commodities. Therefore, the growing trend of Taiwan's agricultural exports to the ASEAN is likely to be affected by this regional free trade arrangement. Although the current level of intra-regional trade in agricultural products is low in the region, there exists considerable potential for increasing the level of such trade flows. On the other hand, if one of the goals of AFTA is to diversify imports away from the other countries, then an enhanced preferential trading arrangement might accomplish this goal to a certain extent.

Although up until now AFTA has had little impact on primary agricultural trade in the ASEAN region, the results of the study show that intra-regional trade will expand sharply if it is liberalized. Nevertheless, the nature of trade in agricultural goods is changing quickly over time (Josling, Tangermann, and Warley, 1996, chapter 9). As trade in differentiated products, such as fruits and vegetables, is now becoming much more important to world trade, the relevance of natural endowments in determining the export comparative advantages decreases. The growing mobility of technology, management, and marketing skills is also making it possible to transform primary food products for world markets. Not only should the countries in the region seriously consider expanded regional cooperation, more efforts have to be made to expand the trading relationship with other Asian Pacific countries for agricultural commodities.

NOTES

[1] Like Brunei, Vietnam, Cambodia, and Laos are not incorporated into the following empirical analysis due to data limitations.

[2] Using trade data to reveal whether a country has a comparative advantage in certain goods is to some extent misleading, for the trade figures are surely distorted by regulation, protection purported policies, such as tariff, quota or even strategic export restriction. For example, beginning in the early 1990s, Indonesia has prohibited the export of wood in an attempt to develop wood-processing and related down-stream manufacturing sectors. As a result, any calculation derived from post-trade data will indicate a downturn of its comparative advantage in its wood export, despite the fact that the export prohibition policy has nothing to do with its resource endowment and technology. Consequently, the extent and intensity of competitiveness/

complementarity could be higher than shown by the results of this chapter.

[3] The Asian financial crisis and large currency depreciation in Indonesia and Thailand have disrupted the upward trend in agricultural trade in the region. However, according to the reports from USDA (1998) and OECD (1998), they appear to have had little overall effect on either total domestic livestock inventories or feed gain import demand throughout most of the region. The prospect for a return to pre-crisis growth trade levels varies by country. Although there exists considerable uncertainty regarding the strength and timing of the economic recovery, the effects of these downturn effects on agricultural trade are expected to be temporary.

[4] The RCA indices cannot capture the potential 'future' comparative advantages since they are based on actual trade data. However, the RCA results over time can show the general direction to which the pattern of comparative advantages is moving.

[5] The outbreak of foot-and-mouth disease in March 1997 led to a ban on Taiwan's pork export. Although the disease has been under controlled, the pork production in Taiwan is expected to remain at the self-sufficient level. Therefore, its comparative advantage will no longer be revealed by trade statistics.

[6] Furthermore, Verdoon and Schwartz (1972) apply a more complex RP term to allow for substitution between imports from partners and non-members as well as substitution between imports and domestic products.

[7] The GTAP assumes that for each commodity, all countries or regions display the same substitution elasticities between domestic products and imports. The source of these substitution elasticities are taken from the SALTER model (Jomini *et al*, 1991) which is based on preferred estimates from the econometric literature with some upward adjustment (McDougall, 1997).

REFERENCES

Aggarwal, M. R. and P. R. Pandey (1992), 'Prospects of Trade Expansion in the SAARC Region', *The Developing Economies*, 30(1): 3–23.

Asian Development Bank (1997), *Key Indicators of Developing Asian and Pacific Countries*, Manila.

Balassa, B. (1965), 'Trade Liberalization and Revealed Comparative Advantage', *Manchester School of Economic and Social Studies*, 33(2): 99–123.

Ballance, R., H. Forstner, and T. Murray (1985), 'On Measuring Comparative Advantage: A Note on Bowen's Indices', *Weltwirtschaftliches Archiv*, 121(2): 346–50.

Ballance, R., H. Forstner, and T. Murray (1987), 'Consistency Test of Alternative Measures of Comparative Advantage M', *The Review of*

Economics and Statistics, 69(1): 157–61.

Barten, A.P., G. D'alcantra, and G. J. Cairn (1976), 'COMET: A Medium-term Macroeconomic Model for the European Economic Community', *European Economic Review*, 7(1): 63–115.

Bowen, H. P. (1983), 'On the Theoretical Interpretation of Indices of Trade Intensity and Revealed Comparative Advantage', *Weltwirtschaftliches Archiv*, 119(3): 464–72.

Deppler, M. C. and D. M. Ripley (1978), 'The World Trade Model: Merchandise Trade', *International Monetary Fund Staff Papers*, 25(1): 147–206.

Houthakker, H. S. and S. P. Magee (1969), 'Income and Price Elasticities in World Trade', *Review of Economics and Statistics*, 51(2): 111–25.

Jomini, P., J. F. Zeitsch, R. McDougall, A. Welsh, S. Brown, J. Hambley, and J. Kelly (1991), *SALTER: A General Equilibrium Model of the World Economy, Vol 1. Model Structure, Database, and Parameters*, Canberra, Australia: Industry Commission.

Josling, T. E., S. Tangermann, and T. K. Warley (1996), *Agriculture in the GATT*, New York: St. Martin's Press.

Kim, K. S. and A. Weston (1993), 'A North American Free Trade Agreement and East Asian Developing Countries', *ASEAN Economic Bulletin*, 9(3): 287–300.

Krenin, M. (1964), 'On the Dynamic Effects of a Customs Union', *Journal of Political Economy*, 72(2): 193–95.

Krenin, M. E. (1973), 'The Static Effects of EEC Enlargement on Trade Flows', *Southern Economic Journal*, 39(4): 559–68.

Kunimoto, K. (1977), 'Typology of Trade Intensity Indices', *Hitotsubashi Journal of Economics*, 17: 15–32.

Llewellyn, J., S. Potter, and L. Samuelson (1985), *Economic Forecasting and Policy: The International Dimension*, London; Boston: Routledge Kegan Paul.

Liesner, H. H. (1958), 'The European Common Market and British Industry', *The Economic Journal*, 68: 302–16

Mayes, D. G. (1978), 'The Effects of Economic Integration on Trade', *Journal of Common Market Studies*, 17(1): 1–25.

Mayes, D. G. (1988), 'The Problems of the Quantitative Estimation of Integration Effects', in El Agraa (ed), *International Economic Integration*, 2nd edition, Hong Kong: The Macmillan Press.

McDougall, R. A. (1997), *Global Trade Assistance and Protection: The GTAP 3 Data Base*, West Lafayette: Center for Global Trade Analysis, Purdue University.

OECD (1998), *The Economic and Policy Aspects of Livestock Versus Feed Grain Imports in Selected Asian Countries.*

http://www.oecd/agr/publications/index1.htm.

Robertson, D. (1997), 'East Asian Trade and the New World Trade Order', in D. Robertson (ed.), *East Asian Trade After the Uruguay Round*, Cambridge: Cambridge University Press, 1–20.

USDA (1998), 'Financial Crisis Dents Certain Asian Livestock and Feed Sectors: Trade Impact Marginal', International Agricultural Trade Report, 18 August.

Verdoorn, P. J. (1960), 'The Intra-Bloc Trade of Benelux', in E. A. G. Robinson (ed.), *The Economic Consequences of the Size of Nations*, New York: Macmillan, 291–329.

Verdoorn, P. J. and A. N. R. Schwartz (1972), 'Two Alternative Estimates of the Effects of EEC and EFTA on the Pattern of Trade', *European Economic Review*, 3(3): 291–335.

Viner, J. (1950), *The Customs Union Issue*, New York: Carnegie Endowment for International Peace Press.

Vollrath, T. I. (1991), 'A Theoretical Evaluation of Alternative Trade Intensity Measures of Revealed Comparative Advantage', *Weltwirtschaftliches Archiv*, 127(2): 265–80.

Webster, A. (1991), 'Some Issues in the Measurement of Comparative Advantage', *Applied Economics*, 23(5): 937–48.

6. Assessment of demand-side factors affecting global food security

Wen S. Chern

1. INTRODUCTION

The objectives of this chapter are to present the estimated income elasticities of food, particularly of grain and meat, in China and Japan using the almost ideal demand system (AIDS), to show the sensitivity of these estimates, and to discuss the implications of these demand parameters for global food security. The importance of providing reliable estimates of income elasticity lies in its essential role in projecting the future long-term demand for grains and the conflicting econometric results obtained in the literature. China and Japan are two large countries in Asia and the world in terms of population, economy, and current and potential agricultural trade; yet, they are in different stages of economic development. Hence, these two countries offer interesting comparisons in their food demand structures and food security concerns. Particularly, their future food supply/demand balances will most definitely affect global agricultural trade and food security. By the same token, the global food security will also directly impact the food security concerns in these two countries.

This chapter is organized as follows. The issues on global food security and declining self-sufficiency in food are addressed in the following section. The importance of dealing with the uncertainties in demand projection, the questions about whether grain, particularly rice, is an inferior good and the relative magnitudes of income elasticities between grain and meat will be discussed next. The performance of the linear approximate AIDS (LA/AIDS) and the original AIDS model will be compared. The econometric results obtained using the household data from China and Japan are then presented. The chapter will be ended with a discussion of the implications of these econometric results for projecting future food demand, and concluding remarks.

2. FOOD SECURITY ISSUES

What are the prospects for long-term food security in the world? Can the world feed itself? By most accounts, long-term food security is achievable despite the fact that presently 800 million people do not have adequate food and 185 million children are malnourished (Pinstrup-Andersen, 1996). The recent Vision 2020 Project conducted by the International Food Policy Research Institute (IFPRI) called for strengthening agricultural investment, particularly in developing countries, and expanding international development assistance to alleviate the malnutrition problem in the world (Pinstrup-Andersen, 1996; Rosegrant, Agcaoili-Sombilla, and Perez, 1995). Mitchell, Ingco, and Duncan (1997) show from their simulation result one of the most optimistic views by far that the world can feed twice as many in 20 years. These optimistic assessments have driven many analysts to predict a declining trend of future of food prices. Tweeten (1998) is somewhat more pessimistic about the future of food prices. His analysis concludes that, during the next several decades (up to 2050), the growth in global food demand may exceed growth in yield, causing food prices to rise. Under his scenario, higher food prices may be needed in order to draw additional land and other conventional resources into agricultural production for meeting the global food supply/demand balance.

Besides these moderately optimistic assessments, there is the distinctly pessimistic view expressed by Brown (1994) in his projection of the future grain import demand of China. He claims that China would need to import more than 230 million tons of grains in 2030 and that all the grain-exporting countries combined would not be able to satisfy this demand. Therefore, grain prices will skyrocket. Most analysts including those cited above tend to dismiss Brown's pessimistic assessment. Overall, the consensus is that the global long-term food problem is likely to be a disparity problem caused by income inequality between the rich and the poor; it will not be a problem caused by either the growing food demand or the stagnation of food production.

If the world can feed itself, as the logic goes, then individual countries should not have to worry about food availability. Unfortunately, the matter is not so simple. For low-income countries, the problem is the lack of income or more specifically foreign currencies to import food. Other countries, like those in Asia with high income, limited arable land and high labour cost, have growing concerns about the declining self-sufficiency in food, particularly grain (Chern, 1998). As projected by IFPRI, Asia as a whole will be the dominant net importer of meats, and its net cereal import requirement will continue to surpass Africa by 2020

(Rosegrant, Agcaoili-Sombilla, and Perez, 1995).

Whether or not self-sufficiency in food should be a national security concern is a controversial topic. As pointed out by Sicular (1989), food security and particularly self-sufficiency in rice have been the policy goals for many Asian countries in their formulation of food price policies. However, these goals are often in conflict with other policy objectives of maintaining low food prices and high farm income. There was and still is a complex political economy of food policy in most Asian countries. For countries with the ability to import food, agricultural trade has undoubtedly contributed to lowering food prices and raising the standard of living. However, there is a risk associated with large dependency on the foreign supply of food.

Perhaps, the recent currency crisis in Indonesia is a very good example. As Indonesian rupiah devaluated from 2800 rupiahs to 1 US dollar in March 1997 to 8600 rupiahs on 24 March 1998 (*Wall Street Journal*, 26 March 1998), the price of imported food increased threefold. The panic buying of food in Indonesia that occurred during the currency crisis must be viewed as the vulnerability of any country highly dependent upon foreign imports of food. Despite the abundance of the world's food supply, the collapse of a country's currency value can bring about a crisis in food security similar to what happened in Indonesia. It is therefore reasonable to be concerned about food security, particularly for food-importing countries.

3.   DEMAND-SIDE FACTORS

For assessing the long-term food balances globally or regionally, the point of debate often rests on the supply side rather than the demand side. The most pervasive reason for this disparity is twofold. First, many analysts and policy makers view the growing food demand as an inevitable but beneficial result of economic development and, thus, tend to adopt the prescription that all we have to do to solve the food problem is to increase yield and production. Secondly, analysts tend to think that there is little, if any, uncertainty about food demand projection because income elasticity can be easily assumed, and projections of income and population are often accessible. A recent study by Fan and Sombilla (1996) reviewing various projections of grain supply/demand balance in China confirmed this assertion. They found that there were more disagreements on supply than demand projections.

Chern (1997b) pointed out several uncertainties often ignored in food demand projections for China. First, the historical data on the consumption of meats can not be validated, casting doubts on the econometric estimates of demand elasticities and various baseline consumption figures used for future projection. Furthermore, the conflicting evidence on the relative magnitudes of the estimated income elasticities for grain versus meats was obtained from various econometric models. There are also methodological issues for estimating food demand in China. For Chinese rural households, a large proportion of food is supplied from their own production, making it difficult to observe and estimate their consumption behaviour. For Chinese urban households, grain and edible oil were under rationing nationwide for a long period of time up to 1993. Therefore, the demand elasticities can not be estimated in the conventional demand system without considering the effects of food rationing. This study represents a follow-up investigation of the earlier paper by Chern (1997b), addressing these same issues but also providing some answers.

4. THE PUZZLE OF INCOME ELASTICITY

The aggregate deficit or surplus in cereals or grains in a country, region or the world are common measures of food security. The definition of cereals used by the Food and Agriculture Organization (FAO) includes maize, wheat, rice, millet, and other coarse grains. Since the term 'cereals' covers both their direct use as food and indirect use as feed, it is more convenient to use the term 'grain' in this study for distinguishing food grain from feed grain. In China, the official definition of 'grain' includes wheat, rice, coarse grains, potatoes, and soybeans. In this study, we define food grain to include mostly wheat and rice, and feed grain to include mostly coarse grains, such as corn. Note that the empirical portion of the study deals with only the demand for grain for direct consumption by humans.[1]

Food prices and weather conditions are the most important factors affecting the short-term fluctuation of the food demand/supply balance in a country, region, or the world (Pacific Economic Cooperation Council, 1997). For projecting food security in the long run, population, income elasticity, and yield projections are the key determinants (Tweeten, 1998). Income is of course a demand-side variable. It is often overlooked that the income elasticity of aggregate grain demand is actually not directly attainable from consumer demand even though it has been so estimated. Consumers only reveal their income elasticities for food grain and animal products, such as meats and poultry. Their demand for meats and poultry will then generate the derived demand for various feed grains. In computing the impacts of changes in income on the demand for feed grain, one needs to know the meat–feed conversion factors that vary greatly depending upon products and regions.

For assessing the future aggregate demand for cereals in a country or globally, analysts often have to adopt or assume composite income elasticity for all grains (food and feed). For example, for his global assessment of cereal demand, Tweeten (1998) adopted the income elasticities for all cereals to be 0.6 for low-income countries, 0.3 for middle-income countries, and 0.1 for high-income countries for 1994, based on the estimates obtained by Mellor (1996). Tweeten further assumed that these elasticities would change to 0.5, 0.2, and 0.05 respectively for 2050 in his scenario analysis. In assessing the growing grain deficit in China, Perkins (1992) adopted an income elasticity of 0.5 estimated for Taiwan by Peng (1992). These income elasticities seem to be 'reasonable' because they produce explainable and seemingly acceptable projections. But they can not be rigorously validated.

For a more credible projection of grain demand, it is necessary to distinguish the grains used for food versus those used for feed. Therefore, at the consumer level, we need to estimate income elasticities for food grains as well as for those foods produced with feed mainly meats, poultry, and eggs.

Based on the economics literature, the following two basic issues related to income elasticity remain unresolved:

1. whether or not grain is an inferior good?
2. whether or not meat and poultry should always have higher income elasticity than grain?

The reminder of this paper is devoted to analysing these two questions.

4.1   Is Grain an Inferior Good?

Numerous studies have found negative income elasticities for food grain, an indication of grain being an inferior good. Rice is the most important staple grain in Asia. Using aggregate time series data, Ito, Peterson, and Grant (1989) found that the income elasticities for rice demand are all negative in Japan, Malaysia, Nepal, Singapore, Thailand, Taiwan, and Bangladesh. Furthermore, the elasticities are positive but very small (less than 0.14) in India, South Korea, Sri Lanka, Burma, China, Indonesia, and the Philippines. Kanai, Sawada, and Sawada (1993) reviewed many studies estimating food demand in Japan and found, in most cases, that rice or cereals are inferior goods in Japan. For China, Lewis and Andrews (1989), Wu, Li, and Samuel (1995), and Gao, Wales, and Cramer (1996) also obtained a negative income elasticity for grain demand by urban households.

If grain is indeed an inferior good in so many countries, particularly those populous ones like Japan and China, we should not have to worry about the shortage of food grain in the future. But is it really so? Huang and Bouis (1996) argued that most estimated income elasticities from aggregate time series data tend to reflect simply the correlation between declining per capita grain consumption and increasing per capita income, not a true demand relationship. They pointed out the real cause for the declining per capita consumption of grain is the rural−urban migration, not the negative income elasticity. Over the last 2−3 decades, rapid urbanization has occurred in many countries. Tables 6.1 and 6.2 show such examples in Japan and China. In Japan, urbanization occurred most rapidly during the 1950s and 1960s. After 1980, urbanization seemed to slow down substantially in Japan. In China, urbanization did not take off until the late 1970s when it began economic reforms. Since 1980, population migration from rural to urban areas has been very steady. As documented in Huang and Bouis (1996) and Chern (1997b), Chinese urban households consumed much more meat and poultry but much less grain than rural households. Therefore, an increasing proportion of urban population would certainly affect the aggregate per capita consumption of grain in China and elsewhere.

Table 6.1 Population and urbanization in Japan

Year	Total population (millions)	per cent of urban population
1950	83.2	37.5
1955	89.3	56.3
1960	93.4	63.5
1965	98.3	68.1
1970	103.7	72.2
1975	111.9	75.9
1980	117.1	76.2
1985	121.0	76.7
1990	123.6	77.4
1994	125.0	

Source: Statistics Bureau, *Japan Statistical Yearbook 1996*, Management and Coordination Agency, Japan, 1996.

Table 6.2 Population and urbanization in China

Year	Total population (millions)	per cent of urban population
1955	614.6	13.48
1960	662.1	19.75
1965	725.4	17.98
1970	829.9	17.38
1975	924.2	17.34
1980	987.1	19.39
1985	1058.5	23.71
1990	1143.3	26.41
1991	1158.2	26.37
1992	1171.7	27.63
1993	1186.2	28.14
1994	1198.5	28.62
1995	1211.2	29.04
1996	1223.9	29.37

Source: State Statistical Bureau, *China Population Statistics Yearbook 1995*, Beijing, China, 1995.

If grain is an inferior good, then we should observe a tendency for grain consumption to be negatively associated with the household income level at any given point in time. Historical data do not provide much evidence of this negative association. Table 6.3 compares per capita rice consumption by income level in Japan for 1986, 1990, and 1995. The data clearly indicate that higher-income households consume more rice has a given year. It is true that the per capita consumption of rice has been declining over time, from 150 kg in 1986 to 105 kg in 1995. However, this declining trend may have been caused by the urbanization mentioned earlier and/or other demographic factors, such as the aging population, changing labour force structure (particularly the increasing employment in the service sector), and the increasing westernization of the Japanese diet. Based on these data (table 6.3), it is difficult to rationalize that rice has become an inferior good in Japan.

The comparisons of per capita consumption of grain by income level (approximated by the total living expenditure) shown in tables 6.4—6.6 also indicate very similar relationships in China. High-income households in both urban and rural areas generally consumed larger amounts of grain

Food security in Asia

Table 6.3 Comparison of per household rice consumption by income level in Japan

Unit: kg/household/year

Year	Income level [a]					Mean
	I	II	III	IV	V	
1986	141.13	139.16	146.68	164.09	163.73	150.96
1990	110.98	111.38	124.74	133.91	137.17	123.64
1995	92.19	96.38	99.94	115.09	119.10	104.54

Notes: [a] Category I denotes the lowest income group and V the highest income group.

Source: Statistics Bureau, 'Annual Report on the Family Income and Expenditure Survey 1995', Management and Coordination Agency, Government of Japan,1996.

Table 6.4 Comparison of per capita grain consumption of urban households by income level in China

Unit: kg/Person/Year

Year	Income level [a]							Mean
	I	II	III	VI	V	VI	VII	
1992	109.2	110.5	107.7	109.0	110.2	116.2	130.1	111.5
1993	93.7	97.2	96.8	98.2	98.2	102.8	105.0	97.8
1994	100.2	100.1	102.3	101.9	101.9	104.7	106.4	101.7
1995	93.1	98.9	96.2	97.1	97.1	98.9	103.6	97
1996	95.6	94.6	93.3	95.7	95.7	94.4	98.7	94.7

Notes: [a] Category I denotes the lowest income group and VII the highest income group. The distributions of households among these groups are I (10 per cent), II (10 per cent), III (20 per cent), VI (20 per cent), V (20 per cent), VI (10 per cent), and VII (10 per cent).

Source: Unpublished data obtained from State Statistical Bureau, Beijing, China, 1997.

Table 6.5 Comparison of per capita food consumption of rural households by total living expenditure per capita, China, 1992

Unit: kg/person/Year

Item	> 100 Yuan	100– 150	150– 200	200– 250	250– 300	300– 400	400– 500	500– 600	600– 700	<700 Yuan
				Income level						
Grain	105.7	155.2	159.7	192.5	209.1	230.3	252.3	269.3	277.9	284.8
Meats	1.99	3.58	4.19	5.02	6.37	8.22	10.34	12.35	14.17	17.76

Source: State Statistical Bureau, *China Rural Household Survey Yearbook 1992*, Beijing, China, 1993.

Table 6.6 Comparison of per capita food consumption of rural households by total living expenditure per household, Jiangsu Province, China, 1994

Unit: kg/Person/Year

Item	>3500 Yuan	3501–5000	5001–7000	7001–12 000	<12 001
			Income Level		
Grain	239.0	264.5	272.0	261.6	276.5
Pork	6.00	7.53	10.1	11.96	18.15

Source: Computed directly from the 1994 Rural Household Survey data base in Jiangsu Province, provided by the State Statistical Bureau, 1997.

than those of low-income households. Even though there has been a declining trend in per capita grain consumption over time (table 6.4), it may have been caused by increasing diversification of the Chinese diet (substitution effects) and other demographic changes. Again, these data provide no credible bases to speculate that grain has become an inferior good in China.

It should be noted, however, the use of household expenditure survey data may also bias the estimate of income elasticities for food staples as shown by Bouis and Haddad (1992) and Bouis (1994). In this case, the income elasticity is biased upward. They pointed out that the food expenditure survey data overstate the effect of income in many developing countries because, among other things, high-income households tend to serve more meals to non-household members, resulting in an overestimation of per capita food expenditure. For low-income households, there is an underestimation of food eaten outside the household, resulting in an underestimation of per capita food expenditure. We have no evidence that this pattern of food consumption also occurred in China. This phenomenon is definitely not prevalent in Japan.

4.2 Grain versus Meat

Historical experience has shown that as income increases, people would substitute animal products for grain products. Therefore, the demand for grain will decrease while the demand for meats and poultry will rise. When Brown (1994) made his prediction for future grain imports in China, he assumed that China would follow the pattern of meat consumption observed in Taiwan, Japan, and Korea. An implicit assumption in his assessment is that the income elasticities in meats and poultry should be very high in China. It seems indisputable that the income elasticity in meat demand should be high or, at least, higher than the elasticity for grain.

Recent consumption trends in China and Japan, however, did not vertify this assertion about the income effect on meat demand. Consider first the recent trends observed in China. Chern (1998, 1997a) has documented that the per capita total meat consumption by rural households decreased in 1993–95, and, furthermore, the per capita consumption of pork in 1995 was smaller than that during 1989–92. In short, these survey results show several counter-intuitive trends in Chinese meat consumption. In fact, there are two puzzles in recent household survey data for China. First, it is not obvious why meat consumption did not increase as household income in urban and rural areas continued to increase in recent years. Secondly, why did grain consumption not decline much despite the skyrocketing rise in grain prices for urban households in recent years? Note that grain prices have increased at much higher rates (more than 20 per cent per year during 1992–95) than household income.

In Japan, the survey data also show that per household consumption of pork and poultry has been decreasing while that of beef has been increasing during the 1980s and 1990s (Statistics Bureau, 1995). For total meat consumption in Japan, the trend has been declining. Specifically, per household consumption of total fresh meat in Japan has remained about 44 kg during 1990–95. With both meat and rice exhibiting a declining consumption trend in Japan, the puzzle is whether or not the income elasticity of meat should always be higher than rice in Japan.

Given that both price and income affect demand,. it is not straightforward to sort out their separate effects by examining the historical trends when both factors were undergoing drastic changes. Econometricians would let the model speak for itself regarding the relative impacts of prices and income. However, the problem arises when different models yield different sets of estimates, drawing different implications for the future food demand outlook. Consider the following example. Chern (1997a) used Chinese urban household survey data at the provincial level from 1992 to 1995 to fit two demand systems. The linear-approximate almost ideal demand system (LA/AIDS) produced the estimates of expenditure elasticity of 1.30 for grain, 0.46 for pork, and 0.10 for poultry while, with exactly the same set of data, the linear expenditure system (LES) yielded estimates of 0.15, 1.28, and 2.37, respectively. The contrasts between these two models are striking. Note that these are expenditure elasticities. But the relative magnitudes between grain and meats will remain unchanged when these expenditure elasticities are converted to income elasticities.[2] The LES was justified on the basis of his earlier study showing similar results between LES and the quadratic expenditure system (QES). LES was used in this comparison simply because it converged more quickly.

The results obtained from the LA/AIDS are disturbing because it is difficult to accept that the expenditure (and thus income) elasticity for grain could be so much higher than for meat. As noted by Chern (1997a), it is not implausible for a set of data to be represented equally well by more than one demand system. Furthermore, given the recent dramatic increases in grain prices in China and the substantial magnitude of the estimated price elasticity of −0.43, it requires a very high expenditure elasticity to rationalize the relatively constant grain consumption trend observed in recent years. But the truth of the matter is that an income elasticity of 0.15 versus 1.30 would produce dramatically different projections for future grain demand in China, especially under the assumption of no dramatic changes in grain prices. The following econometric analysis is intended to deal with these puzzles related to the observed food consumption patterns and the expected income effects in Japan and China.

5. ECONOMETRIC ANALYSIS

One key motivation for this econometric analysis is the repeated experiences with the LA/AIDS model showing higher expenditure elasticity for grain than for meat in China, using recent household survey data (Chen, 1996; Chern, 1997a; Chern, 1997b). Wu, Li, and Samuel (1995), using 1990 urban household survey data, also obtained relatively high expenditure elasticity of 0.98 for rice as compared to 1.17 for pork. It is essential to emphasize the significance of using the data from recent years due to the particular characteristics of the grain market in China. National grain rationing was imposed for Chinese urban households until May 1993. With grain rationing in place, the demand relationship for grain was not directly revealed by the consumption decisions made by urban households. Income could hardly play any significant role in affecting the consumption of grain during the earlier years of economic reforms in the 1980s and earlier 1990s. Therefore, it would not be surprising to obtain low or even negative expenditure (income) elasticities in the studies using data from the 1980s and earlier 1990s (Wang and Chern, 1992; Chern and Wang 1994).

With respect to rural demand for grain, it is important to note that rural households supplied almost 100 per cent of the grain they consumed. The grain market was tightly controlled by procurement and contractual arrangements for most of the 1980s and earlier 1990s (Zhou, 1997). When farmers could not be actively involved in the grain market, their adjustments in grain consumption would be affected more by weather conditions than by changes in prices or income. Therefore, one may not be surprised to obtain low expenditure elasticities for grain when they are estimated using data from the 1980s and earlier 1990s (Fan, Cramer, and Wailes, 1994; Halbrendt, *et al.*, 1994; and Fan, Wailes, and Cramer, 1995). More recently Gao, Wailes, and Cramer (1996), using 1990 rural household survey data from Jiangsu Province, obtained an estimate of expenditure elasticity of 0.52 for grain which is lower than 1.15 for pork and 0.78 for beef, but higher than 0.29 for poultry. Since they used a mixture of a quadratic expansion of AIDS and generalized LES in a two-stage budgeting framework, it is not clear whether the low expenditure elasticity for grain could be credited to the use of AIDS in the mixed model. In any case, their low expenditure elasticity for poultry may raise some concerns if it is used for projecting the future demand for feed grain in China.

5.1   The Model

This study attempts to examine the validity of the estimates obtained from the LA/AIDS model, one of the most widely applied and extensively examined demand systems in the literature. For estimating a LA/AIDS model, researchers typically used the Stone index for the approximation, following the suggestion by Deaton and Muellbauer (1980). Green and Alston (1990) were perhaps the first to suggest various ways to compute the price elasticities. Later, Buse (1994) showed that the seemingly unrelated regression (SUR) estimator for LA/AIDS is inconsistent, but a consistent estimator cannot be constructed. He also showed that, based on a Monte Carlo investigation, the elasticities suggested by Green and Alston are no better than the conventional elasticity formula. Although the focus of our study is on income elasticity, not price elasticity, our experiment with various elasticity formulas reveals only minor differences. With respect to the Stone index, Moschini (1995) showed that this index is not invariant to changes in the unit of measurement and thus its use may seriously affect the approximation properties of the model. He suggested it would be more desirable to use other indexes such as Tornqvist index or the log-linear analogue of the Paasche index. In fact, we have found that these indexes produced more plausible results than the Stone index. However, these findings are not reported here. Hahn (1994) investigated the theoretical property of the LA/AIDS and concluded that the approximation violated the symmetry condition. He suggested that if we wish to use AIDS, we should use the original model, not its linear approximations. Of course, historically the popularity of using the LA/AIDS has been primarily due to the difficulty in estimating the highly non-linear AIDS. With advancements in computation, the AIDS can be more easily converged, as is witnessed in this study.

As recognized, income elasticity can be best estimated with cross-sectional data. Therefore, in this study, we use either purely cross-sectional or pooled cross-sectional and time-series data. Specifically, the food demand systems are estimated for both rural and urban households in China and for households in Japan. The coverage of these models and data are detailed in table 6.7.[3]

The econometric procedure is more complex to estimate the model for rural households in Jiangsu Province, China than the other two models. First, data from 976 households were used for estimation. Since many households had zero consumption in various foods, especially beef and mutton, and poultry, we have to deal with the censored regression problem. We adopt the two-stage procedure used by Heien and Wessells (1990) with one important modification. In the first stage, we estimate a Probit model and compute the Mills' ratios for six food items having a significant number of households with zero consumption. However, in the second stage, we include these Mills' ratios in all the budget share equations, not just the respective share equations as specified by Heien and Wessells. During the course of this study, many extreme observations were detected in this database. Several scholars from Jiangsu Province helped us identify the specific causes for these extreme consumption figures. They include various situations such as households with brewing activities (for very large grain consumption figures), possibly being

Food security in Asia

Table 6.7 Food items and data used in estimation

Country	household	Year/ Data	Food items[a]
China	Rural	1994 976 Households in Jiangsu Province	(1) grain, (2) oil, (3) vegetables, (4) bean products, (5) pork, (6) beef and mutton, (7) poultry, (8) eggs, (9) aquatic products, (10) fruits
China	Urban	1993–96 30 Provinces (120 observations)	(1) grain, (2) vegetable oil, (3) pork, (4) poultry, (5) aquatic products, (6) eggs, (7) vegetables, (8) fruits
Japan	All	1986–95 10 age groups (100 observations)	(1) rice, (2) fish, (3) meat, (4) vegetables, (5) fruits

Note: [a] Numbers correspond to the subscripts in eq. (6.1).

watermelon producers (for very large fruit consumption figures) or special festivities of weddings or funerals (for very large consumption of aquatic products, meats, and poultry). In addition, some extremely small consumption figures in the database remain unexplained. We do not discard these observations but use various dummy variables to account for these abnormalities. Finally, in order to account for variations across households, several demographic variables are included in the model.

The AIDS model for rural households in China can be expressed as

$$w_i = \alpha_i + \sum_j \gamma_{ij} P_j + \beta_i \log (X / P)$$

$$and \quad \log P = \alpha_0 + \sum_k \alpha_k \log P_k + 1/2 \sum_j \sum_k \gamma_{kj} \log P_k \log P_j$$

$$(6.1)$$

where P_i is price and w_i budget share. For LA/AIDS, log P was replaced by the Stone index. The linear translation is used to incorporate Mills' ratios and other demographic and dummy variables

$$\alpha_i = \alpha_i {}^* + \sum_j d_{i,j} D_j + \sum_k \sigma_{i,k} M_k$$

where all these variables are defined in table 6.8. In estimating the model for urban households in China, we encounter a severe problem in convergence. As a result, several food items with a small budget share (beef and mutton, other meats, milk and milk products) are excluded from the model. Also, no demographic variables are included in the urban model because of the degrees of freedom problem. The use of provincial level data tends to reduce the need to include demographic variables.

The model for Japan includes only five food groups because of the limited degrees of freedom. Three demographic variables are incorporated into the model through demographic translation

$$\alpha_i = \alpha_i * + d_{i,1} D_1 + d_{i,2} D_2 + d_{i,3} D_3$$

These demographic variables are defined in table 6.9.

5.2 Regression Results

The models are estimated by the non-linear iterative SUR in SAS. The theoretical restrictions of homogeneity and symmetry are imposed in the estimation. The adding-up restriction is automatically satisfied since the dependent variables are in share form. However, due to the singularity condition, one equation has to be dropped from the SUR estimation. Since the AIDS is highly non-linear, it often can not converge with the default initial values of parameters. In this case, the estimated parameters obtained from the LA/AIDS are used as initial values except for α_0, which is not estimated in the LA/AIDS. For α_0, either the default value or the minimum total expenditure from the sample is used as the initial value in estimation.

The regression results for both AIDS and LA/AIDS are presented in Appendix tables 6.A, 6.B, and 6.C for China-rural households, China-urban households, and Japan, respectively. In the China-Rural model, nine equations with 244 parameters are estimated. R^2 values in the LA/AIDS range from 0.12 for beef and mutton to 0.62 for vegetables. Given that these are household data, R^2 values tend to be low. The goodness of fit for the China-urban model is similar to that of the rural model. The R^2s are much higher for the Japan model, ranging from 0.65 for rice to 0.95 for meat. Notice that in all three cases, the AIDS model produces vastly different coefficient estimates from the LA/AIDS model. It is more appropriate to compare the estimated elasticities than the coefficients.

Table 6.8 Definitions of Mills' ratios, demographic and dummy variables
included in the rural model, Jiangsu, China, 1994

Variable	Parameter	Description
D_1	$d_{i,1}$	Number of persons in household
D_2	$d_{i,2}$	Proportion of family members aged under 12
D_3	$d_{i,3}$	Proportion of family members aged between 12 and 17
D_4	$d_{i,4}$	Dummy variable for the highest level of the labour force in each household (elementary school or lower)
D_5	$d_{i,5}$	Dummy variable for the highest level of the labour force in each household (middle school)
D_6	$d_{i,6}$	Ratio of the amount of food away from home to total food expenditure
D_7	$d_{i,7}$	Dummy variable for wine-brewing households
D_8	$d_{i,8}$	Dummy variable for extremely large consumption of oil
D_9	$d_{i,9}$	Dummy variable for extremely large consumption of vegetables
D_{10}	$d_{i,10}$	Dummy variable for extremely low consumption of vegetables
D_{11}	$d_{i,11}$	Dummy variable for extremely large price of poultry
D_{12}	$d_{i,12}$	Dummy variable for extremely large consumption of aquatic products
D_{13}	$d_{i,13}$	Dummy variable for extremely large consumption of fruits
D_{14}	$d_{i,14}$	Dummy variable for the counties in southern province
M_1	$\sigma_{i,1}$	Mills' ratio for oil
M_2	$\sigma_{i,2}$	Mills' ratio for bean products
M_3	$\sigma_{i,3}$	Mills' ratio for beef and mutton
M_4	$\sigma_{i,4}$	Mills' ratio for poultry
M_5	$\sigma_{i,5}$	Mills' ratio for eggs
M_6	$\sigma_{i,6}$	Mills' ratio for fruits

Table 6.9 Demographic variables, Japan

Variable	Parameter	Description
D_1	$d_{i,1}$	Household size
D_2	$d_{i,2}$	Age of household head
D_3	$d_{i,3}$	Time trend

Table 6.10 Estimated expenditure and own-price elasticities for rural households, Jiangsu Province, China, 1994 [a]

Food	Budget share	LA/AIDS Expenditure	Own-price	AIDS Expenditure	Own-price
Grain	0.443	1.214	−0.673	0.729	−0.368
Oil	0.071	0.469	−0.574	0.782	−0.580
Vegetables	0.167	1.251	−0.541	0.822	−0.481
Bean products	0.013	0.767	−0.680	0.892	−0.682
Pork	0.108	0.415	−0.632	1.536	−0.657
Beef and mutton	0.008	0.268	−0.365	1.479	−0.376
Poultry	0.035	0.789	−0.484	1.586	−0.499
Eggs	0.051	0.520	−0.900	0.925	−0.912
Aquatic products	0.061	0.632	−0.224	2.163	−0.349
Fruits	0.045	1.596	−0.912	1.406	−0.940

Note: [a] All elasticities were computed at sample means.

Table 6.10 presents expenditure and own-price elasticities estimated at sample means from the China-Rural model. In computing the price elasticities for the AIDS, the sample means of Mills' ratios and demographic variables are used, while the extreme consumption dummy variables are set to zero. The focus of our comparison is on grain and meats (pork, beef and mutton, and poultry). Dramatic differences between the two models are observed for the estimated expenditure elasticities. As mentioned before, the LA/AIDS model produces an expenditure elasticity for grain (1.214), which is much higher than those for pork (0.415), beef and mutton (0.268), and poultry (0.789). Surprisingly, the AIDS model reverses the order, giving much higher expenditure elasticities for meats than grain, as normally expected. In addition, the AIDS model shows that the main staple foods of grain, oil, vegetables, and bean products all have lower expenditure elasticities than non-staple foods. These results are

Food security in Asia

consistent with our usual expectation. With respect to price elasticities, both models produce very similar estimates for all foods except grain, having a smaller own-price elasticity in absolute value in the AIDS model. As one can see, the differences between the linear approximate and original AIDS models are dramatic and the original model appears to be much more plausible.

Table 6.11 compares the estimated elasticities obtained from the China-urban model. The LA/AIDS specification results in many unreasonable estimates of expenditure elasticities, including very large magnitudes for grain and oil, and negative values for poultry and aquatic products. The use of AIDS removes all those peculiarities, reducing the expenditure elasticity to only 0.115 for grain, and changing the signs and magnitudes of the elasticities for poultry and aquatic products. Under the AIDS model, the demands for pork and poultry have much stronger income effects than grain, as expected. Again, the AIDS model appears to produce far more plausible results than the LA/AIDS model for estimating food demand elasticities for urban households in China.

Unlike those found in the China-rural and China-urban models, the estimated expenditure elasticities for food demand in Japan are very similar between LA/AIDS and AIDS (table 6.12). Surprisingly, rice has the highest expenditure elasticity. Furthermore, fish and meat have higher expenditure elasticities than fruits and vegetables. Despite the similarities in the estimated expenditure elasticities, the LA/AIDS yields all own-

Table 6.11 Estimated expenditure and own-price elasticities for urban households, China, 1993–96 [a]

Food	Budget share	LA/AIDS Expenditure	LA/AIDS Own-price	AIDS Expenditure	AIDS Own-price
Grain	0.239	1.879	−0.578	0.115	−0.155
Vegetable oil	0.064	1.785	−0.454	0.377	−0.409
Pork	0.186	0.294	−2.073	1.691	−1.586
Poultry	0.068	−1.187	−1.394	3.142	−1.283
Aquatic products	0.095	−0.575	−0.272	3.434	−0.667
Eggs	0.067	1.761	−1.752	0.549	−1.808
Vegetables	0.178	1.389	−0.671	0.200	−0.428
Fruits	0.103	1.476	−1.046	0.207	−0.875

Note: [a] All elasticities were computed at sample means.

Table 6.12 Estimated expenditure and own-price elasticities, Japan, 1986–95 [a]

Food	Budget share	LA/AIDS		AIDS	
		Expenditure	Own-price	Expenditure	Own-price
Rice	0.182	1.369	−0.999	1.308	−0.140
Fish	0.216	1.078	−0.999	1.067	−0.232
Meat	0.229	0.975	−1.000	1.022	−0.710
Vegetables	0.236	0.790	−0.999	0.802	−0.326
Fruits	0.137	0.788	−0.999	0.790	−0.417

Note: [a] All elasticities were computed at sample means.

price elasticities close to unity for all food groups. This result is peculiar and it is apparently caused by the very small magnitudes of the estimated price coefficients ($\gamma_{ij}s$ in Appendix table 6.C). Note that Japanese data are based on cell averages by age group, computed from household data. The sample size is relatively small. This may be one of the problems in estimating food demand parameters for Japanese households. Overall, the AIDS model appears to perform much better than LA/AIDS for estimating the food demand structure in Japan.

6.   INCOME ELASTICITIES IN CHINA AND JAPAN

As mentioned previously, expenditure elasticities estimated from different demand systems cannot be compared if they covered different sets of foods. These expenditure elasticities need to be converted to income elasticities (that is, the elasticities defined with respect to total living expenditures) for comparison and use in projecting future demand for food in general, and grain in particular. The most appropriate procedure would be to estimate the first-stage demand system, including the aggregate of the foods included in the food system (as the second stage) along with other foods and non-food items of living expenditures. Due to data limitation, this procedure was not attempted in this study. Instead, the income elasticity of aggregate food demand was estimated by an Engel function and it is used to derive the income elasticity from expenditure elasticity.

Specifically, the Engel functions for food are estimated for Chinese rural and urban households as well as Japanese households. The

Food security in Asia

expenditure of the foods included in the model is regressed on the total living expenditure. For rural households in China, the dummy variables for nine of ten counties in the Jiangsu Province are included in the Engel function. The yearly dummy variables are included in the Engel function for urban households. For Japan, the Engel function also includes four age dummy variables. Four functional forms based on log-log, semi-log, Working-Leser, and quadratic specifications are used. The estimated income elasticities for aggregate food expenditure are presented in table 6.13. For rural households in China, all functional forms yield very similar elasticities of income for aggregate food. Similar results are also obtained for urban households. However, the estimated income elasticities for aggregate food are much higher in the urban model (near unity) than in the rural model (around 0.4). Although these differences appear to be counter-intuitive, they may reflect the fact that urban households have to purchase all their food while those in rural areas produce most of the food they consume. Therefore, the propensity to consume food would be higher for urban residents in China as their income increases. On the other hand, rural households have a lower propensity to consume food because many of the foods are produced by themselves and additional income would not be required to purchase them. Thus, there would be a stronger propensity to consume non-food goods when their income rises.

The income elasticities for aggregate food vary more notably among functional forms estimated for Japan. The log-log, Working-Leser, and quadratic forms yield much lower elasticities (0.38, 0.37, and 0.40, respectively) than the semi-log form (0.897).

Table 6.13 Estimated income elasticity for total food expenditure included in the model [a]

	China		
Model	Rural	Urban	Japan
Log-log	0.408	0.990	0.381
Semi-log	0.435	1.082	0.897
Working-Leser	0.439	0.993	0.365
Quadratic	0.412	1.031	0.397

Note: [a] All elasticities were computed at sample means.

Since the Working-Leser form has better theoretical properties, it is used to convert the expenditure elasticities obtained from the AIDS and LA/AIDS models to income elasticities for individual food items (table 6.14). For food grain, the estimated income elasticities from the AIDS model are 0.32 for rural households and 0.114 for urban households in China. For comparison, the LA/AIDS model produces much higher income elasticities for food grain in China, especially for urban households (1.866). Furthermore, based on the AIDS model, animal products of pork, beef and mutton, and poultry all have higher income elasticities than grain in China, especially for urban households.

Table 6.14 Estimated income elasticities by food items, China and Japan[a]

| Food | China | | | | Japan | |
| | Rural | | Urban | | | |
	LA/AIDS	AIDS	LA/AIDS	AIDS	LA/AIDS	AIDS
Grain or rice	0.533	0.320	1.866	0.114	0.500	0.477
Oil	0.206	0.343	1.773	0.377		
Meat					0.356	0.373
Pork	0.182	0.674	0.292	1.679		
Beef and mutton	0.118	0.649				
Poultry	0.346	0.696	−1.179	3.120		
Eggs	0.288	0.406	1.749	0.545		
Fish or aquatic products	0.277	0.950	−0.571	3.410	0.393	0.389
Vegetables	0.549	0.361	1.379	0.199	0.288	0.292
Fruits	0.701	0.617	1.466	0.206	0.287	0.288

Note: [a] Based on the aggregate income elasticities obtained from the Working-Leser form presented in table 6.13. Blanks indicate that the elasticities were not estimated in the model.

For Japan, the estimated income elasticities for individual food items are very similar between the two models. Rice has slightly higher income elasticity than meat. Can this be acceptable? Furthermore, is it reasonable to have a higher income elasticity for rice in Japan than for grain in China? In assessing these elasticity estimates, we must realize that rice is a very important staple food in Japan. But it is not a cheap staple. Rice has been very expensive in Japan. In 1995, the average price of one kg of non-glutinous rice was 496 Yen compared to 1,572 Yen/kg for fresh meat and 906 Yen/kg for poultry. Many Japanese feel that they can not afford to buy Koshihikari rice, the best kind in Japan which is expensive and often in short supply. In comparison, grain is much cheaper than meat in China. For example, in 1996, grain was priced at only 2.87 Yuan/Kg for urban households, compared to 12.56 Yuan/Kg for pork, 14.09 Yuan for beef, and 15.28 Yuan for live chicken. Even though China has a lower income elasticity for grain than Japan, the grains such as rice consumed by Chinese were of much lower quality than those consumed by Japanese. There is no indication that the quality of grain in China will ever reach the level currently consumed by the Japanese. With respect to the demand for quality, it is not simply a matter of income, but, more importantly it is a matter of taste and preference.

7. DISCUSSION

This study obtains several important findings. First, it is found that neither grain nor rice is an inferior good. More interestingly, the income elasticity for high-quality rice in Japan is larger than the income elasticities for grain in both urban and rural areas in China. Thus, higher household income would induce higher demand for high-quality rice in Japan. This result should not contradict the declining trend for per capita consumption of rice observed in Japan. Notice that the model constructed in this study covered only the high-quality rice used for at-home consumption. The uses of lower-quality rice by manufacturers and the food service sector and those for non-food purposes may continue to decline in the future. More importantly, other factors, such as urbanization and westernization of the Japanese diet, may cause the overall per capita consumption of rice to decline in the future. But the pure income effect on rice demand is positive and highly elastic. In projecting the future demand for rice in Japan, income effect alone would not yield a definite declining trend. Of course, given the current economic downturn in Japan, household income may stagnate for many years to come. In this case, the effects of income on rice demand would not be of any significant magnitude despite its large income elasticity. Other factors related to taste and preference may be more important predictors of Japanese rice demand in the long run. They are reserved for further investigation.

   Our second important finding is that the income elasticity for meat does not always have to be greater than that for grain. In Japan, both elasticities are high and the elasticity for meat is slightly lower that that for rice. In China, however, pork, beef, and poultry all have much higher income elasticities than grain, as generally expected. Since household income is expected to rise at a much higher rate in China than in Japan, income will play a much more significant role in determining the future demand for grain in China. The estimated income elasticities for grain and meats suggest that as Chinese household income continues to increase, the demands for grain and meats will have a positive growth but with a higher rate of increase for meats than grain.

The third major finding is that Chinese rural households have a larger income elasticity for grain but much lower income elasticities for pork, beef and mutton, and poultry than urban households. These structural differences in food demand would make the migration from rural to urban areas the most important predictor of future food demand in China. As China's household income increases, the aggregate per capita consumption of grain may or may not decline, depending on how rapidly urbanization takes place in the future.

8. CONCLUSIONS

This study shows that the LA/AIDS model is inferior to the AIDS model for fitting the food consumption data in China and Japan. The estimated elasticities obtained from the AIDS are more consistent with our prior expectation of higher income elasticities for animal products than for grain in China. Despite the popularity of the LA/AIDS, our econometric results appear to echo the suggestion by Hahn (1994), 'If you wish to estimate the AIDS, estimate it, not one of its linear approximations.' The comparative results presented in this paper are based on the version of LA/AIDS using the Stone index. The alternative indexes, suggested by Moschini (1995), might produce more plausible results similar to those from the original AIDS. The performance of these alternative indexes needs further investigation, especially when there is severe convergence problem for the AIDS, as encountered in running the China-urban model.

Our estimation results indicate that grain in China and rice in Japan are not inferior goods. Higher income will result in a higher demand for food grain in these two countries. However, other demographic factors, such as urbanization in China and westernization of the Japanese diet, are likely to play important roles in shaping the future demand for grain in these countries. For projecting the long-term demand for grain, these additional demographic factors need to be carefully assessed.

In China, meats and poultry have higher income elasticities than grain for both rural and urban households. Furthermore, the elasticities for meats and poultry are all higher for urban than for rural households. Therefore, as China become further urbanized in the future, the aggregate demands for meats and poultry will rapidly increase. How will these

consumer demands for animal products be translated into the demand for
feed grain requires an additional modelling scheme about the meat-feed
conversion. This study only provides useful estimates of income
elasticities for these two important countries. Similar estimations would
be required for other countries in Asia and elsewhere before we can fully
understand the impacts of these demand factors on global food security.

NOTES

[1] The demand for feed grain may be derived from the demand for animal or
aquatic products that use feeds for their production. However, in this study, the
demand for feed grain is not derived explicitly.

[2] In a complete food demand system, the expenditure elasticity is defined with
respect to the sum of expenditures of only those foods included in the model.
These expenditure elasticities need to be converted to income elasticities (that is
with respect to total living expenditures) for comparison.

[3] Even though all data used in this study are based on household expenditure
surveys in China and Japan, only the rural model for China is estimated with
household-level data. For the urban model in China and the model for Japan, the
data are cell averages by provinces and by age group, respectively. Both Chinese
rural and urban household surveys were conducted by the State Statistical
Bureau (SSB) while the surveys in Japan were conducted by its Management
and Coordination Agency.

REFERENCES

Bouis, H. and L. Haddad (1992), 'Are Estimates of Calorie-Income
Elasticities Too High?: A Recalibration of the Plausible Range',
Journal of Development Economics, 39: 333–64.
Bouis, H. (1994), 'The Effect of Income on Demand for Food in Poor
Countries: Are Our Food Consumption Databases Giving Us Reliable
Estimates?', *Journal of Development Economics*, 44: 199–226.
Brown, Lester R. (1994), 'Who Will Feed China?', *World Watch*,
September/October.
Buse, Adolf (1994), 'Evaluating the Linearized Almost Ideal Demand
System', *American Journal of Agricultural Economics*, 76 (November):
781–93.
Chen, Jing (1996), 'Food Consumption and Projection of Agricultural
Demand/Supply Balance for 1996–2005 in China', Unpublished
Master Thesis, Department of Agricultural Economics, The Ohio State

University.

Chern, Wen S. (1998), 'Food Security in Asia: A Demand Side Analysis', in H. Horiuchi and K. Tsubota (ed) *The 4th JIRCAS International Symposium: Sustainable Agricultural Development Compatible with Environmental Conservation in Asia*, Japan International Research Center for Agricultural Sciences, Tsukuba, Japan, March.

Chern, Wen S. (1997a), 'Projecting Food Demand and Agricultural Trade in China', *Asia Pacific Journal of Economics and Business*, 1(July): 53–67.

Chern, Wen S. (199b), 'Estimated Elasticities of Chinese Grain Demand: Review, Assessment and New Evidence', A Report to the World Bank, Institute of Economics, Academia Sinica, Taipei, Taiwan, 31 January.

Chern, Wen S. and Guijing Wang (1994), 'Engel Function and Complete Food Demand System for Chinese Urban Households', *China Economic Review*, 5(Spring): 35–57.

Deaton, A. and J. Muellbauer (1980), 'An Almost Ideal Demand System', *American Economic Review*, 70: 312–26.

Fan, Shenggen and Mercedita Sombilla (1996), 'Why Projections on China's Future Food Supply and Demand Differ?' International Symposium on 'Food and Agriculture in China: Perspectives and Policies', Beijing, China, 7–9 October.

Fan, Shenggen, Gail Cramer, and Eric Wailes (1994), 'Food Demand in Rural Mainland China: Evidence from Rural Household Survey', *Agricultural Economics*, 11; 61–9.

Fan, Shenggen, Eric J. Wailes and Gail L. Cramer (1995), 'Household Demand in Rural China: A Two-Stage LES-AIDS Model', *American Journal of Agricultural Economics*, 77 (February): 54–62.

Gao, X. M., Eric J. Wailes, and Gail L. Cramer (1996), 'Partial Rationing and Chinese Urban Household Food Demand Analysis', *Journal of Comparative Economics*, 22: 43–62.

Gao, X. M., Eric J. Wailes, and Gail L. Cramer (1996), 'A Two-Stage Rural Household Demand Analysis:Microdata Evidence from Jiangsu Province, China', *American Journal of Agricultural Economics*, 78 (August): 604–13.

Green, Richard and Julian M. Alston (1990), 'Elasticities in AIDS Models', *American Journal of Agricultural Economics*, 72 (May): 442–5.

Hahn, William F. (1994), 'Elasticities in AIDS Models: Comment', *American Journal of Agricultural Economics*, 76 (November): 972–7.

Halbrendt, Catherine, Francis Tuan, Conrado Gempesaw and Dimphna Dolk-Etz (1994), 'Rural Chinese Food Consumption', *American Journal of Agricultural Economics*,76 (November):794–9.

Food security in Asia

Heien, Dale and Cathay Roheim Wessells (1990), 'Demand Systems Estimation With Microdata: A Censored Regression Approach', *Journal of Business & Economic Statistics*,8 (July): 365–71.

Huang, Jikun and Howarth Bouis (1996), 'Structural Changes in the Demand for Food in Asia', International Food Policy Research Institute, Washington, DC, March.

Huang, Jikun, Scott Rozelle, and Mark W. Rosegrant (1995), 'China's Food Economy to the 21st Century: Supply, Demand, and Trade', International Food Policy Research Institute Discussion Paper, Washington, DC.

Ito, Shoichi, E. Wesley F. Peterson, and Warren R. Grant (1989), 'Rice in Asia: Is It Becoming an Inferior Good?' *American Journal of Agricultural Economics*, 71(February): 32–42.

Kanai, Michio, Yutaka Sawada, and Manabu Sawada (1993), 'Japanese Consumer Demand', in Luther Tweeten, Cynthia L. Dishon, Wen S. Chern, Naraomi Imamura, and Masaru Morishima (eds), *Japanese & American Agriculture: Tradition and Progress in Conflict*, Boulder, CO: Westview Press.

Lewis, Philip and Neil Andrews (1989), 'Household Demand in China', *Applied Economics*, 21: 793–807.

Mellor, John (1996), *The Economics of Agricultural Development*, Ithaca, NY: Cornell University Press.

Mitchell, Donald O., Merlinda D. Ingco, and Ronald C. Duncan (1997), *The World Food Outlook*, Cambridge: Cambridge University Press.

Moschini, Giancarlo (1995), 'Units of Measurement and the Stone Index in Demand System Estimation', *American Journal of Agricultural Economics*, 77 (February): 63–7.

Pacific Economic Cooperation Council (1997), 'Pacific Food Outlook 1997–1998', November.

Peng, Tso-Kwei (1992), 'Prices, Income, and Farm Policy in Taiwan', in Peter Calkins, Wen S. Chern, and Francis C. Tuan (eds), *Rural Development in Taiwan and Mainland China*, Boulder, CO: Westview Press.

Perkins, Dwight H. (1992), 'The Growing Grain Deficit and Its Implications for China's Development Strategy', in Peter Calkins, Wen S. Chern, and Francis C. Tuan (eds), *Rural Development in Taiwan and Mainland China*, Boulder, CO: Westview Press.

Pinstrup-Andersen, Per (1996), 'Designing Long-Term Scenarios: Prospects for Global Agriculture', International Food Policy Research Institute, Washington, DC.

Pollak, R.A. and J.J. Wales (1978), 'Estimation of Complete Demand Systems from Household Budget Data: The Linear and Quadratic

Expenditure Systems', *American Economic Review*, 68 : 348–59.

Rosegrant, Mark W., Mercedita Agcaoili-Sombilla, and Nicostrato D. Perez (1995), 'Global Food Projections to 2020: Implications for Investment', International Food Policy Research Institute, Discussion Paper 5, Washington, DC, October.

Shi, H., R. Mitttelhammer, and T. I. Wahl (1995), 'Aggregate Food Demand Analysis for a Transitional Economy: An Application to Chinese Household Expenditure Data', *Journal of Food Distribution Research*, 26 (2) (September): 20–7.

Sicular, Terry (1989), *Food Price Policy in Asia*, Ithaca, New York: Cornell University Press.

State Statistical Bureau (1992), 'Yearbook of Chinese Rural Household Survey', Beijing, China.

State Statistical Bureau (1994), 'Rural Statistical Yearbook of China', Beijing, China.

State Statistical Bureau (1996), 'Statistical Yearbook of China', Beijing, China.

Statistics Bureau (1996), 'Annual Report on the Family Income and Expenditure Survey 1995', Management and Coordination Agency, Government of Japan, Tokyo.

Tweeten, Luther (1998), 'Dodging a Malthusian Bullet in the 21st Century', *Agribusiness: An International Journal*, 14 (January/February): 15–23.

Wang, Zhi and Wen S. Chern (1992), 'Effects of Rationing on the Consumption Behavior of Chinese Urban Households during 1981– 1987', *Journal of Comparative Economics*, 16: 1–26.

Wu, Yamrui, Elton Li, and S. Nicholas Samuel (1995), 'Food Consumption in Urban China: An Empirical Analysis', *Applied Economics*, 27 : 509–15.

Zhou, Z. Y. (1997), *Effects of Grain Marketing Systems on Grain Production: A Comparative Study of China and India*, New York: The Haworth Press.

Food security in Asia

Appendix

Table 6.A Comparison of regression results of LA/AIDS versus AIDS, rural households, China, 1994

Parameters	LA/AIDS		AIDS	
	Coefficient	t-ratio	Coefficient	t-ratio
α_0			8.041	1.05
α_1	−0.032	−0.35	0.544	0.62
α_2	0.312	8.26	0.031	0.27
α_3	−0.070	−1.26	0.167	0.75
α_4	0.041	4.09	0.018	1.65
α_5	0.482	8.36	0.095	0.22
α_6	0.052	4.21	0.017	0.61
α_7	0.064	2.30	0.032	0.21
α_8	0.216	5.55	0.040	1.24
α_9	0.100	1.80	0.030	0.06
β_1	0.095	7.68	−0.120	−9.57
β_2	−0.038	−7.50	−0.015	−2.89
β_3	0.042	5.42	−0.030	−3.64
β_4	−0.003	−2.24	−0.001	−1.00
β_5	−0.063	−8.24	0.058	7.24
β_6	−0.006	−3.47	0.004	2.18
β_7	−0.007	−1.99	0.020	5.39
β_8	−0.024	−4.69	−0.004	−0.70
β_9	−0.022	−2.93	0.071	9.20
$d_{1,1}$	0.003	0.95	0.024	8.03
$d_{1,2}$	0.020	1.08	0.012	0.64
$d_{1,3}$	0.019	0.86	0.028	1.27
$d_{1,4}$	0.021	2.22	0.010	1.11
$d_{1,5}$	0.013	1.78	0.009	1.22
$d_{1,6}$	−0.064	−1.19	−0.069	−1.29
$d_{1,7}$	0.071	6.64	0.141	13.98
$d_{1,8}$	0.022	2.21	−0.045	−2.05
$d_{1,9}$	−0.161	−9.56	−0.091	−5.56
$d_{1,10}$	0.118	11.91	0.073	7.49
$d_{1,11}$	−0.008	−0.30	−0.017	−0.61

Table 6.A Comparison of regression results of LA/AIDS versus AIDS, rural households, China, 1994 (cont.)

Parameters	LA/AIDS Coefficient	t-ratio	AIDS Coefficient	t-ratio
$d_{1,12}$	−0.312	−5.64	−0.167	−2.98
$d_{1,13}$	−0.148	−8.53	−0.074	−4.44
$d_{1,14}$	−0.058	−7.65	−0.046	−6.01
$d_{2,1}$	0.001	0.88	−0.002	−1.22
$d_{2,2}$	0.004	0.53	0.001	0.07
$d_{2,3}$	−0.002	−0.18	−0.006	−0.63
$d_{2,4}$	−0.005	−1.39	−0.005	−1.36
$d_{2,5}$	−0.012	−3.88	−0.011	−3.76
$d_{2,6}$	0.010	0.43	0.008	0.34
$d_{2,7}$	−0.005	−1.12	−0.015	−3.47
$d_{2,8}$	−0.033	−8.29	0.144	15.38
$d_{2,9}$	0.007	0.95	−0.004	−0.61
$d_{2,10}$	−0.028	−6.85	−0.023	−5.43
$d_{2,11}$	−0.005	−0.42	−0.004	−0.30
$d_{2,12}$	−0.018	−0.78	−0.013	−0.56
$d_{2,13}$	0.002	0.24	−0.011	−1.59
$d_{2,14}$	−0.004	−1.05	−0.005	−1.35
$d_{3,1}$	−0.006	−3.02	0.002	1.15
$d_{3,2}$	0.023	1.90	0.024	1.97
$d_{3,3}$	0.010	0.69	0.016	1.12
$d_{3,4}$	−0.005	−0.77	−0.007	−1.07
$d_{3,5}$	−0.009	−1.83	−0.009	−1.84
$d_{3,6}$	0.041	1.20	0.044	1.25
$d_{3,7}$	−0.048	−7.06	−0.024	−3.71
$d_{3,8}$	−0.017	−2.73	−0.038	−2.65
$d_{3,9}$	0.176	16.35	0.201	18.83
$d_{3,10}$	−0.142	−22.16	−0.157	−24.52
$d_{3,11}$	0.007	0.40	0.005	0.26
$d_{3,12}$	−0.102	−2.87	−0.062	−1.71
$d_{3,13}$	−0.047	−4.20	−0.021	−1.94
$d_{3,14}$	0.033	6.79	0.041	8.03
$d_{4,1}$	0.000	0.43	0.000	−0.10
$d_{4,2}$	−0.011	−5.43	−0.011	−5.55
$d_{4,3}$	−0.002	−0.66	−0.002	−0.79
$d_{4,4}$	−0.001	−0.54	−0.001	−0.53
$d_{4,5}$	−0.001	−1.79	−0.001	−1.75
$d_{4,6}$	−0.007	−1.26	−0.007	−1.27

Food security in Asia

Table 6.A Comparison of regression results of LA/AIDS versus AIDS, rural households, China, 1994 (cont.)

Parameters	LA/AIDS Coefficient	t-ratio	AIDS Coefficient	t-ratio
$d_{4,7}$	−0.002	−1.44	−0.002	−2.20
$d_{4,8}$	0.001	0.66	−0.001	−0.41
$d_{4,9}$	−0.003	−1.53	−0.004	−2.03
$d_{4,10}$	0.003	2.45	0.003	2.86
$d_{4,11}$	−0.004	−1.42	−0.004	−1.38
$d_{4,12}$	−0.008	−1.33	−0.007	−1.23
$d_{4,13}$	0.000	0.13	−0.001	−0.45
$d_{4,14}$	−0.010	−10.42	−0.010	−10.31
$d_{5,1}$	0.003	1.36	−0.010	−5.21
$d_{5,2}$	−0.022	−1.85	−0.019	−1.62
$d_{5,3}$	−0.019	−1.40	−0.026	−1.88
$d_{5,4}$	− 0.005	−0.86	0.000	−0.02
$d_{5,5}$	0.007	1.54	0.009	1.91
$d_{5,6}$	−0.023	−0.68	−0.022	−0.67
$d_{5,7}$	0.021	3.10	−0.019	−3.04
$d_{5,8}$	0.015	2.44	−0.017	−1.24
$d_{5,9}$	0.007	0.71	−0.033	−3.19
$d_{5,10}$	0.011	1.76	0.036	5.83
$d_{5,11}$	0.022	1.26	0.026	1.51
$d_{5,12}$	0.013	0.38	−0.061	−1.72
$d_{5,13}$	0.024	2.17	−0.019	−1.77
$d_{5,14}$	0.041	8.03	0.032	6.20
$d_{6,1}$	0.001	2.29	0.000	−0.05
$d_{6,2}$	−0.001	−0.34	−0.001	−0.29
$d_{6,3}$	−0.003	−1.02	−0.004	−1.22
$d_{6,4}$	0.000	0.26	0.001	0.58
$d_{6,5}$	0.001	0.61	0.001	0.76
$d_{6,6}$	−0.007	−0.96	−0.007	−0.95
$d_{6,7}$	0.000	−0.12	−0.003	−2.47
$d_{6,8}$	−0.003	−2.05	−0.001	−0.30
$d_{6,9}$	0.004	1.62	0.000	0.19
$d_{6,10}$	−0.005	−3.62	−0.003	−2.11
$d_{6,11}$	0.000	0.03	0.000	0.13
$d_{6,12}$	−0.003	−0.45	−0.008	−1.12
$d_{6,13}$	0.001	0.47	−0.002	−1.00
$d_{6,14}$	−0.005	−4.57	−0.006	−5.10
$d_{7,1}$	0.000	0.45	−0.002	−2.61

Table 6.A   *Comparison of regression results of LA/AIDS versus AIDS, rural households, China, 1994 (cont.)*

Parameters	LA/AIDS Coefficient	t-ratio	AIDS Coefficient	t-ratio
$d_{7,2}$	−0.009	−1.61	−0.008	−1.34
$d_{7,3}$	−0.009	−1.40	−0.010	−1.55
$d_{7,4}$	−0.004	−1.28	−0.002	−0.80
$d_{7,5}$	0.000	−0.06	0.000	0.15
$d_{7,6}$	−0.006	−0.40	−0.006	−0.37
$d_{7,7}$	−0.004	−1.33	−0.013	−4.20
$d_{7,8}$	−0.001	−0.21	−0.014	−2.12
$d_{7,9}$	−0.003	−0.66	−0.012	−2.39
$d_{7,10}$	0.003	0.84	0.008	2.73
$d_{7,11}$	−0.021	−2.48	−0.020	−2.40
$d_{7,12}$	−0.035	−2.12	−0.057	−3.40
$d_{7,13}$	−0.002	−0.41	−0.011	−2.08
$d_{7,14}$	0.014	5.72	0.012	4.89
$d_{8,1}$	0.002	1.64	0.000	−0.23
$d_{8,2}$	−0.007	−0.89	−0.009	−1.11
$d_{8,3}$	−0.006	−0.66	−0.009	−0.95
$d_{8,4}$	0.000	0.05	0.000	0.09
$d_{8,5}$	−0.004	−1.14	−0.003	−1.11
$d_{8,6}$	0.055	2.42	0.054	2.34
$d_{8,7}$	−0.008	−1.88	−0.017	−3.78
$d_{8,8}$	0.002	0.50	−0.007	−0.74
$d_{8,9}$	0.023	3.22	0.014	2.03
$d_{8,10}$	0.000	0.06	0.005	1.18
$d_{8,11}$	0.005	0.43	0.006	0.50
$d_{8,12}$	−0.013	−0.55	−0.016	−0.67
$d_{8,13}$	0.006	0.80	−0.004	−0.57
$d_{8,14}$	−0.031	−8.67	−0.032	−8.98
$d_{9,1}$	0.002	1.05	−0.007	−3.73
$d_{9,2}$	−0.039	−3.27	−0.033	−2.90
$d_{9,3}$	−0.003	−0.20	−0.005	−0.38
$d_{9,4}$	0.000	0.01	0.005	0.95
$d_{9,5}$	0.004	0.91	0.006	1.34
$d_{9,6}$	−0.026	−0.78	−0.023	−0.71
$d_{9,7}$	−0.001	−0.20	−0.030	−4.87
$d_{9,8}$	0.012	1.96	−0.015	−1.14
$d_{9,9}$	−0.016	−1.54	−0.044	−4.41
$d_{9,10}$	0.029	4.61	0.048	8.12

Table 6.A Comparison of regression results of LA/AIDS versus AIDS, rural households, China, 1994 (cont.)

Parameters	LA/AIDS		AIDS	
	Coefficient	t-ratio	Coefficient	t-ratio
$d_{9,11}$	0.004	0.25	0.008	0.47
$d_{9,12}$	0.512	14.84	0.437	12.88
$d_{9,13}$	-0.008	-0.75	-0.036	-3.51
$d_{9,14}$	0.020	4.09	0.013	2.83
$\sigma_{1,1}$	-0.078	-3.55	0.005	0.53
$\sigma_{1,2}$	-0.021	-2.10	-0.015	-1.55
$\sigma_{1,3}$	-0.012	-0.91	-0.016	-1.25
$\sigma_{1,4}$	0.025	3.05	0.004	0.51
$\sigma_{1,5}$	0.016	1.72	-0.002	-0.17
$\sigma_{1,6}$	0.030	2.71	0.006	0.57
$\sigma_{2,1}$	0.141	15.60	-0.032	-7.66
$\sigma_{2,2}$	0.021	5.11	0.022	5.21
$\sigma_{2,3}$	0.001	0.16	-0.001	-0.17
$\sigma_{2,4}$	0.011	3.35	0.012	3.50
$\sigma_{2,5}$	-0.002	-0.49	-0.001	-0.19
$\sigma_{2,6}$	0.001	0.22	0.002	0.51
$\sigma_{3,1}$	-0.048	-3.39	-0.023	-3.66
$\sigma_{3,2}$	0.009	1.35	0.010	1.54
$\sigma_{3,3}$	0.015	1.85	0.020	2.34
$\sigma_{3,4}$	0.013	2.65	0.009	1.72
$\sigma_{3,5}$	0.006	1.01	0.001	0.19
$\sigma_{3,6}$	0.009	1.24	0.002	0.27
$\sigma_{4,1}$	-0.001	-0.55	0.001	0.79
$\sigma_{4,2}$	-0.005	-4.90	-0.005	-4.80
$\sigma_{4,3}$	-0.004	-3.04	-0.004	-3.06
$\sigma_{4,4}$	-0.003	-3.92	-0.003	-3.82
$\sigma_{4,5}$	0.000	0.17	0.000	0.27
$\sigma_{4,6}$	0.003	2.25	0.003	2.33
$\sigma_{5,1}$	0.000	-0.02	0.024	3.94
$\sigma_{5,2}$	0.014	2.32	0.012	1.88
$\sigma_{5,3}$	-0.019	-2.39	-0.020	-2.45
$\sigma_{5,4}$	-0.019	-3.71	-0.008	-1.59
$\sigma_{5,5}$	0.003	0.55	0.012	2.10
$\sigma_{5,6}$	-0.008	-1.21	0.004	0.58
$\sigma_{6,1}$	0.000	0.09	-0.002	-1.46
$\sigma_{6,2}$	0.000	-0.01	0.000	-0.14
$\sigma_{6,3}$	-0.009	-5.20	-0.009	-5.20

Table 6.A Comparison of regression results of LA/AIDS versus AIDS, rural households, China, 1994 (cont.)

Parameters	LA/AIDS		AIDS	
	Coefficient	t-ratio	Coefficient	t-ratio
$\sigma_{6,4}$	−0.001	−0.81	0.000	−0.10
$\sigma_{6,5}$	−0.001	−0.89	0.000	−0.32
$\sigma_{6,6}$	−0.001	−0.96	0.000	−0.32
$\sigma_{7,1}$	−0.009	−1.29	0.002	0.51
$\sigma_{7,2}$	−0.004	−1.45	−0.005	−1.79
$\sigma_{7,3}$	0.003	0.88	0.004	0.97
$\sigma_{7,4}$	−0.026	−10.83	−0.024	−9.78
$\sigma_{7,5}$	−0.003	−1.13	−0.001	−0.34
$\sigma_{7,6}$	−0.006	−1.67	−0.003	−0.75
$\sigma_{8,1}$	−0.007	−0.76	0.004	0.86
$\sigma_{8,2}$	0.001	0.13	0.001	0.20
$\sigma_{8,3}$	0.002	0.36	0.001	0.10
$\sigma_{8,4}$	0.001	0.42	0.003	0.76
$\sigma_{8,5}$	−0.030	−7.51	−0.029	−7.11
$\sigma_{8,6}$	−0.006	−1.22	−0.004	−0.85
$\sigma_{9,1}$	0.003	0.25	0.020	3.39
$\sigma_{9,2}$	−0.006	−1.04	−0.010	−1.68
$\sigma_{9,3}$	0.005	0.67	0.008	0.97
$\sigma_{9,4}$	0.002	0.48	0.011	2.24
$\sigma_{9,5}$	0.006	1.03	0.014	2.47
$\sigma_{9,6}$	−0.006	−0.79	0.005	0.77
$\gamma_{1,1}$	0.187	14.23	0.243	1.71
$\gamma_{1,2}$	−0.012	−2.30	−0.019	−0.99
$\gamma_{1,3}$	−0.053	−9.01	−0.044	−1.23
$\gamma_{1,4}$	−0.002	−1.36	−0.003	−1.17
$\gamma_{1,5}$	−0.038	−4.80	−0.067	−0.98
$\gamma_{1,6}$	−0.001	−0.76	−0.003	−0.70
$\gamma_{1,7}$	−0.021	−5.48	−0.028	−1.14
$\gamma_{1,8}$	−0.014	−2.60	−0.020	−2.81
$\gamma_{1,9}$	−0.028	−4.09	−0.040	−0.48
$\gamma_{2,2}$	0.028	4.22	0.029	4.08
$\gamma_{2,3}$	−0.003	−1.02	−0.004	−0.66
$\gamma_{2,4}$	−0.005	−3.38	−0.005	−3.19
$\gamma_{2,5}$	−0.010	−1.63	−0.008	−0.71
$\gamma_{2,6}$	−0.001	−0.41	−0.001	−0.32
$\gamma_{2,7}$	−0.003	−0.76	−0.002	−0.42
$\gamma_{2,8}$	0.014	2.99	0.014	3.02

Food security in Asia

Table 6.A *Comparison of regression results of LA/AIDS versus AIDS,
rural households, China, 1994 (cont.)*

Parameters	LA/AIDS Coefficient	t-ratio	AIDS Coefficient	t-ratio
$\gamma_{2,9}$	−0.008	−1.91	−0.006	−0.56
$\gamma_{3,3}$	0.084	16.40	0.083	8.33
$\gamma_{3,4}$	−0.003	−3.12	−0.003	−3.01
$\gamma_{3,5}$	−0.002	−0.49	−0.006	−0.32
$\gamma_{3,6}$	0.000	−0.30	0.000	−0.31
$\gamma_{3,7}$	0.002	0.98	0.001	0.23
$\gamma_{3,8}$	0.001	0.44	0.001	0.24
$\gamma_{3,9}$	−0.025	−6.19	−0.026	−1.26
$\gamma_{4,4}$	0.004	4.70	0.004	4.70
$\gamma_{4,5}$	0.006	2.84	0.006	2.70
$\gamma_{4,6}$	0.003	3.47	0.003	3.57
$\gamma_{4,7}$	0.001	1.30	0.001	1.31
$\gamma_{4,8}$	0.000	0.31	0.000	0.33
$\gamma_{4,9}$	−0.005	−4.52	−0.005	−3.35
$\gamma_{5,5}$	0.033	2.90	0.049	1.41
$\gamma_{5,6}$	−0.003	−1.27	−0.002	−0.69
$\gamma_{5,7}$	−0.005	−1.03	−0.001	−0.06
$\gamma_{5,8}$	−0.001	−0.16	0.002	0.24
$\gamma_{5,9}$	0.012	2.03	0.017	0.41
$\gamma_{6,6}$	0.005	3.70	0.005	3.69
$\gamma_{6,7}$	0.001	0.55	0.001	0.60
$\gamma_{6,8}$	−0.002	−1.36	−0.002	−1.23
$\gamma_{6,9}$	0.000	0.22	0.001	0.23
$\gamma_{7,7}$	0.018	5.22	0.019	3.46
$\gamma_{7,8}$	−0.003	−0.85	−0.002	−0.63
$\gamma_{7,9}$	0.004	1.40	0.005	0.35
$\gamma_{8,8}$	0.004	0.61	0.004	0.67
$\gamma_{8,9}$	0.003	0.76	0.005	1.05
$\gamma_{9,9}$	0.046	6.99	0.048	0.99

Table 6.B Comparison of regression results of LA/AIDS versus AIDS, urban households, China, 1993—96

Parameters	LA/AIDS		AIDS	
	Coefficient	t-ratio	Coefficient	t-ratio
α_0			9.449	2.76
α_1	-0.894	-3.63	0.084	0.26
α_2	-0.322	-3.95	-0.072	-1.10
α_3	1.287	5.65	0.493	2.27
α_4	0.971	5.56	0.284	1.25
α_5	0.841	3.17	0.418	1.18
α_6	-0.402	-3.72	-0.193	-3.50
α_7	-0.198	-1.40	0.054	0.24
β_1	0.210	5.09	-0.211	-6.29
β_2	0.051	3.83	-0.040	-3.32
β_3	-0.131	-3.61	0.128	4.26
β_4	-0.149	-5.10	0.146	5.83
β_5	-0.150	-3.15	0.231	6.77
β_6	0.051	2.82	-0.030	-1.82
β_7	0.069	2.83	-0.142	-7.95
$\gamma_{1,1}$	0.101	3.35	0.484	1.70
$\gamma_{1,2}$	-0.039	-3.77	0.037	0.65
$\gamma_{1,3}$	0.090	3.16	-0.193	-1.05
$\gamma_{1,4}$	-0.001	-0.04	-0.264	-1.34
$\gamma_{1,5}$	-0.060	-3.34	-0.417	-1.40
$\gamma_{1,6}$	-0.018	-1.46	0.025	0.53
$\gamma_{1,7}$	-0.048	-3.63	0.203	1.09
$\gamma_{2,2}$	0.035	4.06	0.048	3.15
$\gamma_{2,3}$	0.046	3.32	-0.007	-0.17
$\gamma_{2,4}$	0.006	0.57	-0.044	-1.08
$\gamma_{2,5}$	-0.012	-1.82	-0.080	-1.33
$\gamma_{2,6}$	-0.003	-0.38	0.002	0.22
$\gamma_{2,7}$	-0.012	-1.87	0.037	0.94
$\gamma_{3,3}$	-0.200	-4.76	0.038	0.29
$\gamma_{3,4}$	-0.080	-3.65	0.108	0.85
$\gamma_{3,5}$	-0.032	-1.98	0.194	1.03
$\gamma_{3,6}$	0.068	4.58	0.051	1.53
$\gamma_{3,7}$	0.064	4.13	-0.121	-0.99
$\gamma_{4,4}$	-0.027	-1.10	0.150	1.06
$\gamma_{4,5}$	-0.002	-0.14	0.246	1.19
$\gamma_{4,6}$	0.062	5.02	0.038	1.09
$\gamma_{4,7}$	-0.001	-0.06	-0.173	-1.30
$\gamma_{5,5}$	0.069	3.10	0.452	1.40
$\gamma_{5,6}$	0.016	1.91	-0.037	-0.73
$\gamma_{5,7}$	-0.016	-1.44	-0.255	-1.27
$\gamma_{6,6}$	-0.051	-4.72	-0.050	-3.87
$\gamma_{6,7}$	-0.026	-3.34	0.003	0.09
$\gamma_{7,7}$	0.058	5.04	0.227	1.76

Table 6.C Comparison of regression results of LA/AIDS versus AIDS, Japan, 1986–95

	LA/AIDS		AIDS	
Parameters	Coefficient	t-ratio	Coefficient	t-ratio
α_0			−57.36979	−1.19
α_1	−0.10549	−1.49	−3.24879	−1.09
α_2	−0.05207	−0.95	−0.98883	−1.89
α_3	0.24552	4.73	−0.09409	−0.13
α_4	0.64361	14.54	3.39032	1.45
β_1	0.06738	4.09	0.05614	3.94
β_2	0.01690	1.34	0.01447	1.43
β_3	−0.00571	−0.46	0.00493	0.49
β_4	−0.04954	−5.01	−0.04682	−6.14
$d_{1,1}$	−0.01878	−3.33	−0.01691	−3.21
$d_{1,2}$	−0.00109	−3.15	−0.00086	−2.69
$d_{1,3}$	−0.00301	−5.27	−0.00346	−6.23
$d_{2,1}$	0.00226	0.52	0.00255	0.69
$d_{2,2}$	0.00111	4.18	0.00105	4.63
$d_{2,3}$	0.00081	1.84	0.00329	7.69
$d_{3,1}$	0.01904	4.47	0.01419	3.90
$d_{3,2}$	−0.00294	−11.55	−0.00270	−11.49
$d_{3,3}$	0.00145	3.40	0.00161	4.20
$d_{4,1}$	−0.00853	−2.49	−0.00736	−2.55
$d_{4,2}$	0.00068	3.14	0.00046	2.79
$d_{4,3}$	0.00207	6.04	0.00052	1.44
$\gamma_{1,1}$	0.00022	6.99	−0.04540	−0.22
$\gamma_{1,2}$	0.00000	0.10	−0.12137	−4.36
$\gamma_{1,3}$	−0.00001	−1.27	−0.02736	−0.64
$\gamma_{1,4}$	−0.00017	−6.30	0.11575	0.75
$\gamma_{2,2}$	0.00011	10.15	0.15468	7.03
$\gamma_{2,3}$	−0.00003	−4.89	−0.01907	−1.85
$\gamma_{2,4}$	−0.00005	−4.51	−0.01415	−0.47
$\gamma_{3,3}$	0.00009	16.02	0.06607	9.92
$\gamma_{3,4}$	−0.00003	−6.72	−0.01150	−0.33
$\gamma_{4,4}$	0.00029	6.74	0.00069	0.01

7. Economic development and food security issues in Japan and South Korea

Toshiyuki Kako

1. INTRODUCTION

Japan and South Korea have achieved rapid economic growth in the last 30–40 years. The rapid economic growth in both countries has been marked by unbalanced growth between the industrial and agricultural sectors. Both countries suffered substantial losses of comparative advantage in agriculture relative to other industrial countries (Hayami, 1988, p. 11; Kim, 1997, p. 6). The decline in comparative advantage in agriculture, coupled with progress in trade liberalization and substantial changes in food consumption patterns resulted in sharp increases in imports of agricultural products and significantly reduced food self-sufficiency rates in both countries.

Although consumers are satisfied with the rapid improvement in food consumption, they are anxious about future food security. They feel uncertain whether or not they will be able to acquire enough food if the global food supply–demand balance experiences a sharp deterioration. The need for re-examining current food security policies is increasing in both Japan and South Korea. Especially, the need to maintain food security is felt strongly in South Korea where a military outbreak with North Korea is possible, and where concern increased after the financial and currency crisis in 1997.

This chapter will identify some common experiences shared by Japan and South Korea with respect to changes in food supply and demand, agricultural trade and food self-sufficiency through an analysis of historical data from these two countries.[1] More specifically, the objectives of this study are: (a) to describe how per capita food supply and the PFC calorie ratio have improved in the last 30–40 years;[2] (b) to describe the correlation between the increases in food imports and the decreases in the food self-sufficiency rate; (c) to make projections of supply and demand for rice, and discuss the implications for the future self-sufficiency of food; (d) to examine the impact of beef import liberalization on the domestic market in Japan; and (e) to discuss how to minimize the risks involved in achieving food security.

2. FOOD CONSUMPTION AND SELF-SUFFICIENCY IN FOOD

2.1 Economic Development and Position of Agriculture in the National Economy

Japan and South Korea achieved rapid economic growth after World War II, and the per capita GNP of these countries has increased greatly. Japan's per capita GNP increased by 21.1 times from $1948 in 1970 to $41 185 in 1995, while South Korea's per capita GNP increased much faster than Japan's, reaching 39.8 times from $252 to $10 037 during the same period.

One of the characteristics of rapid economic growth in Japan and South Korea has been their unbalanced growth. The growth rate of the manufacturing sector has been far greater than that of the agricultural sector. As a result of unbalanced growth, the relative share of the agricultural sector in the national economy has declined in the process of rapid economic growth. In Japan, the share of the agricultural sector accounted for 4.2 per cent of GDP in 1970, and it declined to 1.4 per cent by 1995. In South Korea, it fell much faster, from 23.3 per cent in 1970 to 5.6 per cent in 1995, reflecting the fact that South Korea started its high economic growth about ten years later than Japan.

The decline in the share of the agricultural sector in the national economy is related to lower productivity in the agricultural sector relative to the non-agricultural sector and the small and declining income elasticity of agricultural products. In Japan, the ratio of the net labour product of the agricultural sector relative to that of the non-agricultural sector was 28.8 per cent in 1965. It rose gradually to a peak of 36.7 per cent in 1975. Since then it has been falling, down to 28.1 per cent by 1995. In South Korea, labour productivity of the agricultural sector was about a third of that of the non-agricultural sector in 1972. Although the difference in labour productivity between the two sectors has lessened over time, a large gap still exists. In 1996 the ratio of agricultural labour productivity relative to that of the non-agricultural sector was just 44 per cent.[3]

Since agricultural products are mostly necessity goods, the income elasticity in middle-income countries is less than one, and the value tends to decline as income increases. Therefore, the expenditure share of agricultural products in final consumption expenditure has declined in the process of economic growth. This results in a decline in the share of the agricultural sector in the national economy. Increasing imports of agricultural products was also responsible for the declining share of the agricultural sector in both countries.

2.2 Trends in Food Consumption

Food consumption patterns have changed significantly throughout the period of high economic growth in Japan and South Korea. Traditionally, the Japanese diet consists of mainly rice and a few dishes derived from vegetables, soybeans, and fish. It is characterized by relatively low calorie intakes, a high proportion of starch, a good animal/vegetable protein balance, and a high proportion of seafood in the animal protein intake (Higuchi, 1991, p. 98). Japanese dietary habits underwent drastic changes during the 1955–72 period. Consumption of cereals, potatoes, and soybeans declined considerably, while concurrently the consumption of meat, eggs, milk, dairy products, and oils and fats increased.

Korean meals in the 1960s consisted mainly of rice, barley, wheat, and a few dishes derived from vegetables and soybeans. A high proportion of calorie intake came from cereals, potatoes, and pulses, and daily per capita calorie intake levels were relatively low. Korean dietary habits have also undergone significant changes in the last 25 years. Consumption of cereals and starchy roots has decreased considerably, while consumption of animal products, fruits, and vegetables has increased. Figure 7.1 shows the annual average changes in per capita food consumption for Japan, South Korea, and Taiwan from 1970 to 1995. Similar changes in food consumption patterns occurred in all three countries. Basically, per capita cereal consumption declined and the per capita consumption of meat, milk, fish, shellfish, and oils and fats increased. These changes in food consumption patterns were one of the major causes for the decline in the food self-sufficiency rates in these countries. This point will be discussed in more detail later.

2.3 Trends in Calorie Intake

Calorie intake from food increased in parallel with the changes in food consumption patterns in Japan. Specifically, daily per capita calorie intake increased at high rates during the period of high economic growth, from

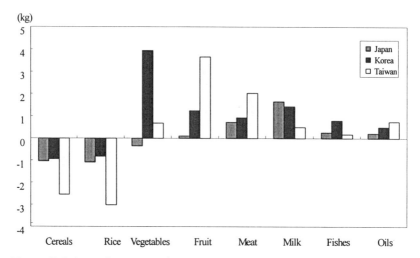

Figure 7.1 Annual average change in per capita food intake: 1970—95

2291 kcal in 1960 to 2569 kcal in 1973. However, per capita calorie intake approached the saturation point by the middle of the 1980s, and flattened out from the end of the 1980s, reaching 2638 kcal in 1995 (figure 7.2). The increase in calorie intake from 1965 to 1995 can be largely attributed to increases in the use of animal products (by 270 kcal) and oils and fats (by 209 kcal). The calorie intake from rice decreased by 430 kcal during the same period.

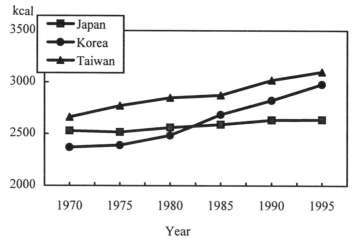

Figure 7.2 Daily per capita calorie intake

The sum of the increases in calorie intake from these foods was larger than the decrease in calorie intake from rice.

The PFC calorie ratio was also improved in parallel with the changes in food consumption patterns in Japan. Until the end of the 1960s, the average Japanese consumed an excess of carbohydrates, too little fats, and slightly less proteins compared to the optimal PFC calorie ratio which is 12–13 per cent for proteins, 20–30 per cent for fats and 57–68 per cent for carbohydrates. The decrease in the consumption of rice and increase in the consumption of animal products and oils and fats in the 1960s have led to a more desirable PFC calorie ratio. The optimal PFC calorie ratio was achieved by the early 1970s so that the food consumption pattern in the 1970s was nutritionally well-balanced. The Ministry of Agriculture, Forestry and Fisheries (MAFF) called this dietary pattern 'the Japanese-style Diet' and for a long time promoted its maintenance. In 1995, the PFC calorie ratio of the average Japanese diet was 13.6 per cent for proteins, 29.5 per cent for fats, and 56.9 per cent for carbohydrates, which is still very close to the optimal PFC calorie ratio. Japan has the longest average human life expectancy in the world: 77 years for males and 83 years for females. This may be related to the nutritionally well-balanced Japanese diet.

In South Korea, daily per capita calorie intake increased rapidly from 2189 kcal in 1965 to 2980 kcal in 1995. This increase is much bigger than that of Japan – a 36 per cent increase compared with 7.2 per cent in Japan during the last 30 years. The increase in calorie intake can be largely attributed to increases in the consumption of oils and fats (by 333 kcal), animal products (by 246 kcal) and sweeteners (by 174 kcal). In this same period, calorie intake from rice decreased by 122 kcal which was less than one-third of the decrease in Japan.

In parallel with the increase in calorie intake, the PFC calorie ratio was improved considerably over the 30-year period in South Korea. The average Korean used to consume too much carbohydrate and too little fat and protein compared with the optimal PFC calorie ratio. The decrease in the consumption of cereals and the increase in the consumption of oils and fats and animal products have led to a more desirable PFC calorie ratio recently. The PFC calorie ratio in 1994 was 10.9 per cent for proteins, 17.1 per cent for fats, and 72.0 per cent for carbohydrates.

These rapid improvements in food consumption observed in Japan and South Korea was made possible by increases in domestic agricultural production as well as by the big increase in agricultural imports. The reliance of domestic food supply on imported agricultural products has increased over time.

2.4   Agricultural Trade and the Self-Sufficiency of Food

Agricultural production in both Japan and South Korea has grown rapidly during the period of high economic growth. The production structure has also changed, partly induced by their agricultural policies designed to help producers respond and adjust to rapidly changing food consumption patterns. However, there still exists a wide gap between agricultural production and food consumption, and it has widened over time. This gap was filled by the imports of agricultural products, and as a result imports of agricultural products have been expanding at very high rates in both countries.

The international balance of payments in Japan was in deficit in the 1950s, and there were strict limits on trade and foreign exchange. In 1960, the Japanese government set out a concrete schedule for trade liberalization. In 1964, Japan adopted Article 8 status in the International Monetary Fund (IMF) and article 11 status in the General Agreement on Tariffs and Trade (GATT), a status which requires that a nation imposes neither exchange restrictions nor import restraints. These actions marked the beginning of the Japanese economy's journey towards full domestic and international liberalization (Saeki, 1991, p. 121).

Japanese imports of agricultural products increased 23.2 times from $1.7 billion in 1960 to $39.4 billion in 1995. The growth rate of agricultural imports have accelerated since 1986 due to the sharp fall in import prices derived from the high yen value. The yen exchange rate rose rapidly to almost 2.5 times from 239 yen to the US dollar in 1985 to 96 yen to the dollar in 1995. The agricultural product import price index fell by nearly 44 per cent from 1985 to 1995.

The annual average net imports of agricultural products was $16.6 billion for 1985–86. This was the highest level in the world, followed by the Soviet Union and West Germany. In the 1985–86 period, Japan's agricultural imports comprised a significant portion of the world agricultural trade: 25.2 per cent of maize, 17.7 per cent of soybeans, 6.8 per cent of raw sugar, 5.8 per cent of wheat. Japan's agricultural imports, as a share of the world's total agricultural trade, reached 8.7 per cent in 1993 and by 1995 net imports of agricultural products had risen to $37.6 billion. The largest source of agricultural imports is United States (about 37 per cent in 1989) followed by Australia (about 10 per cent). The import shares from China, Taiwan, and Thailand have increased in recent years.

In South Korea, net imports of agricultural products (including forestry and fishery products) increased from $0.4 billion in 1975 to $7.1 billion in 1995. The rate of increase in net agricultural imports has accelerated since 1988, partly due to the increased demand for foreign agricultural products driven by changes in food consumption patterns. This is reflected in the increases in the imports of feed grain, fruits, livestock products, and processed food. Another reason is the accelerating market liberalization of agricultural products. Owing to the rapid increase in exports and successive surpluses in the balance of payments during the 1986–88 period, South Korea has come to encounter trade frictions with its major trading partners. As a result, the South Korean government has launched many internationalization and open-door policies. For example, South Korea opened its agricultural markets under a series of import liberalization schedules. Korea's agricultural import liberalization has been accelerated to earn its graduation from the GATT Article XVIII;B in 1989 (Lee, 1993, p. 42). The ratio of agricultural import liberalization has been sharply increased in a short period of time. The import liberalization ratio of agricultural and livestock products was 71.1 per cent by 1970, and increased gradually to 76.1 per cent in 1985.[4] The rate of increase accelerated since the middle of the 1980s and grew to 98.5 per cent by 1997.

Since the domestic prices of agricultural products in Japan and South Korea are much higher than international prices it is expected that imports of agricultural products in both countries will increase further in the future under the World Trade Organization (WTO) system.

2.5   Declining Trend of the Self-Sufficiency of Food

The self-sufficiency rates for food in Japan and South Korea have declined in parallel with the expansion of imports of agricultural products. The decline in self-sufficiency rate is conspicuous for cereals, especially for animal feed (table 7.1). The self-sufficiency rate for cereals in Japan declined from 62 per cent in 1965 to 30 per cent in 1995. The self-sufficiency rate for meat was maintained at a relatively high level until the middle of the 1980s. It started a rapid decline since the end of the 1980s and was only 57 per cent in 1995. This was mostly due to the appreciation of the yen against the US dollar and the liberalization of beef trade.

The calorie self-sufficiency rate for food declined rapidly from 73 per cent in 1965 to 42 per cent in 1995. This is the lowest self-sufficiency rate among the major industrialized countries. The calorie self-sufficiency rate of major industrialized countries in 1987 was as follows: the United States, 121 per cent; West Germany, 92 per cent; the United Kingdom, 73 per cent; and France, 141 per cent. The calorie self-sufficiency rates of these countries have not only been high but have also increased

Table 7.1 Self-sufficiency rate of agricultural products

Year	Calorie		Cereals		Meat	
	Japan	Korea	Japan	Korea	Japan	Korea
1965	73		62		90	
1968	65	86	54		83	
1970	60	85	46	78	89	100
1975	54	84	40	74	77	101
1980	53	74	33	53	80	97
1985	52	71	31	49	81	100
1990	47	67	30	44	70	93
1995	42	62	30	30	57	89

Note: Blanks indicate data not available.

Sources: (1) '1995 Food Balance Sheet', Korea Rural Economics Institute.
(2) 'Food Balance Sheet', Ministry of Agriculture, Forestry, and Fisheries, Japanese government, 1997.

consistently over time.

A similar increase in imports of agricultural products and decrease in the self-sufficiency rate for agricultural products were observed in South Korea over the last 25 years. The calorie self-sufficiency rate fell from 85 per cent in 1970 to 62 per cent in 1995. The self-sufficiency rate for cereals declined especially fast, from 78 per cent in 1970 to 30 per cent in 1995. The self-sufficiency rate for meat was nearly 100 per cent until the middle of the 1980s, but it started to fall by the end of the 1980s and was 89 per cent in 1995. It is expected to decline further in the future because of the decline in the domestic prices of imported meat. The absolute value of the calorie self-sufficiency rate in South Korea is 20 points higher than in Japan, but the rate of decline is similar to that of Japan.

3. IMPACT OF AGRICULTURAL TRADE LIBERALIZATION ON DOMESTIC MARKET

It is expected that agricultural trade liberalization in the future will bring about further increases in the import of agricultural products, and decreases in the food self-sufficiency rate in Japan and South Korea. In order to study the impacts of agricultural trade liberalization on domestic markets in both countries, we will focus on rice and beef industries. This section has three parts. The first two are projections of the supply–demand balance for rice in these two countries, with special attention on the impact of the minimum access (MA) for rice imports on food self-sufficiency. The last part examines how liberalization of the beef trade impacts the Japanese domestic market.

3.1 Projections of Supply and Demand of Rice in Japan

Rice is the most important agricultural product in Japan and has been most strongly protected by Japan's agricultural policy. Although the relative importance of rice in agricultural production and food consumption has declined with economic development, rice continues to hold the biggest proportion in Japanese domestic agricultural production. In 1995, the proportion of rice production in total agricultural production was 30.4 per cent (compared to 47.4 per cent in 1960) and per capita calorie intake derived from rice was 25 per cent (compared to 44.3 per cent in 1965).

The situation surrounding the Japanese rice industry has changed in recent years. The biggest change was the partial opening of the rice market in 1995. Subsequent to its acceptance of the GATT Uruguay Round accord, Japan started the minimum access for rice imports in 1995, starting with 4 per cent of domestic rice consumption in 1995, gradually increasing to 8 per cent by 2000.[5]

Besides MA rice imports, the Japanese rice sector faces other challenges. First, domestic rice production costs are far higher than the international level because of small-scale farming, relatively high labour costs, high land costs, and overinvestment in farm machinery. A rapid appreciation of the yen in recent years exaggerated domestic production costs compared to that of major rice exporting countries. Second, rice has become an inferior good in Japan and per capita rice consumption for table use has been in steady decline. Per capita rice consumption of 118.3 kg in the peak year of 1962 had fallen by nearly half to just 67.8 kg in 1995. A trend of slower and gradual decline, which began in the latter half of the 1980s, is expected to persist. This declining trend of per capita rice consumption will be one of the causes of excess rice supply in the future.

It is important to know the future trend for supply–demand balance for rice and the impact of MA rice imports on food self-sufficiency. Since we have made future projections of rice supply and demand in another article (Kako, Gemma, and Ito, 1997), only an outline of the analytical model and projection results are summarized here:

1   The per capita rice demand function is estimated using a partial equilibrium model, which assumes that per capita rice demand is a function of income, rice price, and prices of substitutes for rice. Rice demand is projected based on the assumption that per capita income and the retail rice price will increase at 2 per cent and 1.5 per cent per annum, respectively, in the future;

2   Future rice yields and paddy field areas are projected based on the estimated parameters of the rice yield function and the paddy field function; and

3   Future target rice diversion areas are calculated by using projected values of paddy field areas and rice yields.[6] MA rice imports are assumed to increase at the same rate as that of the 1995–2000 period, that is, an 0.8 per cent increase per annum for the 2001–2010 period or a rise to 1.515 million metric tons (mmt) by the year 2010.

Table 7.2 shows projection results of supply and demand for rice in Japan.[7] According to our estimation results, per capita rice consumption for table use is expected to decline to 60 kg by 2010. Future rice yields are projected to increase at declining rates. This improvement in land productivity will contribute to increasing the potential rice production capacity. In addition, MA rice imports will increase the total rice supply. These two factors, as well as declining future rice consumption, will put pressure on the need to expand rice diversion areas. Using 1994 as a base year, target rice diversion areas are projected to increase to 878 000 ha by the year 2000, rising to 1.021 million ha by 2010, or a 74 per cent increase.

The following conclusions can be drawn from the above analysis: the future annual supply–demand balance for rice is predicted to be positive because of declining rice demand, increasing rice yields, and increasing MA rice imports. Reduction in rice consumption in the past was responsible for declining food self-sufficiency. Rice consumption is projected to decline and this will also be responsible for a further decline in food self-sufficiency in the future. Imported rice under the MA scheme will substitute for domestic rice, and result in a reduction in domestic rice production. This reduction in domestic rice production was one of the causes of the decline in the food self-sufficiency rate. Hence, MA rice imports will further reduce the food self-sufficiency rate in the future.

Table 7.2 Projection results of supply and demand of rice in Japan and Korea

(milled rice)

	Japan			South Korea		
			Annual average change			Annual average change
Year	1995	2010	1995–2010	1995	2010	1995–2010
Per capita rice supply (kg/year)	68	60	−0.83	106	81	−1.79
Total rice demand (10 000t)	937	860	−0.57	526	455	−0.97
Rice yield (kg/10a)	457	477	0.29	462	500	0.53
Rice planted area (10 000ha)	212	145	−2.53	106	78	−2.04
Total rice production (10 000t)	973	692	−2.27	489	393	−1.46
Rice imports (10 000t)	38	152	9.24	5	31	12.16
Rice diversion area (10 000ha)	63	102				

Notes: (1) The values for 2010 are projection results.
(2) Quantity is on milled rice base.

3.2 Projections of Supply and Demand of Rice in South Korea

Rice is a staple food in South Korea and the relative importance of rice in agricultural production and food consumption is much greater than in Japan. The proportion of rice production in total agricultural production was 34.0 per cent and calorie supply derived from rice was 37.0 per cent in 1995.

Rice became an inferior good around the middle of the 1980s. Total rice consumption has been on a continuous decline since 1987 and the rate of decline accelerated around 1990. South Korea entered a rice surplus phase at the end of the 1980s. Rice stocks started to increase in 1990 due partly to a bumper crop in 1988 and partly to declining rice consumption. Year-end rice stocks in 1992 were equivalent to more than four months of national rice consumption. Facing problems of surplus rice management, the South Korean government introduced various measures to increase rice consumption rather than enacting production control measures.

However, rice production in South Korea started to decline continuously from the end of the 1980s because of a rapid reduction in rice acreage. The rice economy shifted from a phase of rice surplus to a phase of rice shortage in the first half of the 1990s. Both supply and demand of rice declined in the 1990s and this trend seems likely to continue into the future.

As in the case of Japan, it is important to know the future trend of the supply–demand balance of rice and the impact of MA rice imports on Korea's food self-sufficiency situation. Since a projection of future rice supply and demand in South Korea is available in another article (Kako, 1997), the analytical model and projection results are briefly summarized here:

1 The analytical model of rice supply projection consists of a rice acreage response function and a rice yield function. It is assumed that rice acreage can be expressed as a function of rice price and input prices, and rice yield can be expressed as a function of farm gate rice price, farm wage rate, technological change and the proportion of high yield rice variety planted areas.

2 Rice acreage and rice yield for the 1995–2010 period are projected based on estimated parameters of the rice acreage and rice yield functions, and assumptions with respect to the future values of explanatory variables of these equations. The future values of these explanatory variables are assumed to follow the trends of the 1988–93 period.[8]

3 With respect to rice demand projection, it is assumed that per capita demand for rice is a function of income, rice prices and prices of substitutes and complements.[9] Future per capita rice demand is projected based on the assumptions that future rice prices and wheat and barley prices will follow the trends of the 1988–93 period. Per capita income of both farm households and non-farm households are assumed to increase at 5.5 per cent for the 1995–2010 period.[10]

4 The South Korean government has also acceded to MA rice imports under the GATT Uruguay Round accord. It started at 1 per cent of total rice consumption (51 000 tons) of the base period (1988–1990) in 1995 and will increase to 4 per cent (205 000 tons) by the year 2004. Rice imports for the 2005–2010 period are assumed to increase at the same rate as for the 1995–2004 period.

According to our projection results, rice acreage is expected to be reduced by 18 000 ha per annum on average and will reach 784 000 ha by 2010 (table 7.2). Rice yield is predicted to increase by 2.6 kg per annum to reach 500 kg (milled rice) per 10 ares by the year 2010. Rice production is predicted to decrease in the future because rice acreage is expected to decline at a higher rate than the rate of increase in rice yield.

This declining trend of rice acreage is the most crucial factor in the projection of future rice production. Total rice production is expected to decrease by 63 000 tons per annum, falling to 3.93 million tons in 2010. Per capita rice demand for direct food use is predicted to decrease by 1.7 kg per annum, slightly slowing down from the 1.9 kg annual reduction during the 1979–95 period. The major reasons for this are the slower growth of per capita income and reduction of the farm population. Total rice use is estimated to decrease by 47 000 tons per annum, eventually falling to 4.55 million tons in 2010. This is 708 000 tons less than the 1995 level.

The following conclusions can be drawn from the above analysis: the annual supply–demand balance is predicted to be negative throughout the projection period of 1995–2010. Ending rice stocks will continue to decline and turn to negative in the future if rice imports are limited to MA imports. Reduction in rice consumption in the past was responsible for declining food self-sufficiency. The projected decline in rice consumption will also reduce the food self-sufficiency rate in the future. Although imported rice was not used as table rice, MA rice imports also reduced the food self-sufficiency rate. MA rice imports will contribute to the decline of the food self-sufficiency rate in the future.

3.3   The Impact of Beef Import Liberalization on the Japanese Domestic Market

The Japanese government attempted to expand the beef industry prior to trade liberalization. Protection was given by an upper limit imposed on beef imports. However, beef import quotas were raised by 60 000 metric tons (mt) each year from 1988 to 1990 in accordance with the Japanese Beef Market Access Agreement signed between Japan, Australia and the United States in 1988. Three years later, beef import liberalization was implemented. Import quotas were replaced by higher *ad valorem* import tariffs. The *ad valorem* import tariff rate was set at 70 per cent in 1991 and will be lowered to 38.5 per cent by the year 2000 as agreed under the GATT Uruguay Round.

As a consequence of the increase in import quotas and the introduction of beef import liberalization, beef imports have expanded from 285 000 mt (boneless prime cut weight) in 1988 to 658 000 mt in 1995. Most beef was imported from Australia and the United States. The rapid increase in beef imports sharply reduced Japan's self-sufficiency in beef. The self-sufficiency rate of 72 per cent in 1985 dropped to 50 per cent in 1990 and then to 39 per cent in 1995.

Since 1988 wholesale prices of imported beef fell by about 50 per cent.

For example, in the case of US frozen striploin, prices dropped from 2305 yen per kg in 1988 to 1296 yen in 1994. This decline is mainly due to the reduction in the *ad valorem* tariff rate and an appreciation of the yen against the currencies of beef-exporting countries.

The sharp drop in imported beef prices, as well as increase in per capita income, stimulated beef consumption because beef has a high price elasticity and a high income elasticity – particularly for imported beef. Per capita beef consumption rose from 6.1 kg in 1990 to 8.3 kg in 1995. Total beef consumption has steadily increased from 766 000 mt in 1990 to 1 068 000 mt in 1995.

Despite a rapid increase in beef imports and a decline in beef price, domestic beef production, as a whole, did not suffer significant disruption until 1994. Most particularly, the high-grade Wagyu beef was only slightly affected because of the big difference in quality. On the other hand, the quality of dairy beef is similar to imported beef and was affected by increased beef imports. Prices of dairy beef declined substantially and dairy beef production declined by 10 per cent from 1988 to 1990 before leveling off (Mori and Gorman, 1995, p. 23). Because some farmers switched from dairy beef production to Wagyu beef production, Wagyu beef production increased constantly at an average annual rate of 5 per cent between 1988 and 1994. The proportion of Wagyu beef in total domestic beef production rose from 35 per cent in 1989 to 45 per cent in 1996.

However, domestic beef production started to decline in 1995. The volume of Wagyu beef production fell by 0.4 per cent in 1995, 2.6 per cent in 1996 and 2.5 per cent in 1997, and the volume of dairy beef production also declined by 1.5 per cent in 1996 and 0.5 per cent in 1997. This downsizing of beef production is mainly the result of the fall in and instability of farm income from beef production.

The average price of dairy feeder calves fell from its record high of 229 000 yen per head in 1989 to 149 000 yen in 1991 and went down further to just 83 000 yen in 1994. The steady decline in wholesale prices of fed dairy beef and weakened future expectations of the meat market contributed to this sharp decline (Mori and Gorman, 1995, p. 25). Also the number of female Wagyu cows for breeding declined from 745 000 heads in 1993 to 654 000 heads in 1997, and resulted in a reduction of the number of Wagyu calves. An aging Japanese work force in beef production and an unstable income from beef production together foreshadow the danger of a steep reduction in beef production in the future. This will result in further decline in food self-sufficiency in the future.

4. FOOD SECURITY ISSUES IN JAPAN AND SOUTH KOREA

As discussed in the previous section, the food self-sufficiency rates of Japan and South Korea have consistently declined over time. The calorie self-sufficiency rate for food was the lowest in Japan among the major industrialized countries, 42 per cent in 1995. The figure was also low in South Korea, 62 per cent. These declining trends in food self-sufficiency rates are expected to continue in the future in both countries because of MA rice imports, beef trade liberalization in Japan, gradual reductions in the tariff rate of agricultural products, changes in food consumption pattern, and widening price gaps between domestic and foreign agricultural products. Reflecting on these declining trends in food self-sufficiency rates in both countries and the greater variability in recent world agricultural production caused by abnormal weather patterns, such as the El Niño effect, increasing numbers of people are anxious about the food supply in the future. A public opinion poll carried out by the Management and Coordination Agency of Japan in 1996 reported that the majority of people in Japan (70.5 per cent of the respondents) were anxious about the supply of food in the future (table 7.3). Since a high

Table 7.3 Result of public opinion poll on food production and food supply in Japan

(%)

Opinion	1987	1990	1993	1996
1. It is better to import food if it is cheaper.	19.9	17.0	17.4	10.8
2. It is better to produce food domestically with continuous effort of reducing production costs even though domestically produced food is more expensive than food produced abroad.	31.9	32.7	32.7	45.9
3. It is better to produce basic food like rice domestically with continuous effort of reducing production cost even though it is more expensive than rice produced abroad.	39.3	40.5	44.7	37.5
4. Others.	0.2	0.3	0.5	0.3
5. I don't know.	8.7	9.5	4.7	5.4

Note: Figures in the table show the proportion of answers to the question 'What do you think about the way of food production and supply in Japan?'.

Source: Management and Coordination Agency of Japan, 'Public Opinion Poll on the Role of Food, Agriculture, and Rural Areas, January 1997.

proportion of people are anxious about food security in the future, it is important to discuss how to minimize the risks involved in achieving food security.

4.1 Possible Food Crises

What kinds of food crises may Japan and South Korea face in the future? There are several kinds of possible food crises that may occur. These crises can be classified into: (a) military crisis, such as war and strife; (b) political and economic crisis, such as embargoes and economic blockade; and (c) crisis in peacetime, such as an atomic power station accident, natural calamities, and abnormal weather.

Military crisis used to be the most frequently cited reason for creating a food security policy because of the experiences of food shortages during and just after World War II. South Korea has been faced with a possible outbreak of a military collision with North Korea for a long time. This possible military crisis is the most important reason for maintaining food security. The Korean people's concern about food security heightened following the financial currency crisis, which occurred in December 1997, and was bailed out by the IMF.

The Japanese people's concern over food security was heightened following the world food crisis in the early 1970s. Poor harvests due to abnormal weather conditions worldwide and large amount of crop imports by the former Soviet Union contributed to this crisis. What worsened this Japanese anxiety was the US embargo on soybean exports in 1973. Soon after this world food crisis, a Japanese DIET resolution to maintain 100 per cent self-sufficiency for rice was passed.

Another example of peacetime food crisis was the atomic power station accident in Chernobyl, the Ukraine. A large amount of food was abandoned because of radioactive contamination, and some farmland in Europe could not be used for food production. After this accident, Germany introduced a new law in 1990 to enhance food security in response to this new type of food crisis.

It is possible that these types of food crises could occur in Japan and South Korea. An outbreak of these crises would cause a decrease in food supply and an increase in food prices and could result in malnutrition and starvation.

4.2 Food Security Policies

What kinds of food security policies should be introduced to cope with these possible food crises? Effective food security policies consist of both supply-side policies and demand-side policies. Supply-side policies are related to the plans to ensure a supply of the required food by a combination of food imports, reserve stocks and domestic production in times of emergency. Japan is the world's largest net importer of agricultural products, and South Korea has been increasing its agricultural imports at very high rates since the middle of the 1980s. Since maintaining stable food imports is crucially important for their food security, it is essential for them to maintain friendly relations with agricultural exporting countries and to make long-term trade contracts for agricultural products. It is also desirable to diversify import sources to avoid overconcentration of imports from only one or two countries.

In discussing the food security problems of net importing countries, like Japan and South Korea, it is necessary to understand the characteristics of world agricultural markets and the contents of international trade agreements, such as the GATT. When a small number of countries have a large share of agricultural exports, there will be a tendency for oligopoly to grow under the WTO system (Pinstrup-Andersen, Pandya-Lorch, and Rosegrant, 1997).[11] It is also important to note that the exporter's responsibility of agricultural supply is not guaranteed, and the embargo of agricultural products and regulation of agricultural exports are not prohibited under the GATT Uruguay Round agreement. When food is in short supply, food-exporting countries tend to introduce export regulations to prevent increases in domestic food prices. The US embargo on soybean exports in 1973 is a frequently cited example. It is natural for a government to give priority to consumers within its own territories, and the possibility is high for exporting countries to introduce export regulations when there are sudden food supply shortages.

In Germany and Switzerland, food imports are not considered a reliable source of food supply in their food security policies because food imports were unstable during World War II. The food security policies in both countries lay emphasis on building food reserves. Food reserves are usually held by the government, as well as by private companies and households. In Switzerland, a six-month food stock is maintained by private companies under contract with the government. The Swiss government also recommends private households to hold a few weeks' worth of food stocks.

The Japanese government holds stockpiles of rice, wheat, feed grain, and soybeans under the national reserve system, and the private sector also holds stockpiles of rice, wheat, and feed grain. The Japanese government considers 1.5 million metric tons (mmt) plus or minus 0.5 mmt as the appropriate level of rice stock. The Korean government and the private sector also hold stockpiles of rice and barley. The Korean government considers 1.0 mmt as the appropriate level of rice stock, in which the minimum amount of government stock is 0.5 mmt. Besides having an adequate quantity of domestic reserves, it is desirable for both countries to cooperate with some kind of international stockpiling programs.

According to the result of the same public opinion poll carried out in 1987 by the Management and Coordination Agency of Japan cited earlier, 71.2 per cent of the respondents felt that it is better to produce food domestically with continuous efforts to reduce production costs even though domestically produced food prices are to some extent higher than international food prices. The percentage of those supporting this view has risen to 83.4 per cent in 1996 (table 7.3). While 19.9 per cent of the respondents in 1987 answered that it is better to import foods if they are cheaper, this percentage has dropped to 10.8 per cent in 1996.

If imports should suddenly halt or be disrupted because of war or strife, agricultural production should be increased by expanding farmland to pastures, idle land, and non-farmland as well as expanding production of crops which can supply more food calories per unit of farmland. As a medium-term measure, it is important to maintain potential production capacity. Seeds, farmland, agricultural inputs, and agricultural technology should be preserved, and manpower mobilization plans must be ready so that the minimum amount of required agricultural products can be produced.

If enough food cannot be acquired, food demand control programs, such as food rationing, will have to be introduced. The government will decide the minimum amount of food required and take responsibility for supplying it. In Switzerland, per capita calorie intake is 3300 kcal in ordinary times; in times of food crises, the government will provide 2300 kcal of food per day per person. Such emergency foods can be obtained only through exchange with a ration coupon.

The majority of people are anxious about the supply of food in the future in both Japan and South Korea, reflecting the changes in the environments of supply and demand of food in the world as well as a consistent decline in food self-sufficiency in both countries. Hence it is necessary for the Japanese and Korean government to re-examine current food security policies and establish new policies so that they can cope with a possible food crisis.

5.   CONCLUSIONS

Food consumption in Japan and South Korea has improved significantly in the last 30–40 years due to the rapid increases in per capita income. Nutritionally well-balanced dietary patterns were achieved based on the increase in the consumption of domestically produced as well as imported agricultural products. The dependence on foreign agricultural products has increased considerably over time, especially since the latter half of the 1980s, and is expected to increase further as agricultural trade liberalization proceeds under WTO.

In Japan, total calorie supply has increased slowly since the end of the 1980s because per capita calorie supply is fast approaching saturation point and population growth has become very slow. Japanese agriculture has to compete with foreign agriculture in a zero-sum game of food supply and the country is losing the game because of relatively high production costs. Cheap imported agricultural products have been substituting for domestic agricultural products, and the absolute size of domestic agricultural production has been declining since the middle of the 1980s. The situation is slightly different in South Korea. Total calorie supply has been increasing due to the increase in the per capita calorie supply and the country has a higher population growth rate than Japan. Nonetheless, the proportion of imported food has increased gradually, because of the higher production costs of domestic agricultural products relative to international prices, and changes in food consumption patterns.

The food self-sufficiency rates in Japan and South Korea have consistently declined over time. The decline in the self-sufficiency rate for cereals has been most significant because of the large and widening price differences between domestic and foreign cereals. This declining trend of the food self-sufficiency rate is expected to continue in both countries because of MA rice imports, beef trade liberalization in Japan, gradual reductions in the tariff rate of agricultural products, changes in food consumption patterns, and widening price gaps between domestic and foreign agricultural products.

Although consumers are satisfied with the improvement in food consumption, they feel uncertain whether or not they will be able to acquire enough food if the global food supply–demand balance deteriorates sharply in the future. The public opinion poll carried out by the Management and Coordination Agency of the Japanese government indicates that public opinion is largely in favour of domestic production and the continued efforts to reduce agricultural production costs. Hence, policies should concentrate on reducing production costs through farm mechanization, land improvement, expanding farm size, as well as technological innovation. Since Japanese consumers' concern for high-quality and good-tasting food is strong, it is very important to develop food with these characteristics. Consumers' interest in food safety, reflected by the growing demand for organic agricultural produce, also calls for further development of less input sustainable agriculture.

It is realistic to establish food security policies for Japan and South Korea by combining domestic production, reserved stocks, and imports because land resources are limited and production costs are far higher than that of agricultural exporting countries. Japan's and South Korea's heavy dependence on food imports makes friendly relations with agricultural exporting countries and long-term trade contracts highly important. It is also desirable to diversify import sources and avoid over-concentration of imports from a few specific countries. Moreover, in building an appropriate level of buffer food stocks, these countries need to consider many factors, including the rising global air temperature, increasing grain yield variability in major agricultural exporting countries, as well as progress in agricultural trade liberalization. Although it is an unlikely possibility, countries like Japan and South Korea need to prepare plans for a safe supply of food when sudden disruptions to food imports occur. As a short-term measure, it is necessary to hold domestic food stockpiles and to prepare administration and legislation for the rationing of food. As a medium-term measure, it is important to maintain potential production capacity. Seeds, farmland, agricultural inputs, and agricultural technology should be preserved, and manpower mobilization plans must be ready so that the minimum amount of required agricultural products can be produced domestically.

NOTES

[1] The period of analysis in this article is 1960–95, and the impact of the IMF crisis on Korean agriculture is not investigated here.

[2] PFC calorie ratio is the proportion of calorie supply from proteins, fats, and carbohydrates.

[3] Major sources of data in this article are 'Portable Size Statistics Book on Agriculture, Forestry and Fisheries', Ministry of Agriculture, Forestry and Fisheries, Japan, and 'Major Statistical Indicator for Agriculture', Ministry of Agriculture and Forestry, Korea.

[4] The ratio of agricultural import liberalization is defined as the ratio of the number of agricultural trade items that can be imported without any regulation to the total number of imported agricultural item.

[5] The current GATT accord allows Japan to be exempted from tariff imposition for the period 1995–2000. In return for this concession Japan started the minimum access rice import in 1995.

[6] Rice production started to exceed domestic rice consumption at the end of the

1960s, resulting in an accumulation of surplus rice in government storage. To prevent the accumulation of surplus rice a series of rice diversion programs have been implemented since 1969. The government decided the nationwide goal for rice diversion acreage. The goal of rice diversion acreage was divided among rice producers. Rice producers were compelled to fulfill rice acreage reduction quotas by both the national government authority and the agricultural cooperatives.

7   The fit of the model is fairly good. The coefficients of determination of the rice demand function and the rice yield function are 0.995, and that of the paddy field function is 0.999. The t-statistics of all parameters are large, and all parameter estimates are different from zero at the 5 per cent significance level. The signs of the estimated parameters are consistent with the economic theory.

8   Real farm gate rice prices are assumed to decrease at 3.1 per cent, and real retail rice prices are assumed to decrease at 2.4 per cent per annum. It is also assumed that farm gate real wheat and barley prices will decrease at 0.2 per cent per annum.

9   The fit of the model is good. The coefficients of determination of the rice acreage response function and the rice yield function are 0.985 and 0.900, respectively. The coefficients of determination of the rice demand function of farm households and non-farm households are 0.968 and 0.955, respectively. The t-statistics of almost all the parameters are large, and parameter estimates are different from zero at the 5 per cent significance level. The signs of the estimated parameters are consistent with the economic theory.

10 These assumptions may have to be re-examined carefully because of the recent IMF crisis of Korean economy. However, there is not enough accumulation of economic data related to this crisis, yet. Therefore, current projection of supply and demand of rice was carried out using these assumptions.

11 Pinstrup-Andersen, Pandya-Lorch, and Rosegrant (1997) projected that net cereal exports will increase by almost 60 per cent between 1993 and 2020, and the United States is expected to capture a large share of the increased export market for cereals.

REFERENCES

Hayami, Yujiro (1988), *Japanese Agriculture under Siege: The Political Economy of Agricultural Policies*, Hampshire: Macmillan Press.
Higuchi, Teizo (1991), 'Japanese Dietary Habits and Food consumption', in the Committee for the Japanese Agriculture Session, XXI IAAE Conference (ed.), *Agriculture and Agricultural Policy in Japan*, Tokyo, Japan: University of Tokyo Press, 87–104.
Kako, Toshiyuki, Masahiko Gemma, and Shoichi Ito (1997),

'Implications of the Minimum Access Rice Imports on Supply and Demand Balance of Rice in Japan', *Agricultural Economics*, 16: 193–204.

Kako, Toshiyuki (1997), 'Projections and Policy Implications of Supply and Demand of Rice in South Korea', *Journal of Rural Economics*, 69(1): 1–13.

Kim, Yong-Taek(1997), 'Structural Adjustments in Korean Agriculture', *Journal of Rural Development*, 20(1): 1–31.

Lee, Jae Ok (1993), 'Trends and Problem of Import Liberalization of Agricultural Markets in Korea', *Journal of Rural Development*, 16(1): 41–55.

Management and Coordination Agency, Government of Japan (1997), 'Public-Opinion Poll on the Role of Food, Agriculture, and Rural Area', January.

Mori, H. and W. D. Gorman (1995), 'The Japanese Beef Market Following Liberalization: What Has and Has Not Happened?', *Journal of Rural Economics*, 67(1): 20–30.

Pinstrup-Andersen, Per, Rajul Pandya-Lorch, and Mark W. Rosegrant (1997), *The World Food Situation: Recent Developments, Emerging Issues, and Long-term Prospects*, IFPRI.

Saeki, Naomi (1991), 'Development of Trade in Agricultural Products and Border Adjustment in Agriculture', by the Committee for the Japanese Agriculture Session, XXI IAAE Conference (ed), *Agriculture and Agricultural Policy in Japan*, Tokyo, Japan: University of Tokyo Press, 121–42.

8. A policy choice of the rice import issue in Taiwan

Min-Hsien Yang and Yu-Hui Chen

1. INTRODUCTION

Food security is one of the most important issues in agricultural production for many countries. It is not surprising that many countries use this as a reason to intervene in their domestic agricultural commodity markets. However, it very often causes disputes between countries in international trade. The trade liberalization of agricultural commodities was one of the main topics in the Uruguay Round Negotiation. The negotiation was completed in 1993. According to the agreement on agriculture, all market distortions, such as tariff and non-tariff trade barriers, price support programs, and subsidies of production factors, should be eliminated within some period of time. It is anticipated that the order of the international trade in agricultural commodities will step into a new era. In general, the agricultural policy reform of our country follows closely the guidelines of the agricultural agreement. However, the rice import issue is a main concern, since it will influence the structure of agricultural production in Taiwan and other rice-producing countries.

 In Taiwan, rice is the most important crop with most farmers and occupies a large proportion of cultivated land. Its production not only relates to the rice growers but also affects the daily lives of the people, resource allocations and the environment of the nation. How to keep production continuing and to maintain its self-sufficient status are always the first priorities of the agricultural policy. Even with less comparative advantage in rice production after 1972, price support and limit import programs were employed to support the domestic rice industry. These policies are still in force now. However, the adequacy of the current price support program has been argued, not only because of concerns of a closed economy but also it conflicts with the agricultural agreement reached in the most recent negotiations of the GATT. Furthermore, it seems that Taiwan has to make some concessions to gain membership into

WTO.

In the agreement on agriculture, open market issues include tariffs, tariffication for non-tariff policy, and limited access. Based upon these open market rules, Taiwan can make a choice between tariffication and limited access at the beginning of the rice import period. The first policy alternative is tariffication along with importing 3 per cent of the consumption level each year. The second one is to import 4 per cent of the domestic consumption level each year without tariffication. In the first six years of reform, the requirements of the two alternatives are quite different. Under the case of tariffication, the lowest import quantity should increase to 5 per cent of the domestic consumption level, while in the limited access case, the import should increase to 8 per cent of the consumption level. Therefore, by the end of the reform period, there is going to be a significant difference in the import levels for the two alternatives. Under the tariffication regime the tariff reduction should increase 2.5 per cent each year, which implies by the end of the reform the total tariff reduction will be 15 per cent of the original tariff level. Since limited access is only related to the import level, at this moment, it is irrelevant to the tariff reduction.

The theory of international trade says that there exists an equivalent relationship between a tariff and a quota. This relationship may not hold, however, under the circumstances of the incomplete competitive market such as price uncertainty, the change of the exchange rate and price support program (Woo, 1993; Yang, 1995; Baldwin, 1989; Bhagwati, 1968; Hossain, Hassan, and Jensen, 1993). Moschini (1991) also mentioned that the use of the tariffication accompanied with the lowest import quantity may reduce the risk of miscalculation of the tariff equivalent. It is not hard to find that tariffication and limited access have different implications both for production and consumption. Their impacts on a domestic aggregate measurement in agriculture are also expected to be different. Although the Taiwanese government tends to adopt the limited access policy on rice import as Japan and South Korea did, it is worth giving some more thought on this policy choice issue under the consideration of rationality.

Neoclassical economic theory points out that a free economy will help economic efficiency, and that free trade will increase social welfare. However, economic theory cannot explain the facts that protection for the domestic market and limiting trade policy prevailed in many countries. According to the political economy point of view, economic efficiency is not the only consideration in the decision-making process. This explains why the phenomena of limited trade still exists. Since the policy choice does not depend entirely on the economic efficiency viewpoint, the purpose of this research is to find a plausible rice policy under the consideration of political economy.

There are five sections in this chapter. The theory of policy choice is stated in section 2. In section 3, a multiplier analysis is employed to examine the economic effects of tariffication and limited access policies. In the fourth section, the political preference function and welfare measures are combined together to order the political preference for three import scenarios. Some policy implications and conclusions are addressed in the last section.

2. THE THEORY OF POLICY CHOICE

In the political economy of trade policy, Baldwin (1989) and Vousden (1990) classified the research methods into two categories: the self-interest approach and the social-concerns approach. These two approaches are used to explain the determinants of the trade policy. The former suggests the policy is determined by the demand side. The decision to adopt a new policy depends totally on the pressure from the lobbyists of different interest groups. The government only plays a minor and passive role in decision making. The only thing that government does is policy enforcement. In the social concerns approach, the policy is decided by the government only. That is, the government's decision will not be influenced by the pressures of interest groups. Since the self-interest and social-concerns approaches depend either on the interest groups or the government's points of view, it is easy to fall into the fallacy of prejudice. In the reality, the decision-making process is affected by both the demand and supply sides of the political market (Chen and Liu, 1993). Baldwin (1989) also showed that the determinants in both analytical models affect the decision making. According to the new political economy approach, neoclassical economics should be taken into account. It suggests that government intervention is determined by the operation of the political market. Decision makers offer a policy to their constituency in return for political support. Interest groups increase their political support if they are helped by the policy and reduce support if they are hurt (Swinnen, 1994). The change in political support is assumed to be proportional, so that policy-makers apply a redistributive policy up to the point where the marginal increase in support from those benefiting is offset by the marginal loss in support from those hurt.

Since the Political Preference Function (PPF) approach assumes that current policies reflect a political economic equilibrium summarizing all the relevant forces, we can integrate the reduced-form political preference

(Love, Rausser, and Burton, 1990; Swinnen and Zee, 1993) to explain the policy formation and reflect the change of political support rating (de Gorter and Tsur, 1991; Yang, 1995). The reduced-form political preference or governing criterion function acknowledges the influence of pressure groups in the policy process by the assumption that an abstract policy maker maximizes a weighted objective function reflecting the welfare of lobbying groups and reveals his preferences through the weights he attribute to the different objectives. Policy preferences are seen as the result of a political-economic game between pressure groups and the policy maker (Swinnen and Zee, 1993). Assuming the political rating is positively related to each group's welfare level, the economic surplus can be used as a proxy to measure the political support rating (Tyers, 1990). The political preference function should include the groups affected by the policy so an economic surplus representing the welfare of each group should also be included in it. The economic surplus is also affected by a policy change. The effect of a policy change will affect the economic surplus directly and influence the political support rating indirectly.

The political preference function can be expressed as

$$\text{Max } V = V\{S[PS(X), CS(X), G(X)]\},$$
$$x$$

where *PS*, *CS*, and *G* are producers' surplus, consumers' surplus and government's gain, respectively. Term *X* represents a vector of policy variables, which are endogenously determined by the political market. Since *PS*, *CS*, and *G* are functions of *X*, these policy variables are directly related to the welfare level of each group.

The political preference function is quasi-concave and ordinal so any monotonic transformation of the function will represent the same order of the political preference. Without loss of generality, it is also assumed that the functional form is additive separable

$$\text{Max } V = PS(X)W_P + CS(X)W_C + G(X)W_G, \qquad (8.1)$$
$$x$$

where the *x*'s are policy instrument variables. Terms W_P, W_C and W_G are the political weights for producers, consumers, and government, respectively. They are the political economic parameters representing the reaction of each group's response to the policy change and the tendency of the government's bias towards or against some interest group. Their values reveal the marginal trade-off of the political influence among the interest groups.

Putting the current structure of the political weights into the political preference function, we can order the political preference for all policy alternatives. Tyers (1990) suggests that in order to have a successful trade negotiation, the strategic trade policy formation should result in the least impact on the original political market. Therefore, the policy choice should follow the guide of policy ordering and Tyers' suggestion.

In the empirical, we try to build up the econometric model for the Taiwanese rice market. The long-run and short-run multiplier analysis is then applied to analyse alternative rice policies. The results later will be used to measure the consumers' surplus, producers' surplus, and the change in expenditures of the government. Combining those welfare measures and the revealed policy weight, the political preference for different policy alternatives can be ordered and then used as the criteria for the policy choice.

3. THE ANALYSIS OF ECONOMIC EFFECTS

In this section, an econometric model of the Taiwanese rice market is developed. According to the model's dynamic nature, two policy alternatives (tariffication and limited access) are analysed by using the multiplier analysis under the short-run and the long-run circumstances.

3.1 Model Specification and Estimation

A seven-equation econometric model is developed and set forth on the nature of the Taiwanese rice market. The model is defined as follows

$$QS_t = f_1 (QS_{t-1}, PS_{t-1}, VPI_{t-1}, WA_t, TT_t, D84_t) \quad \text{Rice production} \quad (8.2)$$

The rice production lagged one period (QS_{t-1}) and the producer's price lagged one period (PS_{t-1}) are included to reflect the adaptive expectation model. They are expected to have positive effects on supply. The price index for vegetables lagged one period (VPI_{t-1}) is used as a proxy for the price of the competitive crop. The cost of labour (WA_t) and technology variable (TT_t) are also included in the function. A dummy variable, $D84_t$, is used to represent the rice land diversion program from 1984. The prices for competitive crop, production cost, and land diversion program are anticipated to have negative influences on rice supply. The technology progress, on the other hand, is expected to have a positive sign.

$$QD_t = f_2 (QD_{t-1}, PD_t, GNP_t, POP_t, D1_t, D78_t, D91_t, QG_t)$$
Rice consumption   (8.3)

where QD_{t-1} is the lagged one period rice demand; PD_t is the retail price of rice; GNP_t represents income; POP_t is the total population of Taiwan; QG_t is the amount purchased by the government; $D1_t$, $D78_t$, and $D91_t$ are binary variables representing oil crises, structural change of consumption, and rice ration policy, respectively. The lagged consumption, total population, and government purchase are expected to have positive signs. According to the economic theory, the retail price is expected to have negative influence on consumption. The impact of income on rice consumption is ambiguous. If the income effect is positive, rice is a normal good, otherwise, it is an inferior good.

$$CSTP_t = f_3 (CSTP_{t-1}, PD_t, CSTG_t, D74_t, D85_t)$$
Private stock change   (8.4)

The private stock change is affected by last period stock change ($CSTP_{t-1}$), retail price (PD_t), government stock change ($CSTG_t$), price support program ($D74_t$) and the structural change of the private storage industry ($D85_t$). The increase of the government stock change is expected to decrease the private stock change. The retail price is also expected to have a negative impact on the private stock change.

$$QG_t = f_4 (R_t, PG_t, PF_t, QS_t)$$
Government purchase   (8.5)

where R_t is the announced quantity that will be purchased by the government per acre; Term PG_t is the target price of rice; PF_t is the farm price of rice. The government purchase per acre, target price, and level of production are expected to have positive impacts on total quantity of government purchase. The farm gate price, on the other hand, is anticipated to have a negative effect on the dependent variable.

$$PF_t = f_5 (PD_t, W_t)$$
Price transmission   (8.6)

The farm price is affected by the retail price (PD_t) and marketing margin (W_t).

$$PS_t = f_6 (PF_t, PG_t)$$
Producer price   (8.7)

The producer's price is affected by the farm price and the price support level.

$$QS_t' = QD_t + QG_t + CSTP_t \qquad \text{Market-clearing condition (8.8)}$$

where the total supply of rice on the market (QS_t') is the rice production minus the rice consumption on the farm. According to this market-clearing condition, the total supply of rice on the market is the sum of the total consumption, government purchase and the private stock change. The variable definitions can be found in table 8.1.

Assume all functional forms are linear and the producer's price is the weighted average of the farm price and price support level. Since the model is a simultaneous equation system, all equations should be estimated at the same time. The two-stage Least Squares method (2SLS) and the 1952–95 annual time series data are employed to estimate the system. The estimated results are presented in table 8.2. Most of the coefficients have the correct signs as expected with significant t ratios. This estimated model then will serve as the basis of the multiplier analysis stated in the following section.

3.2   The Multiplier Analysis for Each Policy Alternative

According to the multiplier analysis, the final form of a dynamic model can be expressed as

$$AY_t + BY_{t-1} + CX_t = U_t$$

where Y_t is a matrix containing endogenous variables in period t, X_t is the matrix of exogenous variables, Y_{t-1} contains the predetermined variables and U_t is the disturbances. Rearranging the above equation, the reduced form can be written as

$$Y_t = D_1 Y_{t-1} + D_2 X_t + V_t$$

where $D_1 = -A^{-1}B$, $D_2 = -A^{-1}C$ and $V_t = A^{-1}U_t$.

Taking the partial derivative of Y_t with respect to X_t, we can obtain the short-run static multiplier

$$M^S = D_2 \qquad (8.9)$$

The short-run static multiplier shows that the impact of the exogenous shock only lasts for one period. It measures the impacts of a tariff decrease (or limited access increase) on endogenous variables each year during the reform period. Assume any exogenous shock continues more

Food security in Asia

Table 8.1 List of variables, definitions, and data sources

Variables	Definition	Data source
Endogenous variables		
QS	Annual domestic rice production (metric ton)	Taiwan Food Statistic Book
QD	Annual domestic rice consumption (metric ton)	Food Balance Sheet
PD	Retail price of rice (NT$ /kg)	Taiwan Food Statistic Book
CSTP	Private stock change (metric ton)	Calculated by market-clearing condition
QG	Government purchase (metric ton)	Food administration in Taiwan
PF	Farm price	Agriculture yearbook
PS	Producer price	Weighted average of farm price and target price
Exogenous variables		
VPI	Wholesale price index of vegetables	Monthly Statistics of Agricultural Commodity Price and Production Cost
WA	Labour cost per acre (NT$/acre)	Monthly Statistics of Agricultural Commodity Price and Production Cost
TT	Time trend	1952 = 1
GNP	Gross national production	Taiwan Statistical Data Book
POP	Total population	Taiwan Statistical Data Book
D84	Binary variable representing rice land diversion program	1 for 1984 and after 0 otherwise
D1	Binary variable representing the oil crisis	1 for 1973, 1974 0 otherwise
D78	Binary variable represents change of the structural change of consumption	1 for 1978 and after 0 otherwise
D91	Binary variable represents change of the food rationing program	1 for 1991 and after 0 otherwise
D74	Binary variable representing the price support program	1 for 1974 and after 0 otherwise
CSTG	Government stock change (metric ton)	Food Balance Sheet
R	The target quantity of purchase announced by the government (kg/ha)	Food administration in Taiwan
PG	Target price of rice ($NT/kg)	Food Administration in Taiwan
W	Index of wage rate for the manufacturing industry	Quarterly Statistics of Economic Tendency

Table 8.2   *Structural parameters of an econometric model of the Taiwanese rice market, estimated using two-stage least squares and time series data 1952–95*

Variable	Parameter estimated	Asymptotic t-ratio
Rice supply (QS_t):		
$CON1$*	–129 284 000	
QS_{t-1}	+0.5921784	8.98
PS_{t-1}	+2 358 459	4.34
VPI_{t-1}	–3 707 233	3.20
WA_t	–25 595.92	3.58
TT_t	+412 720.5	6.28
$D84_t$	–314 972 300	7.48
$R^2 = 0.9857$, $\overline{R}^2 = 0.9833$, DW = 1.8962, h = 0.3774		
Rice consumption (QD_t):		
$CON2$	+53 599 110	
QD_{t-1}	+0.6331060	6.86
PD_t	–5 340 521	1.65
GNP_t	–78.07508	2.37
POP_t	+49.52233	3.22
$D1_t$	+143 911 600	3.13
$D78_t$	–169 576 500	4.93
$D91_t$	+154 010 000	2.48
QG_t	+0.1440108	2.54
$R^2 = 0.9220$, $\overline{R}^2 = 0.9901$, DW = 1.7778, h = 0.89832		
Change of stock ($CSTP_t$):		
$CON3$	–27 892 100	
$CSTP_{t-1}$	+0.2999102	2.88
PD_t	–5 475 339	2.15
$CSTG_t$	–0.4330709	6.25
$D74_t$	+8 598 800	1.78
$D85_t$	–238 777 900	4.40
$R^2 = 0.7456$, $\overline{R}^2 = 0.7112$, DW = 2.0811, h = –0.2674		
Government purchase (QG_t):		
$CON4$	–1 673 246 000	
R_t	+172 021.7	3.25
PG_t	+67 135 330	9.54
PF_t	–50 237 150	5.91
QS_t	+0.7210575	12.24
$R^2 = 0.9574$, $\overline{R}^2 = 0.9474$, DW = 2.0278		
Price transmission (PF_t):		
$CON5$	+0.5346029	
PD_t	+0.7645146	40.05
W_t	–0.01449376	5.05
$R^2 = 0.9935$, $\overline{R}^2 = 0.9932$, DW = 1.8150		
Farm price (PS_t):		
PF_t	+0.6872900	44.72
PG_t	+0.3163046	24.68
$R^2 = 0.9997$, $\overline{R}^2 = 0.9997$, DW = 2.0201		

CON_i represents the constant term for each regression equation.

Food security in Asia

than one period and increases at a fixed rate each year during the period of reform and the values of exogenous variables stay at the last year's level of the reform in the long run. The vector of the long-run exogenous variables is then

$$X_t = (1 + \gamma)^5 X_{t-5} = X_t^*$$

The long-run multiplier is

$$M^L = \partial Y_t / \partial X_t^* \tag{8.10}$$

$$= [D_1^2 + D_1(1 + \gamma) + D_1(1 + \gamma)^2 + D_1(1 + \gamma)^3 + D_1(1 + \gamma)^4 + D_1(1 + \gamma)^5] \\ D_2 / (1 - D_1)$$

Since it evaluates the impact for more than one period, it can show the feedback effects of lagged dependent variables on the endogenous variables. Therefore, the long-run multiplier reflects the aggregate effects of the tariff reduction or limited access increase for the whole reform period.

3.3   Results of Multiplier Analysis

The policy scenarios should be set up under the guideline of the GATT's Agreement on Agriculture to generate the short-run and long-run multipliers. However, the tariff equivalent for each policy scenario must be calculated since the government is still using the non-tariff barriers to prevent rice imports. To calculate the tariff equivalent, the tariff basis should be determined first. On 1 January, 1990, Taiwan applied for membership of GATT and obtained the observer status of GATT two years later. Because of this, the average tariff for the period 1990—92 serves as the tariff basis for the tariffication even though Taiwan will get membership later than that period. The tariff equivalent is calculated by using the average tariff and the price difference between the domestic and foreign market. The calculation looks simple; however, it is not. For example, which price should be used as the domestic price of rice, retail price or wholesale price? What does the foreign rice price mean? Which country's price should be applied here? Is the price based on CIF or FOB? Which period's exchange rate should be used, the base period or current year? How should the quality of rice be defined? The lack of the specific standards for the calculation causes some debates among countries. Because of this controversy, there is also no consistent method to calculate each country's domestic tariff equivalent. In related research on the Taiwanese rice market, the calculated tariff equivalent ranges from 95 per cent to 266 per cent (Yang, 1996). To avoid the variation of results and to analyse the impact of the rice imports, we choose American rice, Long grain, No.2 and FOB as the standard to proceed with the estimation analysis. For the period of 1990–92, the average rice price in the US market was NT$ 8.42/kg. For the same period, the domestic wholesale price of rice was NT$ 23.36/kg. Based on the price difference, the calculated tariff equivalent is NT$14.94 /kg or 177 per cent.

According to the agreement at the Uruguay Round, by the end of the reform period the tariff reduction of any single commodity cannot be lower than 15 per cent. Assuming the reduction is linear in the year, then the tariff reduction is 2.5 per cent per year. That is, the tariff equivalent continues to be reduced NT$ 0.37/kg each year. The agricultural agreement also requires that, by the end of the period, the average reduction cannot be lower than 36 per cent. We also assume the reduction is linear, which means that the tariff falls 6 per cent and the tariff equivalent declines NT$ 0.90/kg. Assume after the tariffication, the domestic wholesale price of rice (*PH*) equals the sum of the world price of rice (*PW*) and the tariff equivalent after reduction. The tariffication links the world price and domestic wholesale price together and then transmits this effect into the retail and farm prices. We found that the domestic price is no longer determined by the market-clearing condition. There is a need to re-examine the relationship between the retail and wholesale prices. After the estimation, the relationship between the two prices is as follows

$$PD_t = 2.302005 + 1.225562 \, PH_t \quad R^2 = 0.9716 \quad \overline{R}^2 = 0.9790 \quad DW = 1.8206$$
$$(35.18) \hspace{7cm} (8.11)$$

According to the above equation, when the tariff is reduced 2.5 per cent or 6 per cent, we know that the wholesale price decreases NT$ 0.37/kg and NT$0.90/kg, and the retail price falls NT$0.46/kg and NT$1.1/kg, respectively.

The estimated parameters of the econometric model and equation (8.11) are plugged into equation (8.9) and (8.10) to generate the short-run and long-run multipliers for different tariffication scenarios. The results of the 2.5 per cent and 6 per cent tariff equivalent reduction scenarios are shown in tables 8.3 and 8.4.

From table 8.3, in the first year of the reform, the production level stays the same, but the private stock change and consumption react immediately to the variation in the retail price. The decrease in farm price enlarges the difference between the support price and farm price, which results in the increase in government purchase. After calculating the excess demand of the nation, we know in the first year of reform we are going to import 25 063 metric tons of rice from the world.

Table 8.3 Tariffication: the long-run and the short-run multipliers (under the scenario of 2.5 per cent tariff reduction per year)

unit: brown rice, metric ton, NT\$/kg

	Short run						Long run
	1st year	2nd year	3rd year	4th year	5th year	6th year	
Production	0	–5673	–14 704	–25 725	–37 924	–50 820	–208 087
Consumption	4976	12 514	21325	30 736	40 403	50 166	92 221
Private stock change	2506	5764	9248	12 799	16 370	19 950	2850
Government purchase	17 581	31 071	42 140	51 774	60 558	68 859	–44 539
Retail price	–0.46	–0.92	–1.37	–1.83	–2.29	–2.75	–2.75
Farm price	–0.35	–0.70	–1.05	–1.40	–1.75	–2.10	–2.10
Producer's price	–0.25	–0.48	–0.72	–0.96	–1.20	–1.44	–1.44

Source: Calculated from the econometric model of the rice market.

Table 8.4 Tariffication: the long-run and the short-run multipliers (under the scenario of 6 per cent tariff reaction per year)

unit: brown rice, metric ton , NT\$/kg

	Short run						Long run
	1st year	2nd year	3rd year	4th year	5th year	6th year	
Production	0	–13 614	–35 290	–61 741	–91 018	–121 970	–499 372
Consumption	11 943	30 035	51 181	73 765	96 967	120 386	221 307
Private stock change	6015	13 834	22 195	30 717	39 288	47 874	68 383
Government purchase	42 194	74 571	101 135	124 256	145 399	165 215	–106 914
Retail price	–1.10	–2.20	–3.30	–4.39	–5.49	–6.59	–6.59
Farm price	–0.84	–1.68	–2.52	–3.36	–4.20	–5.04	–5.04
Producer's price	–0.58	–1.16	–1.73	–2.31	–2.89	–3.46	–3.46

Source: Calculated from the econometric model of the rice market.

The calculated import level of a 2.5 per cent tariff reduction is lower than the limited access quantity of 44 599 metric tons. By continuing the 2.5 per cent tariff reduction until the end of the reform, domestic rice production will decrease 50 820 metric tons and the quantity of rice imports is 189 795 metric tons. This import level is over the minimum access level (74 332 metric tons) and accounts for about 13 per cent of the long-run consumption, which also results in a decrease in the retail price by 2.75 NT dollars per kilogram. Under the tariffication scenario, there are two cases applied here to analyse the long-run impacts. If the tariff stays at the sixth year's level of reform, rice production will decrease 208 087 metric tons in the long run. This is four times the domestic production reduction at the end of reform (table 8.3). The impacts of a 6 per cent tariff reduction each year will be more substantial than those of a 2.5 per cent tariff reduction. The long-run production will decrease 499 372 metric tons, accounting for 30 per cent of the current production. Consumption will increase 221 307 metric tons and the retail price is going to fall 6.59 NT dollars per kilogram (table 8.4).

The implication of a limited access policy is simpler than those of tariffication. The major policy scheme is to control the quantity of rice imports. Owing to the barrier of connecting to the world price, the domestic price is determined endogenously by the market-clearing condition. The average annual consumption level for the base period (1990—92) is 1 486 633 metric tons of brown rice. Therefore, at the beginning of the reform we have to import 4 per cent of the average consumption level, which is 59 465 metric tons. The import level continues to increase by the amount of 11 893 metric tons each year and by the end of reform the import level will be 118 931 metric tons (which is 8 per cent of the average consumption level of the base year).

Table 8.5 shows that during the period of reform, both rice imports and consumption levels will increase but the quantity of production will decrease. The decrease in production is lower than the amount of import increase. The amount of decrease in production is about 30 per cent of the import level. The imported rice will not be consumed entirely by the consumers. It will go to the government stock as well. In the limited access case, the import level is 4 per cent of the average annual consumption, which is larger than that of tariffication with a 2.5 per cent tariff reduction. Under this program, the decrease in price will be substantial as well, but the rate of the price decrease will get smaller. The impact of tariffication is just the other way around, with an increasing influence as times goes on. In the third year of reform, the impact of tariffication on price is more significant than limited access. In the long run, the import level stays at 118 931 metric tons. The import level is

Food security in Asia

Table 8.5 Limited access: the long-run and short-run multipliers

unit: brown rice, metric ton, NT$/kg

	Short run						Long run
	1st year	2nd year	3rd year	4th year	5th year	6th year	
Production	0	−13 459	−21 492	−27 620	−33 011	−38 089	−119 149
Consumption	11 807	17 940	22 192	25 793	29 167	32 467	41 720
Private stock change	5 946	7 758	8 907	10 030	11 200	12 403	11 426
Government purchase	41 712	32 202	30 661	31 702	33 660	35 972	−53 364
Retail price	−1.09	−1.09	−1.20	−1.34	−1.50	−1.65	−2.30
Farm price	−0.83	−0.83	−0.92	−1.03	−1.14	−1.26	−1.75
Producer's price	−0.57	−0.57	−0.63	−0.71	−0.79	−0.87	−1.21

Source: Calculated from the econometric model of the rice market.

almost equal to the amount of decrease in production. Due to the production decrease, the quantity of rice controlled by the government will decrease in the long run. Based upon the analyses stated above, the change in government purchasing will be 50 per cent of the import level. Thus limited access has less negative impacts on the retail and producers' price, and is, therefore, a better alternative for producers.

4. WELFARE EFFECT AND THE ORDER OF POLITICAL PREFERENCE

4.1 Welfare Analysis

From the results of the multiplier analysis calculated in the last section, the social welfare can be evaluated by using the farm price, retail price, and the change in the quantities. According to Bale and Greenshield (1978), the production and consumption gains and the changes in producers' surplus, consumers' surplus, and social welfare can be calculated as follows:

The production gain = $0.5 \times \Delta PS \times \Delta QS$.
The consumption gain = $0.5 \times \Delta PD \times \Delta QD$.
The change in producer's surplus = $\Delta PS \times QS_0 -$ the production gain.
The change in consumers' surplus = $\Delta PD \times QD_0 +$ the consumption

gain.

The change of social welfare = the change in producers' surplus + the change in consumers' surplus + the change in tariff revenue

where QS_0 and QD_0 are the production and consumption levels before the enforcement of the policy. The estimated welfare effects are presented in table 8.6, table 8.7, and table 8.8. The results show that domestic rice production decreases as imports increase, which in turn improves the efficiency of resource allocation and, therefore, increases the production gain. It is 6 per cent tariff reduction per year scenario that stimulates the largest import increase and production gain. The decrease in the retail price alleviates the consumers' expenditures on rice consumption, which in turn increases the consumption gain. The consumption gain will continue to increase as long as the import level increases.

Generally speaking, the social welfare will increase since the gain in consumers' surplus is greater than the loss of producers' surplus. One thing that should be emphasized is that the increase in rice imports will have significant influence on domestic rice growers in the long run. According to the calculated results shown in table 8.7, the long-run producers' surplus will decrease 6.7 billion NT dollars for the 6 per cent tariff reduction scenario. From table 8.6 and table 8.8, loss of producers' surplus caused by limited access and a 2.5 per cent tariff reduction are 2.1 billion NT dollars and 2.6 billion NT dollars, respectively.

Table 8.6 Tariffication: the welfare effects (under the scenario of 2.5 per cent tariff reduction per year)

unit: 1,000 NT$

	1st year	2nd year	3rd year	4th year	5th year	6th year	Long-run equilibrium
Production gain	0	1 364	5 305	12 375	228 064	36 677	150 174
Consumption gain	1 139	5 728	14 642	28 138	46 236	68 902	126 665
Tariff revenue	365 659	702 713	1 009 937	1 290 419	1 547 542	1 784 324	978 074
Change of producer's surplus	−405 645	−812 655	−1 222 241	−1 634 956	−2 051 031	−2 470 988	−2 584 485
Change of consumer's surplus	651 144	1 305 724	1 964 643	2 628 144	3 296 247	3 969 600	4 027 362
Change of social welfare	611 158	119 578	1 752 338	2 283 607	2 792 758	3 282 936	2 420 950

Source: Calculated by this research.

Food security in Asia

Table 8.7 Tariffication: the welfare effects (under the scenario of 6 per cent tariff reduction per year)

unit: 1,000 NT$

	1st year	2nd year	3rd year	4th year	5th year	6th year	Long-run equilibrium
Production gain	0	7 859	30 557	71 279	131 350	211 221	864 785
Consumption gain	6 560	32 996	84 340	162 076	266 318	396 766	729 379
Tariff revenue	848 112	1 570 456	2 167 355	2 648 732	3 024 279	3 301 386	1 809 469
Change of producer's surplus	−973 552	−1 954 963	−2 951 214	−3 965 472	−4 999 095	−6 052 518	−6 706 082
Change of consumer's surplus	1 566 558	3 153 006	4 764 348	6 402 082	8 066 336	9 756 781	10 089 394 384
Change of social welfare	1 441 117	2 768 498	3 980 489	5 085 342	6 091 520	7 005 649	5 192 782

Source: Calculated by this research.

Table 8.8 Limited access: the welfare effects

unit: 1,000 NT$

	1st year	2nd year	3rd year	4th year	5th year	6th year	Long-run equilibrium
Production gain	0	3 858	6 786	9 752	12 976	1 652	71 846
Consumption gain	6 411	9 787	13 335	17 332	21 819	26 813	47 878
Tariff revenue	838 996	816 682	865 905	939 387	1 021 235	1 105 634	−2 873
Change of producer's surplus	−962 438	−970 782	−1 071 799	−1 200 750	−1 338 828	−1 480 221	−2 105 791
Change of consumer's surplus	1 548 602	1 559 178	1 719 905	1 925 755	2 146 352	2 372 213	3 307 047
Change of social welfare	1 425 160	1 405 077	1 514 011	1 664 393	1 828 759	1 997 625	1 198 384

Source: Calculated by this research.

According to conventional welfare economics, the purpose of a trade liberalization policy is to reach the goal of maximize social welfare and find the optimal resource allocations. Since the gains in consumers' surplus is larger than the losses in producers' surplus, for all three scenarios proposed here, the effects on the social welfare are positive. When the tariff revenue is added to this positive effect, the value of welfare will be even more. The government can use a subsidy to compensate for the producers' loss caused by the imports and still have the positive net social welfare. According to this point of view, the policy choice should be based on maximizing the net social welfare. This implies the government should choose the tariffication with a 6 per cent tariff reduction per year as the policy over all other scenarios. This conclusion suggests that free trade should always be chosen by any country.

Assume that there is no cost in bargaining, and that a compensation payment is possible, then the decision process will lead naturally to free trade. However, it is the limits on trade that prevail in the real world. It turns out that the policy consideration based solely on the welfare effect is not persuasive.

On the other hand, Corden (1974) suggests that the policy decision should not result in any sector suffering from obvious and absolute loss. In his opinion, the best way to deal with the rice import issue is not to import. Actually, both the welfare analysis and Corden's suggestion are too extreme. They are not applicable in the real world. The policy choice does not depend entirely on the loss or gain of welfare. More importantly, it depends on the change of political support rating, and, therefore, the political economic point of view should also be taken into consideration.

4.2 The Order of Political Preference for Policy Scenarios

Combining the political preference function with the welfare effect, we can calculate the change of political support rating for different import scenarios. The order of the political preference is shown in table 8.9. The results suggest that the political support rating will decline no matter which scenario is applied. In economic theory, since the loss of producers' benefit can be offset by the gain of consumers' surplus, the rice import policy should win the majority support from the society. However, from the political economic view, producers have greater influence on policy making even though the number of producers are relatively few compared with the number of consumers. Yang (1995) estimated the political weights and found that the value of producers relative to consumers is 1.41. It reflects the fact that current rice policy emphasizes producers' benefit more than the consumers' benefit.

Food security in Asia

Table 8.9 The change of political support rating for different import scenarios

unit: 1,000 NT$

	Support rating						Long-run equilibrium
	1st year	2nd year	3rd year	4th year	5th year	6th year	
2.5 per cent tariff reduction	−160 147	−319 586	−479 839	−641 769	−805 815	−972 376	−1 141 608
6 per cent tariff reduction	−380 546	−756 921	−1 138 080	−1 528 862	−1 931 860	−2 348 255	−3 322 770
Limited access	−376 274	−382 387	−423 692	−475 744	−531 304	−588 230	−904 534

Source: Calculated by this research.

Following the lead of Rausser and Foster (1990) the government choice of a consumer-based PERT (social-welfare-increasing) leads to an increase in the weight on producers in the PPF. Yang also found that the political weight of the rice growers relative to consumers increases to two when facing the rice import issue. It implies that the decision makers will pay much more attention on the producers while considering the rice import policy.

Under tremendous pressure from foreign countries, however, the government indeed has no choice but to open our domestic rice market. It is a dilemma for the policy maker. Although there is a decrease in the political support rating, according to the long-run equilibrium of table 8.9, the min-max rule suggests that the limited access policy should be a better policy over the other alternatives. The tariffication with a 2.5 per cent tariff reduction should also be the second choice followed by the 6 per cent tariff reduction. It is worth mentioning that our results of policy ordering is opposite to the conclusions of the social welfare analysis. The last columns of tables 8.6–8.8 show the welfare effect change of the long-run equilibrium for each policy scenario. Comparing these results, the 6 per cent decrease in tariff each year will generate the most benefit for the society (table 8.7). The limited access, on the other hand, will improve social welfare less (table 8.8), but the results are the other way around for the political preference ordering. The adoption of the PPF is more appropriate to explain why the government tends to use the limited access as a rice import scheme. The above results show explicitly that the tendency of choosing limited access is actually under the consideration of rationality. At this moment, it will be better for the government to provide some compensations to producers. This will not only alleviate considerable impact from the imports, but will also alleviate the political disputes and make the enforcement of this import policy smoother.

5. CONCLUSION

The rice production cost in Taiwan is much higher than those in many countries. This production also consumes the majority of the agricultural resources of the nation. Once the domestic market is open to the world, it is anticipated that the impacts on the rice industry and the entire agricultural sector will be very substantial. Government officials and researchers are trying to find an appropriate policy to avoid or alleviate the impact. Since recent research is solely focused on economic analysis of each policy alternative, the suggestions are not persuasive. Political economics suggest the existence of endogeneity in the policy-making process and the results coming from economic analysis cannot serve as the basis of decision making.

Thanks to the rice imports, the efficiency of resource allocation of the country will be improved and consumer outlays or expenditures will decrease as well. These results match exactly with the theoretical expectations. Moreover, no matter which import policy scenario is adopted, the gain in consumer surplus is larger than the loss in producer surplus and, therefore, the welfare of the entire society will be improved. The tariffication reduction policy is a better policy choice in terms of the social welfare. However, it is the limited access that is less harmful to the producers. From these results, it is not hard to see that the government is facing a dilemma when considering both economic efficiency and the welfare of the rice growers at the same time.

Before adopting a new policy, the government always wants to know of the changes in its political support rating. By using the political preference function, our results suggest that the political support rating will decrease no matter which of the three scenarios is adopted. This implies that it is going to be hard to make people accept any of these policies. Facing tremendous pressure from foreign countries, however, the government indeed has no choice but to open the domestic rice market. This research suggests that a better way to proceed is to choose policy with less impact on the political market. Therefore, the limited access policy should be chosen. It is shown that the obstacles to adopting this policy will be smaller than for the other scenarios.

REFERENCES

Baldwin, R. E. (1989), 'The Political Economy of U.S. Trade Policy', *Journal of Economic Perspectives*, 3(4): 119–35.

Bale, M. D. and B. L. Greenshield (1978), 'Japanese Agricultural Distortions and Their Welfare Value', *American Journal of Agricultural Economics*, 60: 59–64.

Bhagwati, J. (1968), 'More on the Equivalence of Tariffs and Quotas', *American Economic Review*, 58: 142–6.

Chen, T. J. and M. S. Liu (1991), 'The Formation of Trade Protection in Taiwan', *Proceedings of the Political Economics Conference*, Chinese Economics Association, (in Chinese), 189–214.

Corden, W. M. (1974), *Trade Policy and Economic Welfare*, Oxford: Clarendon Press.

de Gorter, H. And Y. Tsur (1991), 'Explaining Price Policy Bias in Agriculture: The Calculus of Support-Maximizing Politicians', *American Journal of Agricultural Economics*, 73: 1244–54.

Gardner, B. L. (1983), 'Efficient Redistribution through Commodity Markets', *American Journal of Agricultural Economics*, 65: 225–34.

Hossain, F., Z. Hassan, and H. Jensen (1993), 'Special Safeguard Mechanisms for the Agricultural Sector: The GATT Negotiations', *GATT Research Paper 93–GATT3*, CARD, Iowa State University.

Love, H., G. C. Rausser and D. M. Burton (1990), 'Policy Preference Functions Grand Themes and New Directions', *Working Paper, Department of Agriculture and Resource Economics*, Oregon State University.

Moschini, G. (1991), 'Economic Issues in Tariffication : An Overview', *Agricultural Economics*, 5: 101–20.

Rausser, G. C. and W. E. Foster (1990), 'Political Preference Function and Public Policy Reform', *American Journal of Agricultural Economics*, 72: 641–52.

Swinnen, J. and F. van der Zee (1993), 'The New Political Economy of Agricultural Policies: A Survey', *European Review of Agricultural Economic*, 20.

Swinnen, J (1994), 'Positive Theory of Agricultural Protection', *American Journal of Agricultural Economics*, 76: 1–14.

Tyers, R. (1990), 'Implicit Policy References and The Assessment of Negotiable Trade Policy Reforms', *European Economics Review*, 34: 1399–426.

Vousden, N. (1990), *The Economics of Trade Protection*, Cambridge: Cambridge University Press.

Yang, M. H. (1995), 'Taiwan's Rice Policy Formation: Estimation of

Policy   Bias   and   Its   Political-Economic   Implications',   *Taiwan Economic Review*, 23(4): 469–92 (in Chinese).
Yang, M. H. (1996), 'Tariffication and Limited Access: The Evaluation of Alternative Rice Import Policy', *Journal of The Land Bank of Taiwan*, 33(2): 165–94 (in Chinese)
Woo, R. J. (1993), '*Tariffication Program for Major Agricultural Products in Taiwan*', Taipei, Taiwan, Department of Agricultural Economics, National Taiwan University (in Chinese).

9. Rice import competition and demand allocation in Hong Kong and Singapore

Tsorng-Chyi Hwang

1. INTRODUCTION

In Taiwan, Japan, and South Korea market access to foreign rice has been a key political and economic indicator of liberalizing agricultural trade. There is a conflict between trade liberalization and the pursuit of food security goals without international competition. A food policy question confronting each of the three governments is how to manage the objective of providing income parity for farmers and a comfortable level of food security at minimum government expense. Other than the commonly used supply control mechanisms, additional policy adjustments for increased import competition and maintained food security are considered necessary.

To maintain farmers' income parity at minimum government cost, supply control programs were subsequently applied to rice in Taiwan, Japan, and South Korea. Those programs tried to reduce government expense from high price support, including land diversification programs in Taiwan and Japan, and a shift from low-to high-quality rice production but with lower yield in South Korea. However, rice imports by Japan and South Korea, as a result of the GATT Uruguay Round negotiations, and anticipated rice imports by Taiwan, as a result of negotiations for WTO membership, have challenged current projectionist and self-sufficiency food policies in these countries.[1] Thus the serious concerns of weakening comparative advantage and instability of the world rice market have to be resolved by new policy mechanisms, at least, under a partially open market framework (Johnson, 1975; Wailes, Young, and Cramer, 1994; Chen, 1994) .[2]

This chapter attempts to clarify two important aspects of rice trade faced by Taiwan when considering the necessary adjustments on food policy mechanisms. First, the reliability of rice export suppliers to meet both food security and consumer interests is assessed. Second, the potential rice imports to Taiwan are of serious concern for maintaining the future competitive position of domestic rice production. Two important rice import possibilities are considered as essential to Taiwan's rice supply control program as well as to the level of food security. It is further argued that the long-run experience of Hong Kong (HK) and Singapore (SG), with diversified rice import sources and increased rice imports, may provide useful evidence on the reliability of rice supplies and the potential competitive structure of the rice trade in the Asian market. Such an analysis of HK and SG is especially important for Taiwan because the negotiated future rice market liberalization will give freer market access than under the Simultaneous Buying and Selling System (SBS) adopted by Japan.[3]

In HK and SG the import structure of various rice varieties may have reflected the nature of world rice production and trade. A large share of the world's production is of the Indica type which is dominated by Thailand. The major rice production and consumption in Taiwan is of the Japonica type, which is also produced in Japan, northern China, Korea, the European Union, the United States, and Australia. Japonica rice accounts for only about 10–15 per cent of world rice production. The United States accounts for less than 2 per cent of global rice production, but its exports exceed 10 per cent of Indica and 20 per cent of Japonica world trade. Past research on the recognition of differentiated rice types investigated the impacts of rice trade liberalization on the prices and traded volumes in the world market (Childs, 1990; Haley, 1992; Cramer, Wailes, and Shui, 1993; Song and Carter, 1996). Other research, however, focused on the competitive structure of the rice trade in Asia, accounting for 90 per cent of world production and 70 per cent of international trade, and in other regions and found a non-competitive rice trade market (Karp and Perloff, 1989; Yumkella, Unnevehr, and Garcia, 1994). None of these studies looked carefully into the supply and competitive structure of free rice imports to HK and SG nor did they conduct any empirical analysis of the reliability of supply and competitive advantage of rice exports to these high-income Asian countries.

This chapter first reviews the characteristics of potentially reliable rice imports in the Asian region. Then a theoretical model of import demand allocation is presented, which allows the derivation of empirical estimation and hypothesis tests. The estimation results for the major groups of rice import sources into HK and SG markets are presented, and their implications for food policy adjustments in Taiwan are discussed to conclude the chapter.

2. RELATIVE RELIABILITY OF RICE IMPORTS

The relative reliability of world rice supply for Asian countries may be highlighted by rice market movements. Regional changes in the rice supply and demand structure have moved towards a more market-oriented rather than traditionally defined thin rice market structure. Moreover the experience of the already free rice-importing countries, such as HK and SG, may provide evidence on existing reliable suppliers in the world or in regional markets for other high-income Asian countries. However, a country's specific preferences for rice types and for a high but uncertain level of self-sufficiency may have created problems when justifying the historical and current rice supply situations.

The world rice disappearance provides information about changing regional and world rice production and trade. Table 9.1 shows world rice production, stocks, use, and trade during the 1986—97 crop years. For Asian rice-producing countries, only Japan and South Korea have decreased domestic rice production, as a result of over-supply and relaxation of restrictions on imports. Asian countries dominate 87 per cent of world rice production. Many developing countries become rice exporters as they increase their production. Much of the rice production in other regions, or countries outside Asia, has also increased over the same time period. Specifically, Australia doubled its rice production while the United States increased its production by 30 per cent. Due in part to export enhancement and supply control programs, US rice stocks have decreased significantly while world rice stocks did not change much. Comparing use and production, total production grew more than total use. As a result world rice trade increased 63.4 per cent between 1987 and 1997.

Part of the expansion of rice supply on the world market has been a response to the market access of rice exports to countries such as South Korea and Japan with high incomes, high production costs, and autarkic market policies. Annual rice consumption in Taiwan is about 2 million tons while South Korea and Japan respectively consume 6.20 and 10.45 million tons. Taiwan has joined Japan and South Korea in agreeing on a schedule to further open their rice markets in coming years. It is expected that more than 15 per cent of market consumption in these markets will be supplied eventually from imports, which is nearly four times the current total HK and SG rice consumption.

The characteristics of stable rice imports to HK and SG may be attributed to satisfactory quantity and quality supplies from various sources and the increasing residual rice supply from Monsoon Asia. During the 1987—96 period, total rice imports fluctuated around the same

Table 9.1 World rice production, stocks, use, and trade in selected countries or regions ᵃ

	Crop year ᵇ							1986–
Country or region	1986/ 87	1988/ 89	1989/ 90	1992/ 93	1994/ 95	1995/ 96	1996/ 97	97 growth (%)
				million				
A. Production:								
Bangladesh	23.1	23.3	26.8	27.5	25.3	26.5	27.6	19.5
Burma	11.8	12.5	13.5	13.4	16.0	17.0	15.5	31.4
China	172. 2	169.1	180.1	186.2	175.9	185.2	195.1	13.3
India	90.6	105.7	110.4	109.3	121.8	119.4	120.8	33.3
Indonesia	39.7	41.7	44.7	48.2	49.7	51.1	49.2	23.9
Japan	14.6	12.4	12.9	13.2	15.0	13.4	12.9	−11.6
Philippines	9.0	9.2	8.9	9.5	10.5	11.2	11.2	24.4
South Korea	7.9	8.4	8.1	7.3	6.9	6.4	7.2	−8.9
Pakistan	5.2	4.8	4.8	4.7	5.2	5.1	6.4	23.1
Thailand	18.9	21.3	20.2	19.9	21.4	21.8	20.8	10.1
Vietnam	14.9	18.2	19.4	21.7	24.6	26.8	27.3	83.2
Subtotal	407.9	426.6	449.8	460.9	472.2	484.0	494.1	21.1
Australia	0.6	0.8	0.8	1.0	1.1	1.0	1.4	133.0
Brazil	10.6	11.1	8.0	9.9	10.9	10.1	9.7	−8.5
European Union	1.9	2.0	2.1	2.2	2.0	2.0	2.5	31.6
All others	39.2	39.1	38.9	39.1	45.0	46.0	45.9	17.1
Total non-US	460.2	479.6	499.6	513.1	531.3	543.0	553.6	20.3
United States	6.0	7.3	7.0	8.1	9.0	7.9	7.8	30.0
World total	466.3	486.9	506.6	526.4	540.2	550.9	561.3	20.4
B. Ending stock: ᶜ								
Total foreign	49.2	48.2	53.2	53.5	48.0	49.3	52.3	6.3
United States	1.7	0.9	0.9	1.3	1.1	0.8	0.9	−47.1
World total	50.8	49.0	54.1	54.8	49.1	50.1	53.2	4.7
C. Total use ᵈ	319.8	327.5	338.2	357.7	366.9	370.1	375.9	17.5
D. World trade ᵉ	–	13.9	11.7	14.9	21.0	19.5	18.3	63.4

Notes: ᵃ Production is rough basis, but ending stocks are milled basis.
ᵇ World rice harvest stretches almost 18 months and timing varies widely across countries and hemispheres.
ᶜ Stocks are based on an aggregate of different local marketing years and should not be construed as representing world stock levels at a fixed point in time. In addition, stocks data are not available for all countries.
ᵈ For countries for which stock data are not available, utilization estimates represent apparent utilization, that is, they include annual stock level adjustments.
ᵉ calendar year basis.

Source: Foreign Agricultural Service, USDA World Grain Situation and Outlook and World Agricultural Production, 1997.

level (350–400 thousand metric tons [tmt]) in HK but increased significantly in SG from 200 to 300 tmt (figures 9.1 and 9.2). The major import sources were Thailand and Australia for HK and Thailand for SG.[4]

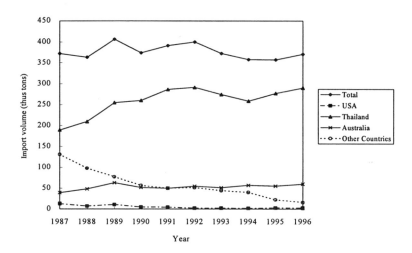

Figure 9.1 Rice import volume of various sources in Hong Kong

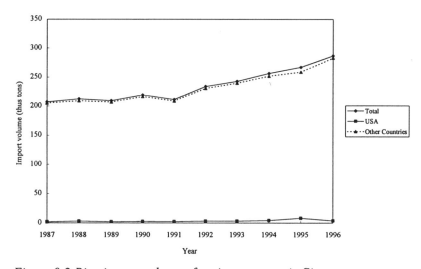

Figure 9.2 Rice import volume of various sources in Singapore

Food security in Asia

Thailand and Australia increased their shares of exports to HK, as the USA, Australia, and India increased their shares slightly to SG (table 9.2). During the 1987—96 period, the combined market share of Thailand and Australia in HK increased from 61.43 per cent to 94.99 per cent, with Thailand accounting for over 70 per cent on average. On the other hand, the combined market share of the USA, Australia, and India in SG increased from 2.07 per cent to 4.41 per cent, as Thailand had nearly 90 per cent of the market share. Even though rice from Thailand and Australia dominated both markets, the significantly larger consumption capacity of Taiwan associated with its gradual relaxation of rice import controls may lead to a recognition that the other rice-exporting countries may become important suppliers and the USA may be an important source for these high-income Asian countries.[5]

Table 9.2 Market shares in volume of rice exporters in Hong Kong and Singapore, 1987—96 (unit: %)

Import market	Year	Import sources				
		Thailand	USA	Australia	India [a]	ROW [b]
Hong Kong	1987	50.87	3.41	10.56	b	35.16
	1988	57.77	1.90	13.34		26.98
	1989	62.73	2.65	15.56		19.06
	1990	69.56	1.29	13.93		15.22
	1991	73.23	1.12	12.82		12.83
	1992	72.81	0.54	13.70		12.95
	1993	73.64	0.60	13.86		11.90
	1994	72.30	0.47	15.98		11.25
	1995	77.52	0.75	15.51		6.22
	1996	78.30	0.64	16.69		4.37
Singapore	1987	88.92	0.95	0.80	0.32	9.01
	1988	89.03	1.53	1.17	0.28	7.99
	1989	90.04	1.13	1.10	0.40	7.33
	1990	88.94	1.28	1.05	0.45	8.28
	1991	90.32	1.23	1.05	0.27	7.13
	1992	84.48	1.41	1.10	0.26	12.75
	1993	88.02	1.38	1.01	0.33	9.26
	1994	86.21	1.72	1.13	0.46	10.48
	1995	91.20	3.07	1.05	0.80	3.88
	1996	88.98	1.34	1.26	1.81	6.61

Notes: [a] Blanks indicate negligible import shares.
[b] The rest of the world including countries mostly in Monsoon Asia.

Sources: Hong Kong Trade Statistics, 1987—96; Singapore Trade Statistics, 1987—96.

Whether these exporters are able to supply Taiwan depends on the market situation and possible political intervention from mainland China. Since the late 1980s, many south and southeast Asian countries have turned from rice importers to self-sufficiency or from self-sufficiency to exporters, such as Indonesia, India, Pakistan, and Vietnam. Consistent rice purchases from HK, SG, and Malaysia have provided incentives for continuous production expansion within or outside of the monsoon Asia economy. As a result there exists enough flexibility for import demand to be shifted to high-income Asian countries with reliable strength in rice supply on the world market. However the political threat from mainland China may lead to cautious treatment of self-sufficiency and food security in Taiwan. The tendency to lower government price support, associated with the promised rice imports, provides significant incentive for the possible relaxation of the food self-sufficiency level, which will in turn guide policy measures to decreasing production and increasing imports for Taiwan.

The increasing dominance of Thailand's and Australian rice in HK and SG raises concerns that they may have exercised market power and gained much of the competitive advantage away from other exporting countries, including the USA. Yumkella, Unnevehr, and Garcia (1994) found that Thailand could only exercise limited market power on high-quality long grain rice in HK and SG markets during the 1980s. The international rice pricing structure of various exporting countries can be shown from the differences among the average import prices by import sources (table 9.3). Thailand and Australia had similar average import prices in SG but Australia received significantly higher prices than Thailand in HK. It seems that Thailand did not exercise much influence on the pricing to market (PTM) strategy for the two markets, as Australia practiced different pricing or export strategies and accounted for only a small market share with a lower price level than the USA in SG. It is interesting to note that Australia exported rice with the price set between Thailand and the US prices and in the meantime gained a significantly better market share in HK than the USA. As a result the higher-quality US rice exports into the two markets provided less competition in terms of market share as compared to Thailand and Australia. India exported to HK the highest price basmati aromatic rice, which commands a price premium above regular milled non-aromatic high-quality rice, but earned a trivial market share. Indian market share increased in SG with exports of its lower-price (non-aromatic) rice in the 1990s. Moreover other countries competed in HK at price levels similar to Thailand and at prices lower than Thailand in SG. Accordingly it is more difficult for rice exporters to exercise the PTM strategy in the SG market. The USA did not find the

Food security in Asia

Table 9.3 Average rice import prices of Hong Kong and Singapore by import sources   *(unit: USD/Ton)*

Import market	Year	Import sources				
		Thailand	US	Australia	India	ROW [a]
	1987	287	332	407	1111	247
	1988	382	485	471	1231	334
	1989	379	419	482	1093	367
	1990	384	487	495	948	379
Hong	1991	399	446	483	1257	383
Kong	1992	413	574	496	826	389
	1993	415	607	486	826	377
	1994	481	747	527	869	440
	1995	445	638	545	922	471
	1996	491	838	673	1028	473
	1987	260	403	366	942	259
	1988	347	475	452	996	302
	1989	376	528	477	844	283
	1990	375	503	465	853	276
Singapore	1991	381	532	448	907	305
	1992	408	560	429	1078	254
	1993	408	581	427	702	257
	1994	435	731	447	580	264
	1995	438	437	478	533	315
	1996	486	795	474	436	343

Note: [a] The rest of the world.

Sources: Hong Kong Trade Statistics, 1987–96; Singapore Trade Statistics, 1987–96.

best way, including any possible PTM practice, to compete with Thailand and Australia in the two markets.

The assessment of competitiveness of rice imports into high-income Asian countries is important for various reasons. First, the import preference on different quality and type of rice may be quite different among importing countries. Second, there exists certain substitution possibilities among various rice quality and types. Third, those export source countries with low average export prices have been able to supply high-quality and different types of rice to the world market, given continuously improving technology. Finally, the convenience and lower transportation costs for countries within the economy of monsoon Asia are among the marketing advantages in rice trade for the exporters with large market shares. The differentiated product treatment of imported rice in HK and SG, for the analysis of import demand allocation, may be used to test these hypotheses. The results should provide a reasonable basis to anticipate the implicit import structure of rice in Taiwan.

3.   IMPORT ALLOCATION AIDS MODEL

The theoretical model employed in this chapter is the Almost Ideal Demand System (AIDS) of Deaton and Muellbauer (1980) with the assumption of differentiated import sources. Derived from the Price Independent Generalized Logarithmic (PIGLOG) class of preferences, which permits exact aggregation over consumers, the cost (expenditure) function can be rewritten to approximate the importer's behaviour that differentiates goods from different origins. The complete demand system in share form is then derived from a well-specified[6] flexible expenditure function by Shephard's lemma (Shephard, 1970)

$$w_i = a_i + \sum_{j=1}^{n} \gamma_{ij} \ln p_j + \beta_i \ln(E/P) \qquad i = 1,.., n \qquad (9.1)$$

where w_i is the expenditure share of source i in total imports of the specified commodity, P_j is the import price from source j , E is total import expenditure on all sources, and P is the aggregate price index defined as

$$\ln P = a_0 + \sum_{i=1}^{n} a_i \ln P_i + 0.5 \sum_i \sum_j \gamma_{ij} \ln P_i \ln P_j \qquad (9.2)$$

Since the price index P in equation (9.1) is non-linear and often causes difficulties in empirical estimation, researchers have used the following Stone's index as a linear approximation

$$\ln P^* = \sum_{i=1}^{n} w_i \ln P_i \qquad (9.3)$$

Once the Stone's price index in equation (9.3) is used, this model is called the 'linear approximate almost ideal demand system' (Blanciforti and Green, 1983). However Moschini (1995) showed several other different measurement units, such as Tornqvist, Paasche and Laspeyres indices on P to be more appropriate than Stone's price index. The theoretical constraints imposed on equation (9.1) of adding-up, homogeneity, and Slutsky symmetry, respectively, are

$$\sum_{i=1}^{n} a_i = 1, \quad \sum_{i=1}^{n} \gamma_{ij} = 0, \quad \text{and} \quad \sum_{i=1}^{n} \beta_i = 0;$$

$$\sum_{j} \gamma_{ij} = 0; \quad \text{and}$$

$$\gamma_{ij} = \gamma_{ji} \tag{9.4}$$

Marshallian price elasticities with the linear approximation and imposed restrictions are

$$\in_{ij} = -\delta_{ij} + \frac{\gamma_{ij}}{w_i} - \beta_i(\frac{w_j}{w_i}) \tag{9.5}$$

where $-\delta_{ij}$ is equal to unity if $i = j$ and zero otherwise. The expenditure elasticity is:

$$\eta_i = 1 + \frac{\beta_i}{w_i} \tag{9.6}$$

4.   DATA AND EMPIRICAL RESULTS

Annual data from 1987 to 1996 and statistical tests were used in this study along with the trials of different price indices in the empirical model. It is assumed that rice imports can be differentiated between different origins. The largest six import sources in terms of market share are Thailand, Australia, rest of the world (ROW), China, Vietnam, and the USA for HK; and Thailand, ROW, India, the USA, Australia, and Vietnam for SG. Due to insufficient data in prior years Vietnam is excluded from discussion in this study. Thailand was defined as an important source because of its dominance in the two markets. For a similar reason Australia was defined as an important source in HK. Other individual countries mentioned above were considered as potentially but not necessarily as being important sources due to their low market shares. However the different costs, quality and types of rice exports may lead these individual countries to be an important and separable source in the model. The separability tests using χ^2 statistics suggested by Berndt and Christensen (1973) were applied on models with different price index definitions in Moschini (1995) and all countries not treated as an important separable source were grouped together as ROW.

Given that only ten observations of the sample data were available, the use of more than six independent variables or five separable origins in each equation would have created a problem of full rank. Thus four price indices, deflated prices by the HK or SG consumer price index, and per capita import expenditure are used for separability tests and performance comparison of different price index definitions used in this study. The AIDS model is estimated by iterative seemingly unrelated regression (ISUR) with imposition of homogeneity and symmetry conditions.

The test results for separability are explained by using the likelihood ratio test and system R^2 as shown in table 9.4. The selections of the Paasche index with lagged share weight for HK and the Laspeyres index with initial share weight for SG are based on the likelihood ratio test estimates shown in table 9.5. In table 9.4, most hypothesized groups of import origins are rejected at less than the 5 per cent level of significance, except for one combined origins in the HK market and there are two groups without full rank. However the combination including the USA, Thailand, Australia (or India), and ROW were used as unrestricted cases for the HK and SG markets respectively. The test results on different combinations and more restricted combinations did not reject the unrestricted combination except the second restricted case in the HK market. Nevertheless the unrestricted case was selected for the HK market due to a slightly higher system R^2. The estimated results of the AIDS model using the unrestricted combinations in both markets were then used for the calculation of elasticities (tables 9.6 and 9.7).

Estimated Marshallian price and expenditure elasticities for rice imports in HK and SG are presented in table 9.8. In the HK market the estimated Marshallian own price elasticities for rice were −2.53 for Thailand, −1.91 for Australia, and −4.16 for ROW. This result implies that a 1 per cent increase in export prices to HK would lead to a decrease in rice exports by more than 1 per cent for Thailand, Australia and ROW. Rice from the USA may not be price sensitive in the HK market. Presumably only the USA was able to adopt the PTM strategy to effectively increase export prices of rice without losing any of its share in the HK market. The significant increase of the US export prices of rice to the HK market after 1991 are consistent with this conclusion.

Food security in Asia

Table 9.4 Likelihood ratio test results for separability of rice import sources in Hong Kong and Singapore

Import market	Group of country origins [a]	Likelihood ratio estimates [b]	System R^2
(Unrestricted	combination: Y_1, Y_2, Y_3, Y_4+ Y_5)		0.79
	Y_1, Y_2, Y_4, Y_3 +Y_5	6.28*	0.77
Hong Kong	Y_1, Y_2, Y_3 +Y_4, Y_5	3.37	0.78
(Paasche with lag)	Y_1, Y_3, Y_2, Y_4+Y_5	58.28**	0.59
	Y_1, Y_2, Y_3, Y_4+ Y_5	44.09**	0.71
	Y_1, Y_2, Y_3+Y_4+Y_5	66.40**	0.57
(Unrestricted combination:	Y_1, Y_2, Y_4, Y_3+ Y_5)		0.99
	Y_1, Y_2, Y_3, Y_4+Y_5	274.75**	0.40
Singapore	Y_1, Y_2, Y_3+Y_4, Y_5	256.89**	0.55
(Laspeyres with initial period)	Y_1 +Y_3, Y_2, Y_4+Y_5	291.98**	0.28
	Y_1, Y_2+Y_4, Y_3+Y_5	258.67**	0.69
	Y_1, Y_2, Y_3+Y_4+Y_5	284.22**	0.41

Notes: [a] Country origins are defined as Y_1 for the US, Y_2 for Thailand, Y_3 for Australia, Y_4 for China, Y_5 for the rest of the world (ROW) in Hong Kong; the definition of Y_1~Y_3 are the same, Y_4 for India, Y_5 for Row in Singapore. The test choices on combinations depend much on the significance of market shares in either markets. Those country origins with minimal market shares are not expressed as individual source but are included in the ROW.
[b] Likelihood ratio test statistics is calculated from $Li = - N(1-\tilde{R}^2)$ for each combination and $-2(L_1 - L_2) \sim X_m^2$ is used to obtain the estimates where L_2 is from unrestricted model, L_2 is from restricted model with m restrictions.
* Denotes significance level at 5 per cent level.
** Denotes significance level at 1 per cent level.

Examining the cross-price elasticities indicates that there is a complementary relationship, mostly inelastic, between the USA and ROW and between Australia and Thailand. All other cross price elasticities were positive, indicating a substitutability. Only the USA export price effects on the ROW export quantity was elastic representing significant complementary relationship. It is implicitly clear that the US rice exports to the HK market played an important role in setting the high-quality rice price. The substitution effects existed between the USA and Australia, between Australia and ROW, and between Thailand and ROW rice. The

Table 9.5 Likelihood ratio estimates of import allocation model by different price index definitions

Markets	Price index	Deflated expenditure from [a]	Likelihood ratio test
	1. Tornqvist price	one-year lag share	51.31
		initial share[b]	25.93
Hong	2. Paasche price	one-year lag share	51.36
Kong		initial share	26.08
	3. Laspeyres price	one-year lag share	41.27
		initial share	26.88
	1. Tornqvist price	one-year lag share	15.38
		initial share	41.67
Singapore	2. Paasche price	one-year lag share	15.27
		initial share	43.31
	3. Laspeyres price [c]	one-year lag share	47.41
		initial share	45.45

Notes: [a] Estimation results obtained by using ISUR procedure and used Thailand, USA, Australia (India), and ROW as the sample combination. The likelihood ratio obtained by leaving ROW and India as given for HK and SG, respectively.
[b] Means the expenditure share on import sources of the beginning sample period.
[c] Initial share weight result is selected due to better symmetric coefficients.

Source: Estimated.

highly elastic US export price effects on Australia represented the similar rice type and quality between these two countries and the potential dominance of Australia in the HK market. The elastic relationships of the impact of Thailand export price on ROW exports and the ROW export rice on Australian exports imply the complicated combination of ROW sources. As a result Thailand rice and ROW rice may be substituted by ROW and Australian rice respectively.

The estimated expenditure elasticity by import source is conditional on the expenditure for imported rice. The estimated elasticity indicates the percentage response in quantities demanded from each supplier as a result of a 1 per cent increase in total import expenditure for rice. The expenditure elasticities were 1.35 for both Thailand and Australia in HK. These results indicate that if a larger budget was allocated to imported

Food security in Asia

Table 9.6 Estimation results of the rice import allocation model in Hong Kong (Paasche index with lagged Ws) [a]

Dependent variables	Independent Variables				
	$\ln P_A$	$\ln P_T$	$\ln P_{AU}$	$\ln P_{ROW}$	DEP
W_A	−0.0100	−0.0071	0.0802	−0.0631	−0.0002
	(−0.70)	(−0.13)	(2.88)	(−2.04)	(−0.06)
W_T	−0.0071	−0.8650	−0.1103	0.9824	0.2348
	(−0.13)	(−1.23)	(−0.90)	(1.66)	(14.80)
W_{AU}	0.0802	−0.1103	−0.1463	0.1763	0.0594
	(2.88)	(−0.90)	(−2.27)	(2.32)	(8.99)
W_{ROW}	−0.0631	0.9824	0.1763	−0.446	0.0086
	(−2.04)	(1.66)	(2.32)	(−3.52)	(0.59)

Notes: [a] *W* and ln*P* denote market share of expenses and logarithm of average real price from various sources such that A for the USA, T for Thailand, AU for Australia, and ROW for rest of the world, DEP represents real expenses on rice from various sources.

Source: Estimated.

rice both quantities and market shares for rice imported from Thailand and Australia would increase. Different expenditure elasticities from different rice sources further imply a non-homothetic expansion of rice import among the importing suppliers. The most likely reasons are considered as non-price export promotion efforts by exporters and intrinsic quality characteristics of rice from different sources. The expenditure effects in the SG market represents a beneficiary market expansion for the USA, India, Thailand, and ROW as the total rice expenditure in SG may increase in the future.

In the SG market the estimated Marshallian own price elasticities for rice were −2.33 for the USA, −1.16 for Thailand, −1.51 for India and −1.05 for ROW respectively. Thailand and ROW rice have a smaller own-price elasticities implying that the rice import preference or loyalty of SG for these two sources was stronger than for rice from other countries. As a result Thailand may not exercise any market power in the SG market which can be proved by the continuously increased imports but not market share of Thailand rice.

Table 9.7 Estimation results of the rice import allocation model in Singapore (Laspeyres index with initial Ws) [a]

Dependent variables	Independent variables				
	$\ln P_A$	$\ln P_T$	$\ln P_I$	$\ln P_{ROW}$	DEP
W_A	−0.0276	0.0070	−0.0146	0.0352	0.0110
	(−1.60)	(0.28)	(−2.68)	(4.03)	(9.66)
W_T	0.0070	0.0353	0.0209	−0.0633	0.1952
	(0.28)	(0.76)	(1.44)	(−3.84)	(69.72)
W_I	−0.0146	0.0206	−0.0046	0.0314	0.0039
	(−2.68)	(1.44)	(−2.81)	(6.07)	(11.18)
W_{ROW}	0.0352	−0.0633	0.0314	−0.0033	0.0090476
	(4.03)	(−3.84)	(6.07)	(−0.51)	(8.93)

Notes: [a] Same as table 9.5.
Source: Estimated.

A negative cross-price elasticity greater than unity in absolute value indicates a significant complementary relationship between India and the USA, which provide high-quality rice. On the other hand, a significant substitution relationship exists between rice imports from the USA and ROW and from India and Thailand as their cross price elasticities are positive and elastic. It is interesting to note that the USA was able to make its rice distinctive to major competitors not in HK but in SG where Thailand accounts for nearly 88 per cent market share. The major competitor of the USA in the SG market was ROW implying a potential disadvantage for the USA rice exporters to compete in this monsoon economy.

5. SUMMARY AND CONCLUSIONS

Rice import prospects in Taiwan, Japan, and South Korea under the GATT and WTO negotiations represent significant movements toward agricultural trade liberalization. At the same time there are increasing concerns on how to manage the food policy objectives of providing

Food security in Asia

Table 9.8 Marshallian elasticities for imported rice of Hong Kong and Singapore from restricted AIDS model

Import market	Import price	USA	Thailand	Australia	India[a]	ROW
	P_{US}	−1.61	−0.43	4.91*		−3.86*
	P_{THAI}	0.02*	−2.53*	0.22		1.42**
Hong Kong	P_{AUS}	0.46**	−0.87*	−1.91**		0.98**
	P_{ROW}	−0.45**	6.89	1.23*		−4.16*
	Expenditure	0.99	1.35**	1.35**		1.06
	P_{US}	−2.33*	−0.13*		−0.71**	1.64**
	P_{THAI}	0.003*	−1.16*		0.02*	−0.09**
Singapore	P_{IND}	−1.63**	1.93*		−1.51**	3.44**
	P_{ROW}	0.47**	−0.97**		0.42**	−1.05*
	Expenditure	1.53**	1.22**		1.43**	1.12**

Notes: [a] Blanks indicates these countries being excluded in the model.
* Denotes significant level at 5 per cent level.
** Denotes significant level at 1 per cent level.

income parity for farmers and maintaining adequate food security levels in these increasingly open markets at minimum government expense. Rice imports promised by Taiwan upon joining the WTO under the Taiwan–US trade negotiations has put potential pressure on its rice sector. Consequently current supply control and price support mechanisms in Taiwan are challenged by additional import competition and the expected weakening comparative advantage of domestic rice. Reliable export supply and proper adjustments in domestic policy mechanisms would become especially important for Taiwan to meet various government policy goals under the future freer agricultural trade environment.

The studies on the prospective rice import competition structure for Taiwan and the rice import demand allocation in the relatively free markets, such as HK and SG, are considered as a necessary approach to understand the likely import structure for a high-income country such as Taiwan. Taiwan, located within the major rice production community of monsoon Asia, may become a potential rice importer and thus reduce its rice self-sufficiency in the near future. This chapter discussed the rice import structure including the relative reliability of rice export supply in the world market as well as in the HK and SG markets and the import demand allocation structure by differentiated sources in terms of quality and type of rice and their implications for Taiwan. The data analysis and estimation results are then used for identifying possible adjustments on food policy mechanisms in Taiwan.

This study found a significant increase in the reliability of rice export supply in the world market. It also identified the competitive advantage and substitution effects among differentiated sources in the HK and SG markets. The higher growth in world rice production than world rice use under a stable world stock level yielded more reliable rice supply during the 1986–97 period. During the same time period a 21.1 per cent increase in rice production in the Asian countries associated with the 63.4 per cent increase of world rice trade further proved the tendency toward a more reliable world rice export supply especially in the Asian region. The shifts of many south and southeast Asian countries from importers to self-sufficiency or from self-sufficiency to actual exporters have characterized a market environment of stronger rice export supply than import demand, which is especially true in the economy of monsoon Asia. Moreover HK and SG faced continuously increasing rice imports from Thailand, the USA, and Australia, as they were considered the dominant and reliable rice export suppliers with segmented demand.

The gradual relaxation on import restrictions of high-income Asian countries, such as Taiwan, Japan, and South Korea, may provide more market potential for rice-exporting countries, which in turn have incentives to produce more rice. In this context a country with a small volume of imported rice, like Taiwan, may view those dominant rice exporters for the HK and SG markets as potentially reliable rice suppliers of various quality and types. Once high-quality rice is considered a better choice for Taiwan, the reliability of the US rice export supply is possible because of its competitive advantage in the HK markets. However the existing competitors of high-quality rice from Asian developing countries, other than Australia, may become even more reliable and competitive sources for the Taiwan market.

The potential rice import structure of Taiwan would be different from that of HK and SG because of the significant domestic consumption preference for Japonica-type rice. Although high-quality and high-price

US rice earned the larger market share in the HK market but not in the SG market, it is appropriate to include the USA as one of the potential import sources for Taiwan because HK imported a larger share of Japonica-type rice than SG. The existing substitution effects of rice between the USA and Australia and between Thailand and ROW in HK indicate that the USA may become a more competitive source than Australia in Taiwan and Taiwan may easily import Indica rice from Asian countries other than Thailand. However a significant complementary relationship between the USA and ROW creates a possibility of rice imports from within monsoon Asia rather than from other countries including the USA. It is expected that the production strategy of existing farmers for self-sufficiency in Taiwan depends for much of its future on food policy mechanisms when rice of various quality and types is able to enter into the Taiwan market.

To achieve the government objective of parity income for farmers at minimum government costs, supply control for reducing self-sufficiency and thus for reducing volume under a high-price support program was determined as the most important and effective policy mechanism. When Taiwan's food security operation is relaxed along with the possible existence of reliable suppliers in the world market, the decreased level in self-sufficiency may become acceptable and the government costs for rice support programs may be further reduced. However the elimination of price supports in future trade negotiations may create problems of maintaining farmers' income parity.

Decoupling of payments from the government is a possible alternative to price supports and would leave rice production more market oriented. It is then suggested that encouraging higher-quality rice production with lower yields to gain market competitiveness should be part of the supply control mechanism, especially when price supports are to be terminated. Non-price promotion efforts are also necessary mechanisms to include in the supply control system for domestically produced rice to gain expenditure effects on high-quality rice similar to that of the USA and Australian rice in the HK market.

This study concludes that reducing self-sufficiency is relatively safe with reliable export suppliers of rice and the inclusion of promotion on high-quality rice production. Taiwan needs to strengthen its rice marketing under the supply control program to enhance its market competitiveness when the government price support program is replaced by the decoupling payment mechanism. At least higher-quality rice production in Taiwan would provide the possibility of segmenting its market with likely imported rice from countries like Thailand. It is expected that more competitive rice production will leave more room for the operation of decoupling payments. However, the food security level may become more important than ever before and we may need greater accuracy in estimating rice imports in future research.

NOTES

1   Rice market opening may not be considered as only the state trading format of Japan and South Korea. The author believes that future rice imports of Taiwan, Japan and South Korea will be more market oriented, which will lead not only to import competition but also decreased domestic market share. As a result food security concerns must be re-evaluated.

2   Except for the United States, Australia, Thailand, Argentina and Uruguay the international market for rice is of a highly residual nature. Only about 5 per cent of world production is traded and Asia accounts for about 70 per cent of international trade. Many high income countries have supported the domestic price to achieve self-sufficiency; others have tried to provide a low rice price to consumers. Sharp fluctuations in international prices may be found when poor harvests in major exporting or importing countries lead to sudden shifts of supply and demand in the world market. Taiwan, Japan and South Korea have provided high price supports to offset the high cost of small-scale farms with decreasing comparative advantage. For example, the comparative advantage of rice production in Taiwan evaluated by the domestic resource cost (DRC) has been found to be disadvantageous since 1982.

3   Since 1995 the Japanese government has recognized 34 wholesalers in an operation of SBS with only a small quantity (one to two tons per year). Under SBS operation, the wholesalers determine the import sources and quality and submit a selling price and a buying price to the government. On the other hand trading companies importing rice under the major commitments on minimum access during the GATT negotiations are restricted on import source and quality (Riethmuller, Kobayashi, and Shogenji, 1996). Taiwan was requested by the USA to provide significantly freer market access than Japan upon joining WTO as a formal member. Such a relaxation of the rice import ban is expected to put pressure on the Taiwanese market.

4   Rice exports from China decreased significantly while exports from Vietnam increased but at a relatively unstable rate. In 1996 both sources accounted for only a small share in the Hong Kong and Singapore markets.

5   Reliable rice suppliers are only meaningful in the sense that Taiwan relaxes part of its total rice consumption volume per year because total rice demand in Taiwan is much more than Hong Kong and Singapore. However, the supply from these mentioned sources reflects growing ability to export. Once high-quality and high-price rice is accepted by Taiwan the US rice will be in a good competitive position. A remote concern will be the possible ban of rice exports

to Taiwan from any of these countries, especially Thailand, due to political intervention from mainland China.

6　The well-specified cost function assumes linear, homogeneous and concave function of commodity prices.

REFERENCES

Berndt, R. E. and L. R. Christensen (1973), 'The Internal Structure of Functional Relationships, Seperability, Substitution, and Aggregation', *Review of Economic Studies*, 34: 403–10.

Blanciforti, L. R. and R. Green (1983), 'An Almost Ideal Demand System Incorporating Habits: An Analysis of Expenditures on Food and Aggregate Commodity Groups', *Review of Economics and Statistics*, 65: 511–5.

Chen, Hsi-Huang (1994), 'Economic Liberalization and Adjustment of Rice Policies in Taiwan', Extension Bulletin 379, Food and Fertilizer Technology Center.

Childs, N. W (1990), 'The World Rice Market-Government Intervention and Multilateral Policy Reform', Washington DC: US Department of Agriculture, ERS, Commodity Economics Division.

Cramer, G. L., E. J. Wailes, and S. Shui (1993), 'Impacts of Liberalizing Trade in the World Rice Market', *American Journal of Agricultural Economics*, 75: 219–26.

Deaton, A. S. and J. Muellbauer (1980), 'An Almost Ideal Demand System', *American Economic Review*, 70: 312–26.

Haley, S. L (1992), 'Evaluating Japanese trade liberalization: Results from a Modeling Perspective', *Agricultural Center Research Report* No. 691, Louisiana State University.

Johnson, D. Gale (1975), 'World Agriculture, Commodity Policy, and Price Variability', *American Journal of Agricultural Economics*, 57(1): 823–8.

Karp, L. S. and J. M. Perloff (1989), 'Dynamic Oligopoly in the Rice Export Market', *Review of Economics and Statistics*, 71(3): 462 – 70.

McElory, M. B. (1977), 'Goodness-of-Fit for Seemingly Unrelated Regressions', *Journal of Econometrics*, 6: 381–7.

Moschini, Giancarlo (1995), 'Units of Measurement and the Stone Index in Demand System Estimation', *American Journal of Agricultural Economics*, 77: 63–8.

Riethmuller, P., S. Kobayashi, and S. Shogenji (1996), 'Japanese Agricultural Policies towards 2000: Swimming with the Tide', *Review of Marketing and Agricultural Economics*, 64(1): 3–18.

Shephard, R. W. (1970), *The Theory of Cost and Production Functions*, Princeton, NJ: Princeton University Press.

Song, J. and C. A. Carter (1996), 'Rice Trade Liberalization and Implications for US Policy', *American Journal of Agricultural Economics*, 78: 891–905.

Wailes, E. J., K. B. Young, and G. L. Cramer (1994),'The East Asian Rice Economy after GATT', in Luther Tweeten and Hsin-Hui Hsu (eds), *Changing Trade Environment after GATT: A Case Study of Taiwan*, Council of Agriculture, chapter 2.

Yumkella, K. K., L. J. Unnevehr, and P. Garcia (1994), 'Noncompetitive Pricing and Exchange Rate Pass-through in Selected US and Thai Rice Markets', *Journal of Agriculture and Applied Economics*, 26(2): 406–16.

10. Food security issues in Singapore: implications for East Asian economies undergoing agricultural trade liberalization

Gwo-Jiun Mike Leu

1. INTRODUCTION

The liberalization of agricultural trade has been included in the Uruguay Round of the General Agreement on Tariffs and Trade (GATT) in December 1993. Nations are to replace quotas on agricultural imports with less restrictive tariffs over a ten-year period. Tariffs on agricultural products are to be reduced by 36 per cent in industrial nations and 24 per cent in developing nations. Domestic support for producers is to be reduced by 20 per cent and 13.3 per cent respectively. Expenditure on export subsidies is also to be cut by 36 per cent.

All of these liberalization agreements on agricultural trade are pressuring many East Asian economies to open up their domestic markets for foreign agricultural products and reduce domestic support for agricultural production. For them, it is uncomfortable and yet inevitable to shift emphasis from domestic food self-sufficiency to trade-oriented self-reliance. What would be the food security issues if a country adopt a more trade-oriented self-reliance policy?

Singapore, with limited natural resources, has literally relied on imports for its food consumption needs. Food security in Singapore has been achieved almost entirely through trade. The study of food security issues in Singapore provides a unique and valuable lesson for these economies to understand their prospective food security problems the better to adapt to the new food security arrangements.

The purposes of this chapter are to (1) review Singapore's food security arrangements and its development and (2) draw some implications for East Asian economies undergoing the process of agricultural trade liberalization.

In the next section, production, consumption, and self-sufficiency ratio of essential food produce in Singapore are reviewed. Measures undertaken by Singapore to ensure adequate and safe food supply are then discussed in section 3. Section 4 applies both partial and general equilibrium models to conceptualize Singapore's food demand and supply situation and strategies in achieving food security. Implications for East Asian economies undergoing agricultural trade liberalization are examined in section 5. Section 6 concludes the chapter.

2. FOOD PRODUCTION, CONSUMPTION AND SELF-SUFFICIENCY RATIO IN SINGAPORE

Singapore is a small city-state with 581.5 square kilometres of land and had 1.87 million in population when it became independent in 1965. The high density in population made Singapore use 31 per cent of the land to house people and only 23 per cent of the land to grow food.

Over the last three decades, although Singapore government has tried hard to increase its land stock by reclaiming land from the sea, its land area increased only 11 per cent while the population increased by 63 per cent. The population density has increased from 3.2 thousand persons per square kilometre in 1965 to 4.7 thousand persons per square kilometre in 1996 (table 10.1). In addition, rapid industrial growth and urbanization in Singapore have made the land much more expensive for farming. From time to time, farmland was cleared in stages for redevelopment and many farmers were resettled to live in new public housing, developed by the Housing and Development Board, and to work in other industries. As a result, the farm-holding land decreased from 131.6 square kilometres in 1965 to only 10.8 square kilometres in 1996. The population–farmland ratio increased rapidly from 14.2 to 281.9 thousand persons per square kilometre over the same period. By 1996, Singapore had only 1.7 per cent of the land for farming while 49.7 per cent of the total land area was used for housing, industrial sites, and infrastructure.

With such a high population–farmland ratio, obviously it is impossible to produce enough food to meet demand. Firstly, not all the food crops, wheat and apples for example, can be grown on such a tiny tropical island. Secondly, even if some food crops, like rice, can be produced in Singapore, they may not be produced in Singapore for economic considerations.

Even in 1965, only a handful of fresh primary produce was grown locally. Other food commodities which can be cheaply imported and

Table 10.1 *Population growth and land use in Singapore, 1965 – 96*

	Unit	1965	1975	1985	1995	1996
Total land area	Square kilometres	581.5	596.8	620.5	647.5	647.5
Build-up area	Square kilometres	177.4	228.4	298.8	319.3	321.6
share of total land	%	30.5	38.3	48.2	49.3	49.7
Farm holding area[a]	Square kilometres	131.6[b]	105.9	47.1	9.3	10.8
share of total land	%	22.6	17.7	7.6	1.4	1.7
Population	Thousands	1864.9	2262.6	2482.6	2986.5	3044.3
Population density	Thousands/square kilometre	3.2	3.8	4.0	4.6	4.7
Population farmland ratio	Thousands/square kilometre	14.2	21.4	52.7	321.1	281.9

Notes: [a] Figures refer to farm holding area of licensed farms excluding land occupied by pure rubber and coconut plantations.
[b] Figure refers to land used for agriculture which exclude land used for pig and poultry farming and inland fisheries.

Source: Singapore Department of Statistics, *Yearbook of Statistics*, Singapore, various issues.

stockpiled, such as grain and sugar, had been phased out of local production. By 1975, only chicken, pork, fish and vegetables were still produced domestically in a significant way. Local farms produced 79 per cent of the poultry consumption, 99 per cent of the pork consumption, 29 per cent of the fish consumption, and 26 per cent of vegetable consumption (table 10.2). Although beef, mutton, and fruits were also produced domestically, they accounted for only 1.64 per cent, 0.17 per cent, and 8.74 per cent, of consumption respectively.

Over the last two decades, Singapore's food self-sufficiency ratio has dropped dramatically due to constant increases in consumption as well as decreases in production. As shown in table 10.3, Singapore's per capita consumption of primary produce has continuously increased between 1 to 2 per cent per annum mainly due to the income effect. Together with population growth, the total consumption of food grew about 3 per cent annually (table 10.2). In the same period, domestic production of meat, vegetables, and fish reduced 98 per cent, 80 per cent, and 43 per cent respectively. By 1996, only 1 per cent of meat consumption, 10 per cent of fish, 3 per cent of vegetables, and 36 per cent of eggs were produced locally.

3. MEASURES UNDERTAKEN BY SINGAPORE TO ENSURE AN ADEQUATE AND SAFE FOOD SUPPLY

The massive reduction in domestic production of primary produce was the result of economic and agricultural policies undertaken by the Singapore government to best utilize Singapore's very precious land and further develop Singapore's economy. While ensuring an adequate and safe food supply for Singapore, the Singapore government puts more emphasis on balanced national development through economic growth. Policy to develop Singapore's economy affects resource allocation and thus domestic food production. However, domestic food self-sufficiency is not the policy objective.

3.1   Export Promotion Policy (1966–Present)

Between 1960 and 1965, Singapore attempted import substitution policy as the primary means of domestic economic growth. However, the policy of import substitution was ineffective because it tends to develop inefficient domestic manufacturing industries, especially when the domestic market is limited. The separation of Singapore from Malaysia in 1965 spelled the end of the import substitution phase (Leu, 1996).

Table 10.2 Fresh food production, consumption and self-sufficiency ratio in Singapore, 1975–96

Year		Unit	Meat	Poultry Meat	Chicken	Duck	Red meat	Pork	Beef	Mutton	Fish	Vegetables	Fruits	Eggs[a]
1975	Production	1000 Tonnes	102.63	43.43			59.20	59.09	0.10	0.01	17.56	38.29	14.65	
	Imports	1000 Tonnes	30.08	14.46			15.61	0.82	7.27	7.53	50.56	151.88		
	Supply	1000 Tonnes	132.70	57.89			74.81	59.90	7.37	7.54	68.12	190.17		
	Exports	1000 Tonnes	4.83	2.77			2.07	0.17	1.32	0.58	7.88	44.31		
	Consumption	1000 Tonnes	127.87	55.12			72.75	59.73	6.05	6.96	60.24	145.86	167.58	
	Self-sufficiency ratio	%	80.26	78.78			81.38	98.92	1.64	0.17	29.15	26.25	8.74	
1979	Production	1000 Tonnes	125.36	51.40			73.96	73.87	0.08	0.01	16.44	36.10	9.26	
	Imports	1000 Tonnes	38.69	20.28			18.40	0.51	11.03	6.86	67.40	136.13		
	Supply	1000 Tonnes	164.04	71.68			92.37	74.38	11.11	6.87	83.84	172.23		
	Exports	1000 Tonnes	7.95	4.13			3.82	0.38	2.83	0.60	27.13	34.78		
	Consumption	1000 Tonnes	156.09	67.55			88.54	74.00	8.28	6.26	56.42	137.46		
	Self-sufficiency ratio	%	80.31	76.09			83.54	99.82	0.98	0.16	29.14	26.26		
1995	Production	1000 Tonnes	2.42								10.45	7.79		364.80
	Imports	1000 Tonnes	246.18								87.45	393.31		
	Supply	1000 Tonnes	248.60	132.90	120.00	12.90	115.70	91.70	15.40	8.60	97.90	401.10	446.54	
	Exports	1000 Tonnes	6.69									141.27		
	Consumption	1000 Tonnes	241.91	128.42	113.49	14.93	113.49	89.60	14.93	8.96	104.53	259.83	310.60	1042.29
	Self-sufficiency ratio	%	1.00								10.00	3.00		35.00
1996	Production	1000 Tonnes	2.53								10.05	7.49		368.24
	Imports	1000 Tonnes	257.87								86.45	388.21		
	Supply	1000 Tonnes	260.40	145.90	133.90	12.00	114.50	92.00	13.80	8.70	96.50	395.70	434.80	
	Exports	1000 Tonnes	7.72									146.07		
	Consumption	1000 Tonnes	252.68	140.04	127.86	12.18	112.64	91.33	12.18	9.13	100.46	249.63	307.47	1022.89
	Self-sufficiency ratio	%	1.00								10.00	3.00		36.00

Notes: [a] Unit in 1000 eggs.

Sources: Singapore Ministry of National Development, *Annual Report*, various issues.
Singapore Primary Production Department, *Annual Report*, various issues.

189

Table 10.3 Singapore's per capita consumption of primary produce, 1975–96

Year	Unit	Meat	Poultry meat			Red meat				Fish	Vegetables	Fruits	Eggs[a]
				Chicken	Duck		Pork	Beef	Mutton				
1975	Kilogram	56.5	24.4			32.2	26.4	2.7	3.1	26.6	64.5	74.1	
1979	Kilogram	65.5	28.3			37.1	31.1	3.5	2.6	23.7	57.7		
1995	Kilogram	81.0	43.0	38.0	5.0	38.0	30.0	5.0	3.0	35.0	87.0	104.0	349
1996	Kilogram	83.0	46.0	42.0	4.0	37.0	30.0	4.0	3.0	33.0	82.0	101.0	336

Notes: [a]Unit in number of eggs.

Sources: Singapore Ministry of National Development, Annual Report, various issues.
Singapore Primary Production Department, Annual Report, various issues.

With a limited domestic market and abundant labour supply, the Singapore government started turning to export promotion of labour-intensive goods in 1965. The success in solving the unemployment problem by 1971 motivated Singapore to shift her emphasis toward capital-intensive industries and select investment projects for its value-added content and technical skills rather than employment creation (Singapore EDB 1990/91).

By 1979, the rewards of export promotion began to be realized and wage rate limitations were partially relaxed. Singapore's per capita income took off and savings grew. Capital-intensive industries became the major focus. The Singapore government was looking into various ways to upgrade technology, develop workers' skill for modern industries, and redevelop land for better use. The export promotion strategy, though going through various stages of economic development, is still the guiding principle in Singapore's economic success. The export promotion policy involves exploiting comparative advantage and importing goods costly to produce domestically.

3.2 Farming on Unsubsidized and Fully Commercial Footing

In Singapore, the responsibilities of ensuring safe and adequate supplies of storable food and fresh food rest on the Trade Development Board and Primary Production Department (PPD) respectively. In line with the export promotion policy, Singapore had been importing all the storable food for domestic consumption. By the late 1970s, the changing comparative advantage also demanded adjustments in the production mix of fresh food and industrial goods.

In March 1979, a committee was appointed to review agricultural policy and recommend measures for the productive and efficient use of land for farming. Based on the committee's recommendations, in 1980 the Ministry of National Development (Singapore MND) adopted an agricultural policy under which farming would be placed on an unsubsidized and fully commercial footing (Singapore MND, 1980). To reflect the policy change towards agriculture, the following measures were taken by the PPD to reallocate farm resources while ensuring an adequate and safe food supply.

3.2.1 Phasing out inefficient / pollutive farming activities
Alternative farmland would no longer be offered as part of resettlement benefits. Only viable and efficient farmers would be allowed to apply for land allocated by the PPD at economic rentals. Other farmers with valid farm licences were offered enhanced resettlement benefits and

resettlement grants. New farm licences would only be issued to farmers carrying out farming activities on newly designated permanent agricultural land. This entailed the continuous clearance of squatters in rural areas, resulting in a reduction in the number of farms and the farm holding area. This was different from previous resettlement practices, where farmers were offered licences as well as alternative farmland and encouraged to form commercial farms for intensive farming.

For example, a programme to clear all pig farms from the Kranji water catchment area to abate pollution was launched in September 1979. Some were resettled to the Punggol Pig Farming Estate. Starting in 1980, a pollution levy of $10 was imposed for every pig slaughtered at the abattoirs to abate pollution in the pig farming areas. Because of environment pollution, in 1985 the Singapore government decided to phase out pig farming in Singapore. The exercise was completed when the remaining 22 commercial pig farms in Singapore ceased operations and the last domestic pig was disposed of on 19 November 1990.

3.2.2   Establishing agrotechnical parks
With very little land for agriculture, farming must be geared towards high -tech farming and high-value, high-quality primary produce. Singapore's strategy is to establish Agrotechnology Parks for modern intensive farms, using high-tech farming methods. Since 1986, the PPD has initiated and coordinated the development of 1200 hectares of farmland into Agrotechnology Parks (Singapore PPD, 1996). It is estimated that between 400 and 500 modern, high-tech farms will be housed in six Agrotechnology Parks by the year 2000. In addition, up to 10 per cent of the land has been set aside for high-tech farms to produce safe, high-value and high-quality produce (Singapore MND, 1994).

The Parks are equipped with the necessary infrastructure and designed to have a complementary mix of non-pollutive farms which can coexist in the urban environment. Currently, parcels of land ranging from 2 to 30 hectares are allocated on 20-year leases to farming companies to produce vegetables, orchids, aquatic and ornamental plants, freshwater ornamental and food fish, eggs, milk, and some exotic animals, like crocodiles and birds.

Besides providing part of the food supply to Singapore, the Agrotechnology Parks are aesthetically pleasant, designed to achieve ecological balance, and can serve as tourist attractions and educational areas. The overall aim of the PPD is to develop Singapore into an Agrotechnology Service Centre and regional R&D Centre.

3.2.3 Enhancing food import management

With the phasing out of many farming activities, the decrease in local production of fresh produce was met by increased imports. The high dependence on external sources presents a challenge for the PPD to ensure a continuous and steady supply of fresh farm produce that is safe and fit for human consumption.

To meet this challenge, firstly the PPD adopted an integrated system of accreditation, inspection, and testing to ensure a high standard of food safety. Imports of farm produce is systematically audited to remove hazards at source before they can be introduced into the food chain. For meat imports, for example, the PPD identifies and assesses countries that meet international standards of animal husbandry and hygiene. After carefully assessing their animal health controls, veterinary public health programmes, legislative power, enforcement action, and production capability, Singapore officers would physically inspect their farms, abattoirs, and food-processing establishments to determine their hygiene standards and eligibility to export to Singapore. On the local front, the pre-slaughter and post-slaughter inspections are carried out rigorously at abattoirs by the Meat Inspection Services. In addition, regular and extensive laboratory testing are performed to screen food for pesticide and fungicide residues, contaminants, preservatives, and additives. Above all, the system is reviewed periodically to keep abreast of new developments.

Secondly, the PPD diversifies the external sources of farm produce to avoid disruption in food imports owing to risk and uncertainty. New establishments are approved continuously for exports to Singapore. Sources of imports which become a threat are removed or suspended from the approved list. In 1996, Singapore imported meat and meat products from 27 countries. Twenty-two new establishments were approved for export of specific meat and meat products to Singapore. Following reports of a possible link between Mad Cow Disease and the human Creutzfeldt-Jakob Disease, the PPD took swift action to ban the import of beef and beef products from the United Kingdom. Today, only countries that have been certified free from Mad Cow Disease for the last six years are allowed to export beef to Singapore. Although many countries are allowed to export their farm produce to Singapore, their farm produce, provided it is safe and fit for human consumption, is competing freely in the Singapore market. As a result, imported vegetables come mainly from Malaysia, Indonesia, China, Australia, Taiwan, and India. Live animals are imported mainly from Malaysia, Indonesia, and Australia, while poultry meat is mainly from the USA, Denmark, and the Netherlands.

Thirdly, the PPD to maintain and foster ASEAN goodwill,

understanding and solidarity participates in a supportive and cooperative way in various ASEAN programmes, projects, and meetings on food, agriculture, livestock, and fisheries. Since 1980, PPD has been participating in programmes and activities of the ASEAN Committee on Food, Agriculture, and Forestry. These programmes and activities, which encompass agricultural development planning, technical research in food production and post-harvest technology of fruits and vegetables, have enhanced the understanding and cooperation among member nations.

4. WELFARE ANALYSIS OF SINGAPORE'S STRATEGY IN ACHIEVING FOOD SECURITY

Food security is commonly defined as an adequate supply of food for all people at all times and the ability of food deficit countries/households to meet target levels of consumption on a yearly basis (Zulkifly *et al.*, 1986). Singapore has achieved food security through trade-oriented self-reliance rather than self-sufficiency. For Singapore, there is no hard choice between trade-oriented self-reliance and self-sufficiency to achieve food security.

To conceptualize Singapore's food demand and supply situation and strategies in achieving food security, both partial equilibrium and general equilibrium models will be used to illustrate the welfare consequence of the trade-related self-sufficiency adopted in Singapore.

The partial equilibrium models for fresh food and storable food are represented respectively in panel (a) and panel (b) of figure 10.1. As a small country, Singapore is a price taker in the world food market. If the food imported from the world market is perishable and freshness is a major consideration, the local price, P_d, of the imported fresh food would be high enough to justify local production at Q_p and consumption at Q_c as shown in panel (a). Thus self-sufficiency was high for perishable produce before 1980.

Over the years, owing to increased land prices and stricter pollution regulations, the cost of local production in fresh food has increased substantially and shifted the local supply curve to S_l. At the same time, the local price of the imported fresh goods with acceptable quality also fell to P'_d as technology in transportation and freezing facilities improved. As a result, local production dropped to Q'_p while consumption rose to Q'_c.

To maximize productivity of limited farmland and ensure safe and adequate supplies of primary produce, the Singapore government started setting up 'agrotechnical parks' to grow primary produce intensively

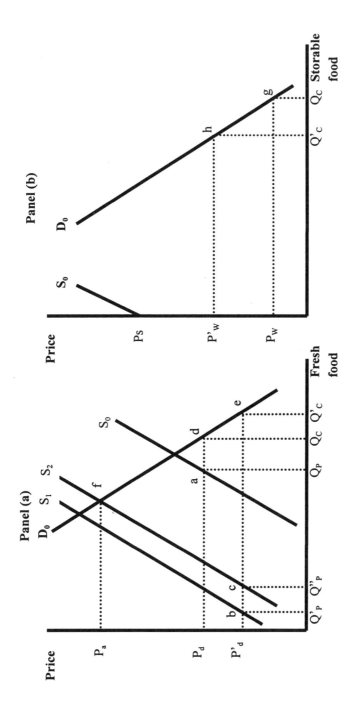

Figure 10.1 The market for fresh and storable food in Singapore

195

since 1985. By 1996, 12 square kilometres of agrotechnical parks have been operational. This has shifted the supply of local fresh produce downward to S_2 and increased the local production slightly to Q''_p. If Singapore were to pursue a self-sufficiency policy, the domestic price would be pushed up to P_a and incur unnecessary welfare loss indicated by area cfe.

If food commodities, like grain or sugar, can be transported into Singapore and stockpiled cheaply, the local price would not be very different from world market prices, P_w, as shown in panel (b). There would be little need for Singapore to produce locally because the start-up price, P_s, of local supply would be too high to justify production locally, even if the world market price occasionally increased up to P'_w. Singapore would simply import all the storable food needed to meet domestic demand at Q_c. Trying to produce this storable food domestically would incur very high production costs and reduce Singapore's financial ability to buy other food from the world market.

To strengthen Singapore's ability to import food to meet target consumption, it is useful to understand the welfare implications of food trade by a general equilibrium analysis as shown in figure 10.2. Because of high opportunity costs in farming, the relative price of food, P_a, would be very high if trade is prohibited. With trade, the lower world relative price of food, P_w, would induce Singapore to import TC quantity of food and export FT quantity of other goods. Singapore would specialize in non-food production, which is where Singapore's comparative advantage lies. For example, besides specializing in industrial goods, Singapore also produces high-value-added crocodiles to replace highly pollutive pig production. As a result, Singapore's utility level would increase from U_a to U_f. Singapore is able to import more food and increase its food consumption because of specialization in industrial goods production and exchange for food at a favourable price. The difference in panel (a) and panel (b) is that the world relative price of storable food in panel (b) is too low to justify any local production of storable food at all. Complete specialization in the production and export of other goods, mainly industrial goods, enhance Singapore's ability to import more storable food to meet its demand.

5. IMPLICATIONS FOR EAST ASIAN ECONOMIES UNDERGOING AGRICULTURAL TRADE LIBERALIZATION

Food security is often confused with food self-sufficiency. Many simply equate food security with food self-sufficiency. However, food self-

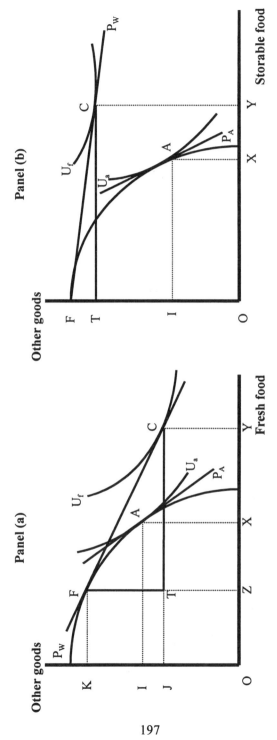

Figure 10.2 General equilibrium analysis of food trade in Singapore

197

sufficiency is a one-dimensional concept (domestic production), while food security has two dimensions (availability of food and ability to acquire food). The case of Singapore is a perfect example to show that the concepts are quite different. By any criterion, Singapore achieves food security, but her food self-sufficiency is less than 10 per cent of food consumption.

In fact, very few countries in the world meet all of their food consumption needs from domestic production. Yet, many countries stress the importance of achieving greater food self-sufficiency, at least in staple foods. The main issue is why forego foreign staple food if it is more competitive? Is it not safe? Not up to the quality? Or simply not affordable? To ensure safe and quality food imports is less a problem if a comprehensive system of accreditation, inspection, and testing, as adopted by Singapore, is applied. The main difficulty of most countries seems to be lack of financial ability to acquire food at market price.

There are many other social, economic, political, and even cultural reasons for maintaining greater food self-sufficiency: protection of domestic agriculture, risk and stability considerations, and pursuit of broader economic goals (Staatz, 1991; Mangahas, 1985). However, most of them are inconsistent with the liberalization agreement on agricultural trade reached in the Uruguay round of multilateral trade negotiations. Many economies in East Asia are either undergoing agricultural trade liberalization or are under tremendous pressure to reduce domestic subsidies for food production and open up their domestic markets for foreign agricultural products. The accelerated rates of urbanization in recent decades also add increasing pressure on policy makers in these economies to rethink their food self-sufficiency approach in achieving food security (Braun *et al.*, 1993). The trend for these economies is to follow the path of Singapore's development in achieving food security in the 1980s. The eventual result may be to farm on an unsubsidized and fully commercial footing and adopt a more trade-oriented self-reliance policy. In that case, Singapore's experience in achieving food security through trade-oriented self-reliance policy may be encouraging to these economies.

As a small city-state and trading nation, Singapore has upheld and benefited from free trade. Her export promotion policy has led to rapid economic growth. In three decades, Singapore's per capita income grew from US$528 in 1965 to US$26 264 in 1996, an average rate of 10.4 per cent per annum growth in real terms. The enviable economic success has given Singapore the financial ability to import more food, even with a certain degree of price uncertainty in the world food market.

The approach of ensuring food supplies by importing food from the best sources in the world not only provides more varieties of food to Singapore consumers, but also at lower and stable prices. Figure10.3 shows the Consumer Price Index (CPI) percentage change for food from 1973 to 1996. It shows that Singapore was severely affected by the food crisis in 1973 and 1974 as were most countries in the world. After that, the CPI percentage change for food has been fairly stable. It is noticeable that the percentage increase in food prices has been lower after Singapore phased out more domestic food production and imported more food from external sources. This outcome is contrary to the common worry that larger price fluctuations would result from relying on the world market for food supply.

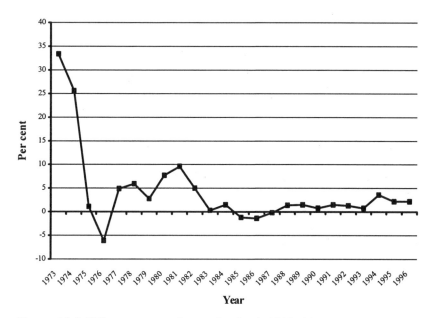

Figure 10.3 CPI percentage change for food, 1973–96

Source: Singapore Department of Statistics, *Yearbook of Statistics, Singapore*, various issues.

Although Singapore depends heavily on imports for food consumption and its value of food imports increased over time, as indicated in figure 10.4, its share of food imports decreased from 20 per cent of total imports in 1965 to only 3 per cent in 1996. The share of food exports and

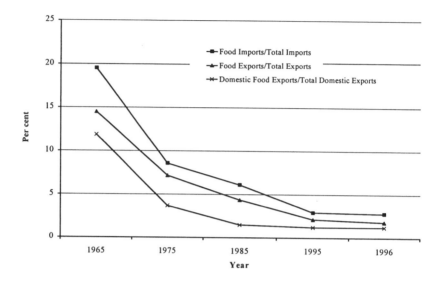

Figure 10.4 Singapore's share of food imports, exports and domestic exports, 1965–96

Source: Singapore Department of Statistics, *Yearbook of Statistics, Singapore*, various issues.

domestic food exports also decreased respectively. It is believed the lower the share of food imports, the smaller the fear that food shortages would lead to social upheaval.

Among all the food traded, vegetables and fruits and fish were the main divisions imported while coffee, fish, and vegetables and fruit were the main divisions exported in Singapore in 1996 (figure 10.5). Staple food accounted for only 11 per cent and 8 per cent of total imports and exports respectively. Trade in staple foods may not be the most important division traded among all food, even if trade restrictions on staple foods in other East Asian economies were relaxed.

6. CONCLUDING REMARKS

Singapore is a small city-state with very limited land resources. The concentration of population has made local production of storable food infeasible. Owing to rapid industrialization and urbanization, by the late

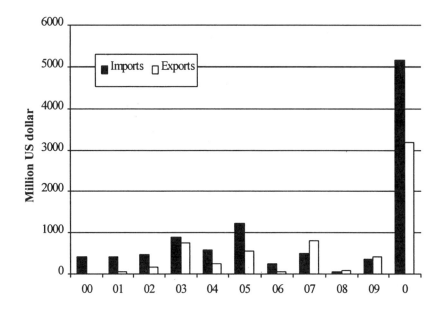

SITC division code

Division: 00: Live Animals; 01: Meat; 02: Dairy Products; 03: Fish; 04: Cereals; 05:
    Vegetables and Fruit;
    06: Sugar; 07: Coffee, Tea, Cocoa; 08: Feeding Stuff; 09:Miscellous Edible
    Products; 0: Food

Figure 10.5 Singapore's food imports and exports by SITC division, 1996

Source: Singapore Department of Statistics, *Yearbook of Statistics, Singapore*, various
    issues.

1970s, local production of fresh food also faced tremendous competition
to yield its land for competing use. To accommodate the changing
comparative advantage, in 1980 the Singapore government decided to put
farming on an unsubsidized and fully commercial footing. This is in line
with the export promotion policy for economic development. The result
was a further drop in food self-sufficiency ratio to less than 10 per cent.
    To ensure an adequate and safe food supply to meet human
consumption, Singapore has enhanced food import management and
established six Agrotechnical Parks for intensive farming of high-value,
high-quality primary produce. The result is high economic growth, more

varieties of food, and low and stable food prices. Furthermore, the share of food trade has been decreasing over the years.

Some East Asian economies, have relied on domestic production for their food consumption needs. Even with the changing comparative advantage and agricultural free trade agreement, they have been reluctant to scale down their inefficient domestic food production for various reasons. They are fearful of the risk and uncertainty involved in food imports. They do not have confidence in agricultural trade and world trading system. Singapore's successful experience in achieving food security through trade-oriented self-reliance should be encouraging to them.

REFERENCES

Braun, J. V, J. McComb, B.K. Fred-Mensah, and R. Pandya-Lorch (1993), *Urban Food Insecurity and Malnutrition in Developing Countries: Trends, Policies, and Research Implications*, International Food Policy Research Institute.

Leu, Gwo-Jiun Mike (1996), 'Singapore's International Trade in Goods and Services', in Lim Chong Yah (ed.), *Economic Policy Management in Singapore*, Addison-Wesley, Chapter 9.

Mangahas, Mahr (1985), 'Relative Emphasis on Domestic Food Self-sufficiency and Trade-oriented Self-reliance', *World Food Security: Selected Themes and Issues*, FAO Economic and Social Development Paper 53, Chapter 1, Food and Agriculture Organization of the United Nations, Rome, Italy.

Singapore Department of Statistics, *Yearbook of Statistics, Singapore*, various issues.

Singapore Economic Development Board, *Economic Development Board Yearbook 1990/91*.

Singapore Ministry of National Development, *Annual Report*, various issues.

Singapore Ministry of National Development (1994), *The MND Network: Shaping the Future*.

Singapore Primary Production Department, *Annual Report*, various issues.

Singapore Primary Production Department, *Agrotechnology Parks*, Singapore.

Staatz, John (1991), 'Conceptual Issues in Analyzing the Economics of Agricultural and Food Self-Sufficiency', in Ruppel and Kellogg (eds), *National and Regional Self-sufficiency Goals: Implications for*

International Agriculture, Lynne Rienner Publishers, Chapter 2.
Zulkifly, Hj. Mustapha; Siwar Chamhuri, and Nik Hashim N M (1986), *Food Economy of Malaysia: Problems and Policies in Food Security*, Malaysia, Penerbit Universiti Kebangsaan.

11. Demand for food safety in Taiwan

Tsu-Tan Fu, Chung L. Huang and Kamhon Kan

1. INTRODUCTION

Food security is commonly regarded as the ability to meet target consumption levels in the face of fluctuating production, prices, and incomes. Although the problem of attaining an adequate food supply is as old as mankind, food security has become a clearly enunciated policy goal for most developing countries only in the last decade or so. Most of the chapters in this book have focused on the themes of achieving food insecurity in terms of stabilizing food supply and prices, improving storage techniques, and projecting food demands with growing population pressures in the Asian region. However, there is another important dimension of the food security problem, namely the quality of food in terms of safety characteristics, which has been largely overlooked in the discussion of food security issues.

Countries at different development stages tend to emphasize different dimensions of the food security issue. Among the low-income developing countries, such as Bangladesh, Myanmar, Cambodia, Laos, Vietnam, Indonesia, and the Philippines, grains (rice mainly) have been and continue to be the primary dietary staples that account for most of the daily intake of calories. Thus, the policy goal for this group of countries has been focused primarily on the quantity dimension of food security. On the other hand, for more developed countries, such as the Asian Newly Industrial Economies (Dragons and Tigers) and Japan, the quality instead of the quantity dimension of food security seems to be the relevant issue that has gained and received increasing importance and attention. As a result of rising real income due to rapid economic growth, consumers in this group of countries have increased their demand for greater diversity in diet and higher quality of foods. Their concerns about the healthiness and wholesomeness of food supplies have tipped the scale of food problems towards the quality aspect of the food security issue in these

Asian countries. Once the real per capita income exceeds the subsistence and poverty level, consumers will turn their attention to the quality of foods and diet that they eat. In particular, this study is designed to address the quality aspect of food insecurity by investigating consumers' concerns and perception of food safety issues in Taiwan.

The field application rate and use of farm chemicals in Taiwan's agricultural sector were found to be substantially higher in the past decade. As shown in figure 11.1, average use of pesticides on agricultural cultivated land in 1988 was about 37.4 kg per hectare in Taiwan, which was greater than the amount used by Japan, Korea, Thailand, and Indonesia combined.[1] The level of pesticide use in agricultural production remains high and even increased in the 1990s. Such a high level of pesticides application in Taiwan can be attributed in part to the substitution of pesticides for labour owing to the decreasing pesticide–labour factor price ratio and the labour shortage experienced since the early 1980s. In addition, farmers were also found to be adopting a strategy of overuse of pesticides on the fields to reduce any loss from yield uncertainty (Huang and Soo, 1991).[2]

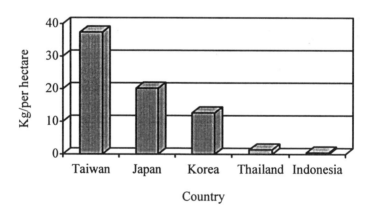

Figure 11.1 Use of pesticides on agricultural cultivated land, 1988
Source: United Nations, 1988.

Public concerns on food safety in Taiwan soared in the 1990s after a series of reported incidences regarding high levels of pesticide residues found in vegetables and fruits in the market. As a result, the demand for safer food with low or no usage of pesticides, such as hydroponically grown and organically grown agricultural products, has become increasingly popular in recent years. To accommodate such public demand for safer foods, the Taiwanese government has increased its budget allocation for food safety research and extension. Since 1994, the government has also promoted the so-called 'Good Agricultural Practice' (GAP) program. A GAP label has been used to certify those farm products with proper application of pesticides. These GAP products plus products such as hydroponically and organically grown products may be found in some supper markets or certain designated shops through special marketing channels. However, the market for these products is generally very thin. Pricing for these products is usually based on a very limited quantity of supply for a few selective foods, which may not be enough to ensure good market potential for these food products. Thus, there is a need to study the demand and market potential for these safer foods in Taiwan.

The objectives of this study are to provide an understanding of Taiwanese consumers' food safety concerns and to evaluate their perception of food safety as well as their willingness to pay for safer foods. The hydroponically grown vegetables (HGV), which are free of pesticide residues, are used in this study to elicit consumer willingness to pay for food safety. More specifically, this study hypothesizes that consumers' food safety preferences and willingness to pay are integrals of a joint decision-making process. Thus, the main objective is to develop an empirical model to estimate simultaneously the interrelationships between the decisions of whether or not to pay more and how much more to pay for a safer food. The findings obtained from this study should provide useful information and important implications for assessing the market potential and for developing marketing strategies to promote the demand for safer foods in Taiwan. Furthermore, the results of this study may provide some insights on and implications for the quality dimension of food patterns to developing countries in Asia as they progress into more industrialized and developed economies.

2. MEASURING WILLINGNESS TO PAY FOR FOOD SAFETY

Food safety is a characteristic of the food products consumers buy, and it is a characteristic that is extremely costly and difficult to assess. It is costly to determine whether a particular food contains a substance that might pose health risks. It is costly to determine just what types of health hazards might be involved. Furthermore, it is extremely difficult for consumers to assess their exposure to risks in each food product, and to accurately articulate their demand for safety. It is because of this problem of insufficient and inadequate information that market mechanisms fail to achieve allocative efficiency and to produce the level of safety or quality that is socially desired. Faced with the task of estimating the demand for goods and services where there is market failure, economists have developed several measurement techniques, such as the travel cost method, for estimating recreation benefits, and the averting expenditure method, for estimating the values of health risks from environmental hazards (Buzby *et al.*, 1998). Others have used contingent valuation methods (CVM) in consumer surveys to elicit respondents' stated preferences or willingness to pay (WTP) for non-market goods.

Conceptually, a consumer's WTP for a health-risk reduction may serve as an indicator of the level of demand for food safety. Randall and Stoll (1980) have discussed the theory of CVM and its applications for measuring willingness to pay. The CVM was developed to place a monetary value on goods, which are not priced in the market. This approach usually requires the use of a bidding procedure with the assistance of trained interviewers. A modified CVM may use a checklist of payment ranges from which the respondents are asked to select their willingness to pay amount. The CVM is less costly than actual market experiments because it circumvents the absence of markets by presenting consumers with hypothetical markets and prices, in which they are asked to make a purchase decision. Although anomalous results have occurred from time to time, substantial supportive evidence has been accumulated to encourage increasing applications after more than two decades of research, testing, and improvement.[3]

CVM have been increasingly used in the US to elicited consumers' WTP for health-risk reduction from pesticides in food. Of these studies, many report that consumers are willing to pay higher prices for residue-free produce (Hammitt, 1993; Huang, 1993; Misra, Huang, and Ott, 1991; Ott, 1990; Weaver, Evans, and Luloff, 1992). While most studies have estimated consumers' WTP for safer food, few studies have estimated WTP for specific risk reductions (Buzby, Ready, and Skees, 1995; van Ravenswaay and Hoehn, 1991). Most recently, Buzby *et al.* (1998) estimate that consumers' WTP are statistically insensitive to the size of the risk reduction associated with shopping at 'government standard' stores versus 'pesticide-free' stores.

Similar concerns about food safety and pesticide residues in food are receiving increasing attention in Taiwan. Fu, Liu, and Hammitt (1997) estimate consumers' WTP for health-risk reductions among Taiwanese women. They find that WTP is positively related to a measure of attitudinal aversion to food risk, and that WTP is significantly related to the measure of risk perception. More importantly, the results suggest that WTP is sensitive to the scope of the goods and is significantly related to the magnitude of risk reductions. However, the difference in WTP was found to be less than proportional to the difference in risk increment. Wan and Wang (1996) also conducted a WTP survey in Taiwan. Their estimates suggest that, on average, consumers in Taiwan are willing to pay a premium between 22 per cent and 44 per cent for selected fresh produce that is marketed with GAP certification. In comparison, consumers in the city of Taipei are willing to pay an even higher premium between 21 per cent and 54 per cent for the same assurance.

3. THEORETICAL FRAMEWORK AND ESTIMATION PROCEDURE

In this study, we adopted a filter design for the purpose of soliciting consumers' WTP for hydroponically grown vegetables. One of the advantages in using the filter approach for collecting WTP information is the reduction in potential biased responses due to presupposition effects (Sterngold, Warland, and Herrmann, 1994). To overcome this presupposition effect, Sterngold, Warland, and Herrmann (1994) suggest that survey questions should be framed in such a manner that a filter question is used to determine first if respondents are particularly concerned about a topic. Then, the degree-of-concern question is asked only to those respondents who indicate that they are concerned.

Following the filter design, it is assumed that a respondent actually has two joint decisions to make: (1) whether or not to pay more, and (2) how much more to pay. Thus, we propose a joint binary and ordinal probit model to estimate consumers' WTP for HGV in Taiwan. More specifically, let us begin with a standard binary choice model where an individual i is said to compare the maximum utility attainable among a set of alternatives $(A, A \in \{1, 2\})$ subject to a budget constraint and then selects one alternative j for which utility U_{ji} is a maximum (that is, $\Delta U_i = U_{ji} - U_{ki} \geq 0; j, k \in \{1, 2\}$). Formally

$$\Delta U_i = U_{1i} - U_{2i} = X_{si}\alpha + \gamma_i, \tag{11.1}$$

and

$$D_i = \begin{cases} 1, & \text{if } \varepsilon_i \geq -X_{si}\alpha \Rightarrow \Delta U_i \geq 0, \\ 0, & \text{otherwise;} \end{cases} \qquad (11.2)$$

where D_i is the dependent variable representing the observed outcome of a binary choice; X_{si} represents a set of s exogenous variables characterizing the decision maker; α is a vector of unknown parameters to be estimated; and ε_i denotes the normally distributed random errors, and j, $k \in A$.

Embedded in equations (11.1) and (11.2) is a threshold concept that choice outcomes are generated by some explanatory variables that cross thresholds in the decision process. An individual responds to some exogenous stimuli with a certain choice when his/her utility function or 'degree of conviction' exceeds some threshold level. In practice, this threshold represents a latent variable which is unobservable, and only the outcome of the decision process is observed. Furthermore, any changes in response are directly related to the estimated probability that a particular decision will be made. The application of this model is particularly attractive from the standpoint of marketing research. Market planners and product developers frequently need to assess the market potential of a product that is not yet available in the marketplace.

Equations (11.1) and (11.2) can be extended to model consumer behaviour in cases where a sequence of choices rather than a single choice is selected in the decision-making process. In many applications, it is often desirable to provide a utility-maximizing rationalization for binary choice problems where the observed outcome reflects a joint choice of two decisions instead of a single decision. The standard Heckman (1979) procedure is not applicable in such a case where both equations in the structure contain a qualitative dependent variable. Poirier (1980) showed that, under the usual normality assumptions, the correct choice of distribution is a bivariate instead of a univariate probit model.

For the purpose of this study, we modified the bivariate probit model discussed by Meng and Schmidt (1985) that exhibits a form of partial observability (censored probit) and extended it to include a probit and an (censored) ordered probit for analysis of consumer demand for food safety. The partial observability referred to the fact that the observation of how much to pay is conditional on the realization of the first decision of 'whether or not to pay more'. Thus, we refer to the observations of the second decision as being censored, because the price premium that a consumer is willing to pay is observed only if a positive response to the filter question is obtained. The structure of the model that is exposed to the partial observability of the non-random sample selection rule is specified as

$$\Delta U_i = X_{si}\alpha + \varepsilon_i, \quad D_i = \begin{cases} 1, & \text{if willing to pay a premium for HGV} \\ 0, & \text{otherwise;} \end{cases} \quad (11.3)$$

$$\pi_i = Z_{ti}\beta + \xi_i, \ P_i = j, \text{ if } \mu_{j-1} < \pi_i < \mu_j, \text{ and } D_i = 1; j = 1, ..., M, \quad (11.4)$$

where D_i and P_i denote the decisions of willingness to pay more and the amount of premium that a consumer is willing to pay for HGV, respectively; X_{si} and Z_{ti} represent matrices of explanatory variables measuring the consumers' risk perceptions, attitudes toward the use of chemical pesticides on food production, and the socioeconomic characteristics associated with the consumers; α and β are vectors of unknown parameters to be estimated; $\mu_0, ..., \mu_M$ are the category thresholds for the underlying response variable, π_i, with $\mu_0 \leq \mu_1 \leq ... \mu_M$; and ε_i and ξ_i are the disturbance terms with zero-mean, and normally distributed as standard bivariate, that is, $\{\varepsilon_i, \xi_i\}$ is distributed as $f(\gamma_i, \xi_i; \rho)$, where $f(\varepsilon_i, \xi_i; \rho)$ is a standard bivariate normal density function and ρ is the correlation coefficient. The cumulative distribution function of $f(\varepsilon_i, \xi_i; \rho)$ is denoted by $F(\varepsilon_i, \xi_i; \rho)$. In addition, the model presented in equation (11.4) is underidentified since any linear transformation applied to the underlying response variable and threshold value μ_j would lead to the same model. For estimation purposes, it can be assumed without loss of generality that $\mu_0 = -\infty$, $\mu_1 = 0$ and $\mu_M = +\infty$.

The specification of equations (11.3) and (11.4) is similar to the standard double hurdle model proposed by Cragg (1971), which emphasizes the importance of participation and consumption as two separate individual choices. The advantage of the double hurdle model is that it allows for a more flexible framework to model the observed consumer behaviour as a joint choice of two decisions instead of a single decision. Nevertheless, when both the participation and consumption choices are observed qualitatively, the conventional double hurdle model may not be applicable.

To illustrate, equation (11.3) which models the decision of whether or not to pay more for HGV, is postulated as a function of consumers' risk perception and attitudes toward use of chemicals in food production. If the consumer has a desire to purchase HGV and is willing to pay more, then the intensity of his/her willingness to pay will be observed. Differences in socioeconomic characteristics are considered the

underlying determinants that influence the extent of consumers'
willingness to pay. Thus, to estimate the likelihood of how much more
they would pay for HGV, equation (11.4), which models the choice among
different premium levels, is hypothesized primarily as a function of
consumers' socioeconomic characteristics.

Note that D_i in equation (11.3) is fully observed, but P_i in equation
(11.4) is observed only among those respondents who chose to pay a
premium for HGV. Although equations (11.3) and (11.4) can be estimated
independently, there will be a loss of efficiency of the parameter estimates
unless $\rho = 0$ (Meng and Schmidt, 1985). More importantly, observations
for equation (11.4) represent a 'choice-based' or censored sample, which
could be subject to potential selectivity bias if estimated separately. Thus,
the appropriate procedure is the joint estimation of equations (11.3) and
(11.4) by the maximum likelihood approach. Accordingly, the log-
likelihood function for the proposed model is specified as

$$
\begin{aligned}
\ln L(\alpha,\beta,\rho) = \sum_i \sum_j & \{(1 - D_i) \times \ln[\Pr(D_i = 0)] \\
& + D_i (1 - C_{ji}) \times \ln[\Pr(D_i = 1, P_i = j)]\} \\
= \sum_i \sum_j & \{(1 - D_i) F(-X_{si}\alpha;\rho) \\
& + D_i (1 - C_{ji}) \times \ln[F(X_{si}\alpha, \mu_j - Z_{ti}\beta;\rho) \\
& - F(X_{si}\alpha, \mu_{j-1} - Z_{ti}\beta;\rho)]\}
\end{aligned}
\tag{11.5}
$$

where $C_{ji} = 1$, if $P_i = j$, and $C_{ji} = 0$, otherwise; $\Pr(\cdot)$ represents the
probability of the event occurring; and $F(\cdot)$ denotes the bivariate standard
normal cumulative distribution function with correlation coefficient ρ.
Efficient parameter estimates for α, β, and ρ that maximize the log-
likelihood function, $\ln L(\cdot)$, in equation (11.5) are obtained by using the
GAUSS program. The joint estimation of these parameters offers
efficiency gains over those obtained in the separate estimation of the
probit and ordered probit equations. More significantly, the joint approach
accounts for potential correlation between equations (11.3) and (11.4),
and thereby corrects for potential sample selection bias that could be
incurred in the separate estimation of the probit and ordered probit
equations.

4.   SURVEY DESIGN AND SAMPLE DATA

The data for this study are obtained from a random sample of approximately 400 female home makers in the city of Taipei selected for in-person interviews. The survey was designed to assess consumers' awareness of potential health risks associated with pesticide residues on food, consumers' evaluation of food quality and safety, and their willingness to pay to reduce exposure to pesticide residues on food. The survey was conducted in the spring of 1995 by the Survey Research Office of the Academia Sinica in Taiwan.

The WTP survey obtained information from participants with respect to food purchasing patterns and behaviour; attitude toward pesticide use in food production and assessment of the safety of food purchased; and willingness to pay for HGV to reduce exposure to pesticide residues in food. With respect to willingness to pay for hydroponic vegetables, the respondents were first asked whether or not they would be willing to pay a higher price. If the responses were positive, the respondents were then queried to indicate how much more they would pay, relative to current prices, from a checklist of price premiums.

Due to refusal and potential misreporting of income, the questionnaires from those who reported zero total household income were deemed unusable and excluded from the empirical analysis. In addition, a few households that provided incomplete information were also deleted from the sample observations. The final sample used for this analysis consists of 323 observations with completed information. In general, the majority of respondents were married women who were the primary food shoppers in the household. More than half of the respondents, 52 per cent, were employed wives. The average household size was about 4.8 persons. Respondents who were 35 years old or younger accounted for 23 per cent of the sample. Approximately 42 per cent of survey participants had high school or above high school education, and 36 per cent had an average monthly household income greater than NT$50 000. The definitions, means, and standard deviations of the variables used in the statistical analysis are shown in table 11.1.

Personal experiences on health risks associated with pesticide residues on vegetables or fruits sold in the market are expected to be an important factor influencing a respondent's willingness to pay for risk reduction. When asked how serious a health hazard do they think that pesticide residues on fresh produce are, 19 per cent and 57 per cent of respondents indicated that pesticide residues on vegetables pose a 'serious' and 'very serious' risk, respectively, on their health (table 11.2). Similarly, more than 70 per cent of the respondents felt that pesticide residues on fruits

Food security in Asia

Table 11.1 Variable definition and sample statistics

Variable	Definition	Mean	Standard deviation
D	= 1, would pay a premium for HGV; = 0, otherwise.	0.8390	0.9160
P	= 1, would pay up to 5% more;	0.2570	0.5069
	= 2, would pay 6%–15% more;	0.3901	0.6246
	= 3, would pay 16% or more.	0.1950	0.4416
AGE	= 1, if the respondent is 35 years of age or younger; = 0, otherwise.	0.2291	0.4786
EDUC	Years of education.	9.2446	10.2198
UNDER12	= 1, children under 12 years old are present; = 0, otherwise.	0.5449	0.7382
SICK	= 1, if any household members has a chronic disease; = 0, otherwise.	0.2291	0.4786
INCOME	= 1, if total household income is more than NT$30 000 per month; = 0, otherwise.	0.6471	0.8044
EATOUT	= 1, if eat out more than 3 times a week; = 0, otherwise.	0.0681	0.2610
PRICE	= 1, if price is important when buying fresh vegetables; = 0, otherwise.	0.1672	0.4089
MEAT	= 1, would pay a premium for 'antibiotic-free' meat; = 0, otherwise.	0.9226	0.9605
BANPEST	= 1, if the respondent indicated that the use of all kinds of pesticides should be banned; = 0, otherwise.	0.0836	0.2891
RISK	= 1, if the respondent perceived pesticide residues in vegetables and fruits pose a very serious health hazard; = 0, otherwise.	0.5077	0.7126
REDUCE	= 1, will reduce consumption of vegetables if there is a report of pesticide contamination; = 0, otherwise.	0.6687	0.8178
NOCHNG	= 1, will not change consumption of vegetables even if there is a report of pesticide contamination; = 0, otherwise.	0.0712	0.2668

Table 11.2 Respondent's evaluation on impact of pesticide residues in vegetables or fruits in the market on her health

Impact	Vegetables	Fruits
	%	
Not serious	4	4
So so	7	9
Somewhat serious	13	16
Serious	19	18
Very serious	57	53

will either have a 'serious' or 'very serious' impact on their health. Overall, the majority of the respondents believed that pesticide residues on fresh produce pose a very serious health hazard.

In the survey, the respondents were twice asked to rate their relative food concerns. The first question asked respondents to rank their first, second, and third food concerns.[4] The concerns listed were: foods grown using pesticides, foods high in salt, foods high in saturated fats, foods high in sugar, foods high in cholesterol, food poisoning, chemical food preservatives, chemical food additives, and foods too low in nutritional value. A rank score was also developed to determine the rank order of concerns. A 3-point score was assigned if the item was selected as the top ranked concern, followed by 2-point and 1-point scores for the second and third ranked concerns, respectively.

Table 11.3 indicates that foods grown using pesticides is the number one food concern among Taiwanese consumers. As shown in table 11.1, 86 per cent of the respondents ranked pesticides as a concern with 59 per cent indicating it was their top concern. The average rank order index for foods grown using pesticides was 2.2, which is much higher than all other rank scores for other concerns. Food poisoning ranked second in food concerns with a rank score of 1.06. About 55 per cent of the respondents ranked food poisoning as a concern with 17 per cent expressing it as their top and second concern, respectively. In addition, chemical food preservatives ranked third followed by chemical additives. To provide an international perspective, the results of a similar study conducted in the US are also presented in table 11.3 for comparison. As shown in the last column of table 11.3, concerns for foods grown with pesticides and food poisoning also received the highest rank scores among Georgia consumers in the US.

Food security in Asia

Table 11.3 Consumer's ranking of food safety concerns

Food concern	Level of concern			Rank score[a]	
	Top concern	Second concern	Third concern	Taiwan	US[b]
	----------------- % ----------------				
Foods grown with pesticides	59	16	11	2.20	1.07
Food poisoning	17	17	21	1.06	0.84
Chemical food preservatives	9	27	20	1.01	0.46
Chemical food additives	5	18	24	0.75	0.39
Foods high in cholesterol	6	11	11	0.51	0.80
Food high in saturated fat	1	5	5	0.18	0.60
Foods too low in nutrition	1	3	3	0.12	0.13
Food high in salt	1	2	3	0.10	0.40
Foods high in sugar	1	1	2	0.07	0.25

Notes: [a] Average score with top concern = 3 points, second concern = 2 points, and third concern = 1 points.
[b] The rank score results are obtained from table 9.1 in Ott, Huang, and Misra (1991).

To further examine consumers' risk perception concerning pesticide use, the second question was designed to compare the relative health risk of eating fresh produce grown with pesticides to foods high in saturated fat, sugar, salt, or cholesterol. The respondents were asked to indicate whether they thought eating fresh produce grown with pesticides had a much lower, somewhat lower, no difference, somewhat higher, or much higher health risk than eating foods with saturated fat, sugar, salt, or cholesterol. A relative risk score ranging from −2 points to 2 points with a 1-point increment was developed to correspond with the responses that varied from 'much lower' to 'much higher'.

Table 11.4 shows that 52 per cent of the respondents rated eating fresh produce grown with pesticides as posing a higher health risk relative to eating foods high in sugar. Similarly, 50 per cent of the respondents considered that eating fresh produce grown with pesticides is riskier than eating foods high in saturated fats, and salt, while 47 per cent considered it has a higher risk as compared to foods high in cholesterol. The relative risk scores in table 11.4 also indicate that the perceived health risk associated with pesticides was much higher than all other food health risks. It is interesting to note that, while the Taiwanese consumers considered eating foods high in sugar as a relatively low risk among other food health risks, their American counterparts viewed it as posing the highest relative risk. On the other hand, while consumers in Georgia considered eating food high in cholesterol as a relatively low health risk, it was perceived to pose the highest relative risk by Taiwanese consumers. This contrast in health risk perceptions may be attributed to cultural differences. Americans, in general, are much more conscious and concerned about calorie intakes and gaining weight than their counterparts in Taiwan.

Table 11.4 Eating fresh produce grown with pesticides relative to other food health risks

Health risk	Relative risk					Relative score[a]	
	Much lower	Somewhat lower	No difference	Somewhat higher	Much higher	Taiwan	US[b]
	---------------------- % --------------------						
Eating foods high in cholesterol	5	18	27	30	17	0.36	0.73
Eating food high in salt	4	18	26	33	17	0.41	0.46
Eating food high in saturated fat	5	18	25	30	20	0.42	0.47
Eating foods high in sugar	4	18	25	32	20	0.46	0.19

Notes: [a] Average score with much lower = –2, somewhat lower = –1, no difference = 0, somewhat higher = 1, and much higher = 2.
    [b] The relative score results are obtained from table 9.2 in Ott, Huang, and Misra (1991).

5. EMPIRICAL RESULTS

For empirical implementation, the explanatory variables of equation (11.3) are specified to include a set of socio-demographic characteristics. In addition, a set of dichotomous variables representing the respondent's risk perception (RISK), general attitude toward pesticides use (BANPEST), attitudes toward the food safety problem (REDUCE and NOCHNG), and the importance of price in making purchase decisions (PRICE).[5] Furthermore, the respondents' willingness to pay a premium for 'antibiotic-free' meat (MEAT) is also hypothesized as a major factor that will influence their willingness to pay for HGV. Specifically, it is expected that consumers would be less willing to pay a higher price for HGV if their consumption behaviours are not affected by media reports of pesticide contamination. Similarly, they would be less likely to pay a premium for HGV if low price was considered as an important attribute in making produce purchases. On the other hand, respondents would be more willing to pay a price premium for HGV if they perceive pesticide residues in fresh produce to pose very serious health hazards and believe that chemical pesticides should be banned. Similarly, one would expect that MEAT and REDUCE to have positive effects on consumer's willingness to pay a higher price for HGV.

Previous studies have identified a variety of socio-demographic characteristics that may affect consumers' willingness to pay for food safety. Wan and Wang (1996) found that number of children, respondent's age, and presence of a patient in the household increased a consumer's willingness to pay for safer fresh produce. Thus, equation (11.4) is specified to include primarily the set of socio-demographic variables representing age, education, income, number of small children, and health status of the household. In addition, it is expected that consumers will be willing to pay a greater amount of premium if they reduced their consumption of vegetables because of report of pesticide contamination. Hence, REDUCE and NOCHNG are also specified to influence the respondents' willingness to pay a higher level of premium for HGV because of their concern about pesticide contamination.[6]

The maximum likelihood estimates of equations (11.3) and (11.4) based on the survey data are presented in table 11.5. The regression model accounts for the interrelationships between the decisions of whether or not to pay more and how much more to pay for HGV. In general, the estimate of ρ that maximizes the likelihood function is 0.488 and is significantly different from zero at the 0.001 significance level, based on the t-test. This suggests that the unexplained residuals of the probit and ordered probit equations are highly correlated, and that joint estimation is appropriate to correct for the potential simultaneity bias and to yield more efficient and consistent estimates.

Table 11.5 Results of joint estimation of the binary-ordinal probit model

Variable	Probit	Ordered
Constant	-1.036^{***}	1.176^{***}
	$(-16.083)^{a}$	(28.818)
AGE	-0.114^{**}	0.169^{***}
	(-2.198)	(3.112)
UNDER12	0.347^{***}	-0.184^{***}
	(6.796)	(-3.900)
EDUC	0.073^{***}	-0.065^{***}
	(12.735)	(-17.110)
SICK	-0.079	0.519^{***}
	(-1.486)	(7.178)
INCOME	-0.032	0.268^{***}
	(-0.572)	(5.847)
EATOUT	-0.628^{***}	
	(-10.967)	
PRICE	-0.403^{***}	
	(-7.926)	
MEAT	1.417^{***}	
	(23.967)	
BANPEST	-0.372^{***}	
	(-6.755)	
RISK	0.139^{**}	-0.188^{***}
	(2.633)	(-3.811)
REDUCE	0.245^{***}	-0.114^{**}
	(4.791)	(-2.569)
NOCHNG	-0.424^{***}	0.381^{***}
	(-7.693)	(7.373)
μ_1		1.253^{***}
		(25.271)
ρ	0.488^{***}	
	(3.270)	
Log-likelihood value	-390.479	
Pseudo-R2	0.230	
Sample size	323	271

Notes: $^{*},^{**},^{***}$ Indicate that the estimated coefficient is statistically significantly different from zero at the 0.05, 0.01, and 0.001 significance level, respectively.

[a] Numbers in parentheses are t-values.

Food security in Asia

Results of the probit equation indicate that, in general, the variables SICK and INCOME have no significant impacts on the likelihood of a respondent's willingness to pay a higher price for HGV. In contrast, Wan and Wang (1996) found that if there is a sick person in the household there are positive and significant effects on WTP for two out of four GAP produce surveyed. The lack of a significant effect on the INCOME variable, perhaps, was not unexpected. Given the relatively high average household income reported in the survey, the insignificant income effect obtained in this study appears consistent with Zind's (1990) finding that low-income consumers were more likely to buy organically grown produce regardless of cost.

More importantly, the results show that those respondents who had small children in their households would be more willing to pay a higher price for HGV. Similarly, the variable EDUC also shows a significant and positive effect, suggesting that the probability of willingness to pay a premium for HGV increases with the level of educational attainment. As might be expected, the effect of RISK on willingness to pay is found to be positive and statistically significantly different from zero at the 0.01 significance level. This result suggests that respondents who considered pesticide residues in fresh produce as posing a very serious health hazard are more likely to be willing to pay a higher price for HGV. Furthermore, the effects of MEAT and REDUCE on willingness to pay are also found to be positive and statistically significant at the 0.001 significance level. The positive coefficients on MEAT and REDUCE suggest that consumers who are willing to pay a premium for 'antibiotic-free' meat and who will reduce their consumption of vegetables because of media reports of potential contamination are likely to be more health conscious and more willing to pay a higher price for HGV than others.

Respondents who are 35 years of age or younger (AGE), eat out more than three times a week (EATOUT), consider price as an important factor in their purchasing decisions (PRICE), and will not change consumption of vegetables (NOCHNG) are found to be less likely to pay a higher price for HGV. The negative sign on the AGE variable suggests that younger respondents are less willing to pay a higher price for HGV than their counterparts. The result is consistent with Wan and Wang (1996), whose study shows that the age of respondents has a positive and significant effect on willingness to pay for some GAP produce. The finding that the coefficient on PRICE is negative and significantly different from zero is consistent with *a priori* expectation. Fu, Liu, and Hammitt (1997) reported that consumers who consider the price of vegetables a very important factor in their purchase decision are less willing to pay more for lower-risk vegetables. However, they found that the respondent's age was not a significant determinant on their willingness to pay more for lower-risk vegetables.

It is somewhat surprising to see that the variable BANPEST also shows a significant and negative effect, suggesting that the probability of willingness to pay a premium decreases if the respondent believes that all pesticides use should be banned.[7] Similarly, using a Likert scale measuring the degree of concern about pesticide residues, WTP for low-pesticide fresh produce in Taiwan was found to be negatively associated with consumer's risk attitude at the 0.10 significance level (Fu, Liu, and Hammitt, 1997). Wan and Wang (1996) also reported a negative but non-significant relationship between a risk attitude variable and WTP for GAP-certified produce, both in the city of Taipei and in Taiwan.

With respect to how much more a consumer would pay, the ordered probit results show that socioeconomic characteristics are the major factors that have significant impacts on the amount of premium that a respondent would be willing to pay for HGV. The results suggest that respondents with small children and higher education are less likely to pay higher premiums for HGV. It is important to note that the negative effects for the variables UNDER12 and EDUC should be interpreted in a relative sense. That is, respondents with small children and higher education are less likely to pay as much as others; they are willing to pay a price premium for HGV nonetheless. It is possible that respondents with young children present in the household were not willing to pay as much premium as their counterparts for risk reduction because of budget constraints.[8]

In contrast, Wan and Wang (1996) found that numbers of children in the household positively affect WTP for GAP produce at the 0.001 significance level. While Wan and Wang (1996) found that education has a positive effect on WTP for GAP produce, the estimated coefficients were not statistically significantly different from zero. Similarly, Fu, Liu, and Hammitt (1997) also found positive but insignificant relationship between education and WTP for low-pesticide fresh produce. Nevertheless, the negative relationship between education and the amount of premiums that a consumer is willing to pay is in agreement with the findings of Misra, Huang, and Ott (1991). They suggested that consumers with higher educational attainment are more likely to have a better understanding of the true risk associated with residue contamination on fresh produce. Therefore, it is possible that consumers with higher education are unwilling to pay a much higher premium for HGV because they believe the benefits derived from HGV may be marginal and do not necessarily justify the additional costs.

The results also suggest that those respondents who are 35 years old or younger, and have family members suffering from a chronic disease are more likely than their counterparts to pay greater premiums for HGV. It seems plausible that older respondents are also likely to be subjected to budget constraints and, thus, would be less willing to pay as much as their younger counterparts for risk reduction. Fu, Liu, and Hammitt (1997) also found that consumers who suffer from a chronic disease have higher WTP for health-risk reduction. However, mixed results were reported by Wan and Wang (1996). They found that having a family member suffering from a chronic disease has a positive and significant impact on WTP for GAP-certified produce among Taiwanese consumers but not among those who reside in Taipei. Furthermore, the results indicate that respondents who perceive pesticide residues to be a very serious health hazard, and will reduce vegetables consumption due to reports of pesticide contamination are less willing to pay as much as others. In contrast, those who would not change their consumption of vegetables are willing to pay much greater premiums for HGV to reduce their exposure to pesticide residues.

It is interesting to note that while income is not a significant factor affecting the probability of willingness to pay, it does have a positive and significant effect on the amount of premiums a respondent is willing to pay. In other words, once a respondent has decided to pay a higher price for HGV, the amount of premium the respondent is willing to pay increases as his/her household income increases. To the extent that higher-income households have the ability and can afford to pay more, it is logical that they would be willing to pay a greater premium for HGV if they have a demand for it. This finding is consistent with Misra, Huang, and Ott's (1991) findings, who reported that consumers with an annual household income below $35 000 were less willing to pay a higher price for certified pesticide residue-free produce than those above the $35 000 income group. Fu, Liu, and Hammitt (1997) also found that income had a positive effect on WTP for low-pesticide produce, but the estimated coefficient was not statistically significantly different from zero.

In general, the results support the notion that whether a consumer will pay more for HGV and the amount of premium that a consumer is willing to pay can be viewed as two different but correlated decisions. The results suggest that socioeconomic characteristics as well as attitudinal inclinations influence whether or not a consumer will pay a premium. In contrast, socioeconomic characteristics appear to be responsible primarily for the determination of the additional amount of premium that a consumer is willing to pay for HGV. More important, the results demonstrate the advantages of modelling the WTP for HGV as a joint decision process. This approach allows for flexibility of parameterizing separately the probability and level of premiums that a consumer is willing to pay for a safer food. It also provides additional insights as to how each explanatory variable may affect the separate decisions differently than would a more restrictive model when only a single probit (Wan and Wang, 1996) or ordered probit (Fu, Liu, and Hammitt, 1997; Misra, Huang, and Ott, 1991) equation was used. In a sense, this is equivalent to decomposing the total effects in a tobit model that may be attributed to market participation and level of consumption. Unlike the single equation approach, the signs and explanatory variables are not restricted to be the same. Thus, it should not be surprising to find out that in most instances that the same factor may have different effects on the two decisions.

6. CONCLUSIONS

This study uses a joint probit and ordered probit model to estimate a consumer's decisions of whether or not to pay a premium and how much more to pay for hydroponic vegetables based on data collected from a consumer survey conducted in the city of Taipei, Taiwan. Based on the empirical evidence, this study finds that those respondents who would pay a premium for 'antibiotic-free' meat are also most likely to pay a premium for HGV. Similarly, respondents who had small children in the household, who would reduce consumption of vegetables as a result of media reports of pesticide contamination, who perceived pesticide residues as posing a very serious health hazard, and who had higher education levels are more likely than their counterparts to be willing to pay a higher price for HGV.

With respect to the amount of premium, the results suggest that socioeconomic characteristics are the major determinants that influence the respondents' choice of the additional premium they are willing to pay. The study shows that family health status appears the most important and significant factor determining the level of premium a consumer is willing to pay. However, the family health status is not a significant factor in predicting the likelihood of a consumer's willingness to pay a higher price for HGV. The results show that, conditional on willingness to pay more, a respondent would be most likely to pay 16 per cent or more for HGV if there is a family member suffering from a chronic disease in the household. Similarly, as household income increases, those consumers who are willing to pay a premium for HGV most likely would pay a price premium at least 16 per cent or more than the prevailing market price.

The findings of this study should be helpful to the produce industry in assessing the market potential for pesticide-free food products, such as HGV, in developing its marketing and pricing strategies. Interpreted as an incentive for new product innovation, this study suggests that HGV seems to have a special appeal to more affluent consumers in Taiwan and its market potential appears promising. This finding is consistent with results obtained from other surveys of WTP for food safety conducted in Taiwan (Fu, Liu, and Hammitt, 1997; Wan and Wang, 1996). It appears that there is a strong demand for food safety by Taiwanese consumers. The findings of this study along with those of previous studies indicate that consumers in Taiwan are willing to pay a higher price for safer food in terms of pesticide-free (HGV), low-pesticide, and government certification (GAP). These results also suggest an urgent need for the government to initiate better food testing and more effective pesticide management programs.

There are additional implications that may be drawn from this study with respect to food security issues among Asian countries. Considering food safety as the quality dimension of the food security problems, it is expected that the provision of and demand for safer foods will become a prevalent and important food policy issue in most Asian countries as they are experiencing rapid economic growth with steady increases in the standard of living. The increasing demand for safer foods among the more developed countries may also create a niche market and provide trade opportunities for some countries to specialize in the production of low or pesticides-free products, such as organically grown produce. For example, Belize is known to produce organic products mainly for export to the US. Last but not least, as consumers in Taiwan become more conscious about the safety attributes of the foods they purchase, they will demand more stringent regulation for food safety standards. Thus, the foreign competition and its impacts from low-quality imports due to trade liberalization upon the domestic producers may be lessened and become less of a political issue and policy concern. The implication that consumers are willing to pay a greater amount of premium for HGV suggests that they will be less likely to trade off safety attributes for lower-priced and less safe foods.

NOTES

[1]   Taiwan is located in a subtropical area which means it has a warmer temperature, longer growing season and more insects than countries like Japan and Korea. Farmers in Taiwan may harvest typically two to three crops a year as compared to one crop in Japan and Korea. Furthermore, higher temperatures also shorten the efficacy of the chemicals, and thus more frequent applications would be

required. With respect to countries like Indonesia or Thailand, most of the crops are grown by tenant farmers, who are generally poor and their purchasing power may be too low to afford the relatively high cost of insecticides. These factors should be taken into consideration when interpreting and making comparisons about pesticides consumption among these countries.

2   Field experiments in Taiwan had found that agricultural production may be reduced by 43 per cent without any application of pesticides. For paddy rice, such damage ranges from 30 per cent to 54 per cent (Lee, 1985 and 1987).

3   Arrow *et al.* (1993) endorse the use of CVM and provide guidelines following which the accuracy of the CVM could be improved. See also Randall (1997) for a recent review.

4   The design for these two questions were first used by Ott, Huang, and Misra (1991).

5   As suggested by an anonymous referee, the RISK variable can be considered conceptually as a measure of risk reduction for purchasing HGV.

6   Initially, other attitudinal variables, such as EATOUT, PRICE, MEAT, and BANPEST, were also included in the specification. However, the preliminary analyses suggest that those attitudinal variables do not seem to have any significant effects on the level of willingness to pay. Multicollinearity is suspected to be the major factor that renders most of the estimated coefficients insignificant. Admittedly, the exclusion of those variables from equation (11.4) appears *ad hoc*, based primarily on the empirical ground.

7   As pointed out by a reviewer, the negative sign on the variable BANPEST could result from a 'protest bid'. In other words, a respondent who believes that pesticides should not be used at all can be expected to refuse to pay any premium for the risk reduction.

8   We thank the anonymous referee for suggesting this explanation as a possible reason accounting for the negative effect that the UNDER12 variable has on the amount of premium that a consumer is willing to pay for HGV.

REFERENCES

Arrow, K., R. Slow, P. Portney, E. Leamer, R. Radner, and H. Schuman (1993), 'Report of the NOAA Panel on Contingent Valuation', *Federal Register*, 58: 4601–14.

Buzby, J. C., J. A. Fox, R. C. Ready, and S. R. Crutchfield (1998), 'Measuring Consumer Benefits of Food Safety Risk Reductions', *Journal of Agricultural and Applied Economics*, 30: 69–82.

Buzby, J. C., R. C. Ready, and J. R. Skees (1995), 'Contingent Valuation in Food Policy Analysis: A Case Study of a Pesticide-Residue Risk Reduction', *Journal of Agricultural and Applied Economics*, 27: 613–

25.

Cragg, J. G. (1971), 'Some Statistical Models for Limited Dependent Variables with Applications to the Demand for Durable Goods', *Econometrica*, 39: 829–44.

Fu, T.-T., J.-T. Liu, and J. K. Hammitt (1997), 'Consumer Willingness to Pay for Low-Pesticide Fresh Produce in Taiwan', *Journal of Agricultural Economics*, 50(2): 220–33.

Hammitt, J. K. (1993), 'Consumer Willingness to Pay to Avoid Pesticide Residues', *Statistica Sinica*, 3: 351–66.

Heckman, J. J. (1979), 'Sample Selection Bias as a Specification Error', *Econometrica*, 47: 153–62.

Huang, C. H. and K. Soo (1991), 'Economic Analysis of Pesticides Use on Paddy Rice in Taiwan', *Taiwan land Financial Review*, 28(3): 1–21 (in Chinese).

Huang, C. L. (1993), 'Simultaneous-Equation Model for Estimating Consumer Risk Perception, Attitudes, and Willingness-to-Pay for Residue-Free Produce', *Journal of Consumer Affairs*, 27: 377–96.

Lee, K. C. (1987), 'Is Pesticide Dangerous or not Dangerous?', *Hsin-Num*, 24: 100 (in Chinese).

Lee, K. C. (1985), 'The Current Pesticides Practices and Problems in Taiwan', Conference Proceedings on Agricultural Chemicals Toxication, 189–203 (in Chinese).

Meng, C. L. and P. Schmidt (1985), 'On the Cost of Partial Observability in the Bivariate Probit Model', *International Economics Review*, 26: 71–85.

Misra, S. K., C. L. Huang, and S. L. Ott (1991), 'Consumer Willingness to Pay for Pesticide-Free Fresh Produce', *Western Journal of Agricultural Economics*, 16: 218–27.

Ott, S. L. (1990), 'Supermarket Shoppers' Pesticide Concerns and Willingness to Purchase Certified Pesticide Residue-Free Fresh Produce', *Agribusiness*, 6: 593–602.

Ott, S. L., C. L. Huang, and S. K. Misra (1991), 'Consumers' Perception of Risks from Pesticide Residues and Demand for Certification of Residue-Free Produce', in J. A. Caswell (ed.), *Economics of Food Safety*, New York, NY: Elsevier Science Publishing Company, 175–88.

Poirier, D. J. (1980), 'Partial Observability in Bivariate Probit Models', *Journal of Econometrics*, 12: 209–17.

Randall, A. (1997), 'The NOAA Panel Report: A New Beginning or the End of an Era?', *American Journal of Agricultural Economics*, 79: 1489–94.

Randall, A. and J. R. Stoll (1980), 'Consumer's Surplus in Commodity Space', *American Economics Review*, 70: 449–55.

Sterngold, A., R. H. Warland, and R. O. Herrmann (1994), 'Do Surveys Overstate Public Concerns?', *Public Opinion Quarterly*, 58: 255–63.

United Nations (1988), *Statistical Book for Asia and the Pacific*, New York: United Nations.

van Ravenswaay, E. O. and J. P. Hoehn (1991), 'Consumer Willingness to Pay for Reducing Pesticide Residues in Food: Results of a Nationwide Survey', Pub. No. 91–18, Department of Agricultural Economics, Michigan State University.

Wan, C. W. and C. S. Wang (1996), 'Consumer Willingness to Pay for Fresh Produce with Good Agricultural Practice (GAP) Certification in Taiwan', *Taiwan Economy*, 239: 50–75 (in Chinese).

Weaver, R. D., D. J. Evans, and A. E. Luloff (1992), 'Pesticide Use in Tomato Production: Consumer Concerns and Willingness to Pay', *Agribusiness*, 8: 131–42.

Zind, T. (1990), 'Fresh Trends 1990: A Profile of Fresh Produce Consumers', *The Packer Focus 1989–90*, Kansas: Vance Publishing Co., 37–68.

12. Forces shaping Asia's demand for vegetable oils and protein meals

Alan J. Webb and Mad Nasir Shamsudin

1. INTRODUCTION

Rising incomes have resulted in major changes in food consumption patterns throughout Asia – a trend which is expected to continue for at least another decade as people in some of Asia's poorest and most populous countries seek to upgrade their diets by shifting some of their consumption away from staples, particularly rice, to animal protein and processed foods. The food source at the heart of this change is oilseeds, including palm oil. Oilseeds not only provide vegetable oils for direct human consumption and for use in the rapidly growing food-processing sector, they are also the source of protein meal for the poultry and livestock sectors. Despite the recent financial crisis, longer-term economic growth throughout Asia will require greater quantities of both vegetable oils and protein meals in order to meet the growing demand for a greater variety of high-quality foods and animal proteins.

The shift in demand away from grains for human consumption towards feed grains and oilseeds is already evident in the region's higher-income countries of Japan, Korea, and Taiwan, where consumption of the main staple, rice, has declined in absolute terms over the past ten years. For China, rice consumption continues to increase but at a slower rate than in the mid-seventies and early eighties while rice consumption in Southeast Asia has continued to grow along its 20-year trend. With rising yields, China is able to devote declining area to rice production and still maintain self-sufficiency. Southeast Asia's rice production has more than kept pace with consumption and the region continues to be a major net exporter. Thus, the region as a whole appears to be capable of meeting its needs with respect to its most important staple. The situation for protein meal and vegetable oil, which is the focus of this chapter, is much different.

Asia produces a large share of its own requirements and is actually a net exporter of vegetable oils – particularly palm oil in Southeast Asia –

but as a whole, Asia is a net importer of oilseeds and oilseed meals (see figure 12.1). Northeast Asia — which includes Japan, Korea, and Taiwan — is already virtually totally dependent on imports of oilseeds or oilseed products for meeting its needs for protein meal and vegetable oil. China is almost self-sufficient in oilseeds and meal but imports nearly half its vegetable oil requirements. Southeast Asia imports a large share of its oilseed and meal requirements but exports large quantities of vegetable oil.

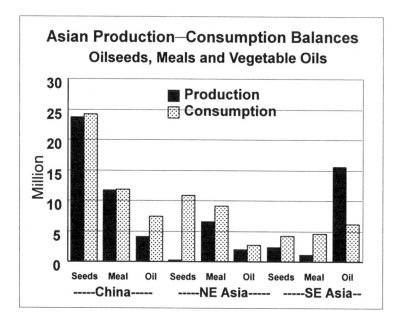

Figure 12.1 Asia is net deficit in oilseed products

Source: ERS, USDA (1998).

This chapter will seek to address three sets of questions related to East Asia's future requirements for vegetable oil and protein meal.

1. How much will Asia's demand for oilseed products grow over the next decade and what is the likely source of that growth? We especially want to determine the extent to which each of the major countries in the region will contribute to demand in the future and

under what economic conditions.

2. The second set of questions relates to the relative rate of growth in demand for the two products — protein meal and vegetable oil. That is, for which of the two products — meal or oil — will demand grow most rapidly? The answer to this question has particular relevance to the region's palm oil-producing countries of Malaysia and Indonesia, because they produce large quantities of vegetable oil but very little of the protein meal.

3. Finally, to what extent is Asia likely to be able to meet demand for these oilseed products from within the region? Given current trends in production of the major oilseeds, is the deficit in protein meal likely to increase or decrease? Likewise, will Asia continue to produce a net surplus in vegetable oil?

A combination of two forces — income growth and the global production mix of oilseeds — will shape the supply—demand balance of Asia's vegetable oil and protein meal markets in the next decade. The focus of this chapter is on East Asia divided into three subregions: Northeast Asia, including Japan, S. Korea, and Taiwan; Southeast Asia, including Malaysia, the Philippines, Thailand, Indonesia, Vietnam, Laos, Cambodia, Myanmar, Singapore, and Brunei; and China as its own region.

2.   THE MAJOR OILSEEDS

Four major oilseeds accounted for 72 per cent of the world's oilseed production in 1996 and more than 80 per cent of trade in the seeds, protein meal, and vegetable oil (table 12.1). Soybeans are by far the most important oilseed and source of protein meal and vegetable oil. For vegetable oil, however, palm oil is a close second to soybean oil in global production and accounts for 11.2 million tons in exports to just 5.7 million tons of soybean oil exports. The 28 per cent of the world's oilseed production not shown in table 12.1 is spread among a number of smaller crops including cottonseed, peanuts, sesame, olives, and coconut among others. These mainly go to specialized uses or are by-products from the production of another commodity, like cotton. The analysis of this chapter focuses on the four major oilseeds because they compete in similar markets and are, therefore, affected by similar economic forces.

A number of key biological characteristics set palm oil apart from the other major sources of oils.   Palm oil comes from the oil palm tree which produces a mass of 1000 to 3000 walnut-sized fruits attached to a large pithy stem which is known as a fresh fruit bunch (FFB). Each of the fruits has a fleshy outside layer known as the mesocarp which contains 90 per cent of the oil, and an inside kernel which is crushed — much like other oilseeds — to produce palm kernel meal and palm kernel oil. An oil palm tree has an economic life of 20 to 30 years and yields continuously throughout the year producing 10 to 12 bunches annually. Oil palm is restricted to tropical lowland climates with an annual temperature range between 20 and 30 decrees Celsius, at least five hours of sunshine per day and 200 cm of rain per year.

Table 12.1 World production and exports of major oilseeds, 1996

	units	Oilseeds		Protein meal		Vegetable oil	
		Production	Exports	Production	Exports	Production	Exports
Total seeds	mmt	258.7	47.0	148.7	49.0	75.0	27.9
Soybeans	mmt	132.1	32.1	89.0	31.8	20.3	5.7
Rapeseed	mmt	30.1	4.4	30.1	4.0	10.5	2.3
Sunflower	mmt	24.6	3.0	9.7	2.5	8.6	3.3
Palm kernel	mmt	na	na	2.6	2.2	2.2	0.8
Palm oil	mmt	na	na	na	na	16.2	11.2
Total major OS.	mmt	186.7	39.5	118.7	40.5	57.7	23.2
Share of world percent		*72.2*	*84.0*	*79.8*	*82.8*	*76.9*	*83.4*

Source: ERS, USDA (1998).

Oil palm is a very efficient producer of vegetable oil but the output of palm kernel meal is relatively small and the quality of the meal is of low quality, normally selling at half the price of soybean meal. Table 12.2 illustrates the point, showing the differences in the yields of oil and protein meal on a per hectare basis in the key producing region for each of the four major oilseeds — soybeans, rapeseed, sunflowerseed, and palm oil. Each oilseed has a different oil and meal extraction rate. On a per hectare basis, for example, oil palm yields almost nine times as much oil as soybeans, while soybeans yield 3.5 times the protein meal output of oil palm. Rapeseed, sunflowerseed, and most other oilseeds fall between these two extremes.

Malaysia and Indonesia now account for 80 per cent of the world's palm oil production and 92 per cent of world exports. Returns to palm oil production — given world prices of $500 per ton and a yield of four tons

Table 12.2 Comparison of the joint product output of the major vegetable oil crops

Items	Units	Soybeans	Rapeseed	Sunflower	Palm oil
Oil extraction rate	%	0.18	0.38	0.41	0.21
Meal extraction rate	%	0.79	0.60	0.48	0.03
Yield per hectare	tons/ha	2.50	2.70	1.50	18.95
Oil per hectare	Tons	0.45	1.03	0.62	3.98
Meal per hectare	Tons	1.98	1.62	0.72	0.57
Value per hectare at world prices	$	$764.80	$862.00	$484.14	$2371.78

Sources: ERS, USDA (1998) for yields and extraction rates except palm oil which is from PORLA (1997); LMC International Ltd (1997) for prices.

per hectare – are over $2000/ha per year. Even at lower prices and lower yields, there are very few alternative uses of agricultural resources in either country that can compete with oil palm. Hence, the area planted to oil palm in both Malaysia and Indonesia is expected to continue to expand and, by early this century, palm oil is expected to surpass soyoil as the world's most important vegetable oil with a 20 per cent share of world consumption (Castaneda and Giordano, 1995; Chow, 1993).

While there is a strong incentive to expand production, there is little incentive in the short or medium term to adjust palm oil production to market conditions. As a perennial, it takes three years from planting for oil palm to begin bearing fruit. Producers must therefore base their decisions on whether to expand or reduce area planted on long-run price expectations for vegetable oil. This means that most of the short-term supply response to vegetable oil price changes are likely to come from the annual oilseeds.

Strong demand for vegetable oils will favour the production of and trade in high oil content seeds, especially palm oil, which comes from within Asia (see figure 12.2) while relatively stronger demand for meat and livestock products will favour production and trade of oilseeds with high protein meal content for use as animal feeds. Oilseeds with a high protein meal component are produced largely outside the region. With the exception of China, most of the Asia's needs for protein and vegetable oil come from soybeans and palm oil (figure 12.2). Although China produces large quantities of soybeans, rapeseed, and sunflowerseeds, it imports soybeans and palm oil to fill its deficits. Northeast Asia relies primarily on soybean imports and Southeast Asia imports soybeans and exports palm oil.

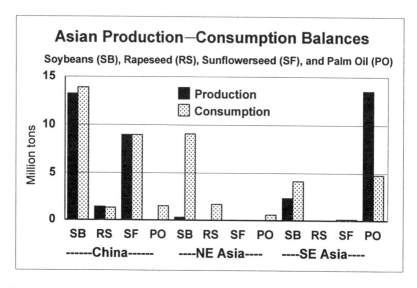

Figure 12.2 Soybeans and palm oil dominate

Source: ERS, USDA (1998).

East Asia has figured prominently in the expansion of oilseed product markets in the past two decades. Consumption of protein meal has increased from 14 per cent of world utilization in 1980 to 26 per cent in 1997, while consumption of vegetable oil in the same period has increased from 16 per cent to 28 per cent of the world total. East Asia has been the driving force behind much of the demand growth in both global markets. Understanding the dynamics of East Asian demand will be crucial to future trade of these products.

For Malaysia and Indonesia, the demand for palm oil within the Asian region will depend on the mix of protein meal and vegetable oil each country needs and how each one chooses to fill those needs. Countries with the greatest net import requirement for protein meal will either import protein meal or oilseeds with a high protein meal content for crushing. Countries with a strong net import demand for vegetable oils and a lesser need for the protein meal can either import high oil content seeds, such as rapeseed, or can choose to import the vegetable oil and protein meal directly rather than develop a crushing industry. Direct import of vegetable oil favours the palm oil industry.

3.   ECONOMIC BACKGOUND

There is a wide diversity of income and population levels and growth rates among the major East Asian countries as shown in table 12.3. Japan had the highest per capita income for the 1990−94 period but the lowest rate of economic growth. All the other key countries with the exception of the Philippines had economic growth rates exceeding 5 per cent. Population growth, as expected, is lower in the higher-income countries of Northeast Asia. Noteworthy is the 1.2 per cent population growth for China which is much lower than for other countries at similar income levels. This reflects the effectiveness of China's population control measures.

We consider demand for each of the two joint products separately because these income and population growth trends affect the vegetable oil and protein meal markets through different mechanisms. For the protein meal market, we study the long-term effects of income growth and population growth on the demand for livestock products. The increase in demand for livestock products leads, in turn, to an increase in demand for animal feeds of which protein meal is a significant component. For the vegetable oil market we forecast the effect of income and population growth on the direct consumption of vegetable oil. In both cases, the analysis focuses on Asia, but within a global context.

Table 12.3 Population and income for major East Asian countries

	Population	Per capita GNP	Growth rates 1990−94	
	mid 1994	1994	Population	Income
	Millions	$/person	per cent	per cent
Northeast Asia	190	17 244	0.5	2.7
Japan	125.0	34 630	0.3	1.2
S. Korea	44.5	8260	0.9	6.6
Taiwan	21.0	10 566	1.0	6.5
China	1191.0	530	1.2	6.8
Southeast Asia	460.2	3544	2.2	3.7
Thailand	58.0	2410	1.0	8.2
Philippines	67.0	950	2.2	1.6
Malaysia	19.7	3480	2,4	8.4
Indonesia	190.4	880	1.6	7.6
Other SE	125.2	921	2.1	

Sources: World Bank (1996a) and *Quarterly National Economic Trends, Taiwan Area, ROC.*

4.   ASIAN DEMAND FOR OILSEED MEALS

Our objective is to project the *additional* quantities of protein meal
required by the East Asian region in the year 2005. A brief outline of the
procedure and key assumptions is as follows. We know that virtually all
of the oilseed meals utilized in Asia are for animal feeds. A wide variety
of fish and animal products are produced and consumed in the region but
the major users of feeds are poultry, pork, and beef and veal.[1] To
determine how much additional protein meal will be required to meet feed
demand in 2005, we first estimate the effect of income growth on per
capita demand for these key livestock products in each of eight East Asian
countries. We use these income elasticities and an extrapolation of
population growth rates to project future demand for animal products
under alternative income growth scenarios.

An increase in demand for animal products will require additional feed
and, consequently, additional protein meal. We use feed conversion rates
(quantity of feed needed to produce a kilogram of meat) to determine feed
requirements and then use the share of protein meal in the appropriate
animal feed ration to compute the protein meal needed. The details of the
methodology including assumptions and justifications are discussed
below.

As with any long-term projection, we need to be cautious not to read
too much into the forecast. The emphasis here is not on the projection
itself, but the implications of alternative income growth scenarios and the
effects on the oilseed complex. This, in turn, will have implications for
the region's feed-livestock and vegetable oil industries.

4.1.   Estimation of Income Elasticities

The first step in developing a set of protein meal projections is the
estimation of income elasticities for poultry, pork and beef for the major
consuming countries of East Asia using a consumer demand function.
Equations estimated were of the form:

$$C_{ij} = f(P_{ij}, P_{ik}, Y_j) \qquad (12.1)$$

where C_{ij} is consumption of the jth livestock product in the ith country;
P_{ij}, P_{ik} are own price (j) and the price of one or more substitute livestock
products (k), respectively, in the jth country; and Y_i is income growth in
the ith country.

The equations are estimated in double logarithm. Data for meat consumption were taken from ERS, USDA (1998) and country sources. Income growth data are from the World Bank (1996b) except for Taiwan which are from country sources. Prices — except for Taiwan — are from FAOSTAT online electronic data for indigenous meats.

Although most of the elasticities are based on annual data for the period from 1975 to 1995, the poultry and beef income elasticities for China were based on shorter periods because of a lack of historical data on consumption. Parameters were corrected for autocorrelation, where it was a problem, using the Cochran—Orcutt procedure. Lack of retail meat price information for Taiwan forced us to estimate a very simple specification of consumption as a function of income alone. Inadequate and inconsistent poultry and livestock data for Other Southeast Asia made direct estimation of the income elasticities for this group of countries impossible. The income elasticities for this region were computed using a population-weighted average of elasticities taken from the Food and Agriculture Organization's global food model.

Table 12.4 shows the income and price elasticities of the estimated relationships. Most of the income elasticities are statistically significant at the 10 per cent level or better and all the signs on the prices are consistent with theoretical expectations. The magnitude of the income elasticities in table 12.4 are also broadly consistent with expectations. The higher-income countries of Northeast Asia have lower income elasticities overall than China or the Southeast Asian countries. All of the estimated elasticities are less than unity.

4.2 Meal Projections

The estimated income elasticities are incorporated into a projection framework based on population and income growth assumptions to the year 2005. The per capita consumption (C_{ijt}) in the ith country of the jth livestock product in the projection year t (2005) is computed as shown in equation (12.2).

$$C_{ijt} = C_{ijb} * ((1 + POPG_i/100 + (INCGR_i * INCEL_{ij})/(1 + ELADJ)) \char`\^ \\ NOYRS) \qquad (12.2)$$

where, C_{ijb} is the same as C_{ijt} but for the base year b (1995); $POPG_i$ is the population growth in country i; $INCGR_i$ is the income growth in country i; $INCEL_{ij}$ is the income elasticity in country i for the jth livestock product; $ELADJ$ is a downward adjustment in the income elasticity as incomes rise; and $NOYRS$ is the number of projection years (10).

Table 12.4 Income elasticity estimation results

Country	Income	Chicken price	Pork price	Beef price	R-SQ	DW	Obs	Period
Japan								
Poultry	0.30 **	−0.89 **	0.73 *	−0.10	0.94	0.99	20	76−95
Pork	0.14		−0.01		0.98	2.19	20	76−95
Beef	0.64 **	0.09	0.15	−0.16 **	0.99	1.59	20	76−95
S. Korea								
Poultry	0.52 **				0.91	1.48	16	75−95
Pork	0.69 **		−0.31 *	−0.01	0.98	1.94	20	76−95
Beef	0.72 **	0.11		−0.36 **	0.93	1.58	20	76−95
Taiwan[a]								
Poultry	0.54				0.96	0.76	21	75−95
Pork	0.35				0.89	0.86	21	75−95
Beef	0.51				0.82	1.84	21	75−95
China								
Poultry	0.34 **	−0.21 *	0.40 *	0.45 *	0.99	2.53	11	82−92
Pork	0.37 **		−0.54 *	0.82 **	0.98	1.79	18	75−92
Beef	0.68	1.17	0.23	−0.20	0.94	2.05	8	85−92
SE Asia								
Thailand								
Poultry	0.51 **	−0.41	0.15	0.40 **	0.95	1.65	21	79−95
Pork	0.18		−0.55 **	0.55 **	0.68	1.33	21	75−95
Beef	0.18 **	0.06		−0.03	0.98	1.54	20	76−95
Philippines								
Poultry	0.45 *	−0.07	0.11	0.14	0.93	2.46	21	75−95
Pork	0.47 **	0.23	−0.06	0.09	0.96	2.31	20	76−95
Beef	0.87 **	0.05	0.27	−0.14	0.23	0.27	20	76−95
Malaysia								
Poultry	0.38	−0.02	0.10		0.98	0.62	20	76−95
Pork	0.46 **	0.17 **	−0.06	0.29	0.99	2.22	14	82−95
Beef	0.82 **	0.04		−0.12	0.96	2.37	14	72−95
Indonesia								
Poultry	0.47 *	−0.24	0.43	0.58 *	0.98	1.94	20	76−95
Pork	0.24	0.99	−1.05 **	0.96 **	0.67	0.22	15	81−95
Beef	0.71	0.83		−0.18	0.30	0.61	15	81−95
Other SE Asia[b]								
Poultry	1.07							
Pork	0.66							
Beef	0.71							

Notes: * Significant at 10 per cent level; ** significant at the 5 per cent level.
     [a] Elasticities for Taiwan estimated without price information.
     [b] Elasticities for Other SE Asia are a weighted average of income elasticities taken from FAO.

Population growth rates are relatively stable over a five- to ten-year period. The major unknown in equation (12.2) is the rate of income growth. We therefore posit three different economic growth scenarios for our projections of protein meal in 2005 – No growth, Moderate growth (3 per cent average annual growth), and High growth (7 per cent average annual growth). The growth assumptions apply to all countries equally. The income elasticities are those shown in table 12.4 and the 1990–94 population growth estimates are shown in table 12.3.

One problem with using historical elasticity estimates to project consumption into the future is that income elasticities for food decline as incomes rise. Therefore, income elasticities need to be adjusted downward with an increase in forecasted GDP growth. The amount of downward adjustment likely depends on the rate of income growth and the initial starting income elasticity. A high rate of income growth and a high beginning elasticity value would have the largest downward adjustment. Our projections assume a 20 per cent annual decline in the income elasticity of demand for all livestock products and countries and, consequently, we use a value of 0.2 for the term *ELADJ* in equation (12.2).

The additional protein meal required to support higher levels of meat consumption are computed using feed conversion ratios and the protein meal share in an efficient feed ration (equation 12.3).

$$PM_{ijt} = (C_{ijt} - C_{ijb}) * FC_j * MSHARE_j * POPG_i \qquad (12.3)$$

PM_{ijt} is the additional protein meal required to support consumption of the *j*th livestock product in the *i*th country in projection year *t* ; FC_j is the feed conversion ratio for the *j*th livestock product; $MSHARE_j$ is the share of meal in the *j*th livestock feed ration.

There are wide differences in feed–meat conversion ratios within and across countries. Any feed conversion ratio we choose can, at best, be only a rough approximation of the feed requirements. Therefore, we choose *not* to estimate the total protein meal requirements for the poultry, pork, and beef sectors in each of these countries, but instead to estimate the minimum additional requirements of protein meal to achieve the consumption levels projected to 2005. This simplifies the assumptions and facilitates the interpretation of the results.

We assume that the increase in the production of these livestock products will have to be achieved at a minimum of feed use, that is, with efficient feed rations. We therefore use feed to meat conversion ratios (*FC_j* in equation 12.3) that are common in the United States –2.6:1 for poultry; 4.35:1 for hogs; and 8:1 for beef – and which represent the operational 'state of technology' in animal feeding. These ratios will generate the overall feed requirements for each of the three animal products. Each animal feed contains different mix of protein meal, grain, and other ingredients. A protein meal share ($MSHARE_j$) converts the overall feed requirements into the protein meal requirements shown in table 12.5. The protein meal shares are again based on an efficient US feed ration – 0.25 for poultry, 0.15 for pork and 0.05 for beef – and are the same for all countries.

Consequently, the protein meal component of feed required to produce one kilogram of chicken ($FC_j * MSHARE_j$) would be 0.65 kg. Likewise, the protein meal component of feed to produce one kilogram of pork would be 0.653 kg and to produce one kilogram of beef it would be 0.4 kg. Although these ratios will vary with production practices, feeding practices for poultry and pork in large production units are relatively consistent across countries, barring major price distortions. Beef cattle feeding practices, however, will depend on the availability of grazing land and the relative cost of feed. This means that the protein meal requirements for beef are probably less accurate than those for poultry and pork. Fortunately, beef is a relatively small portion of the Asian diet (with the exception of Korea and Japan) and so will not have a significant effect on the overall projections.

Table 12.5 shows the protein meal requirements for poultry, pork, and beef for each of the eight major countries in East Asia under the three economic growth scenarios. The 'No growth' scenario assumes that the annual average growth over the decade from 1995 to 2005 is zero. In this case, the increase in protein meal is determined exclusively by population growth and, as a result, the 'No growth' consumption per capita column is equal to per capita consumption in the 1995 base year (not shown to save space). The Moderate and High growth scenarios show the effects of both income growth and population growth.

The projections in table 12.5 show that the protein meal requirements of the High growth scenario (16.1 million tons) are three times as large as the No growth scenario (5.2 mmt). China is the dominant country in generating this increase, with 77 per cent of the 5.2 million ton additional requirement in the No growth scenario. Among the three livestock products, pork accounts for the two-thirds of the increase in protein meal requirements for all three scenarios through 2005; poultry accounts for roughly 25 per cent of meal requirements, and beef makes up the remainder.

Table 12.5 Projected additional meal requirements to meet Asia's livestock feed demand in 2005

Country	Con. 1995	Income elasticity	No growth Cons. Per capita	No growth Add. meal required	Moderate growth (3%) Cons. per capita	Moderate growth (3%) Add. meal required	High growth (7%) Cons. per capita	High growth (7%) Add. meal required
	1000 tons	*per cent*	*kg/person*	*1000 tons*	*kg/person*	*1000 tons*	*kg/person*	*1000 tons*
Japan								
Poultry	1798	0.30	14.38	36	15.50	129	17.11	264
Pork	2093	0.14	16.74	42	17.34	92	18.16	161
Beef	1518	0.64	12.14	18	14.23	126	17.52	295
				96		347		720
S. Korea								
Poultry	452	0.52	10.27	28	11.69	72	13.85	139
Pork	830	0.69	18.86	51	22.38	161	27.99	337
Beef	416	0.72	9.45	16	11.30	51	14.27	108
				94		284		585
Taiwan								
Poultry	627	0.54	29.86	34	34.14	97	40.71	194
Pork	857	0.35	40.81	46	44.23	97	48.54	161
Beef	72	0.51	3.43	2	3.89	7	4.60	13
				83		201		368
China								
Poultry	9582	0.34	8.05	789	8.70	1360	9.52	2078
Pork	36 257	0.37	30.44	2997	33.14	5363	36.57	8360
Beef	4062	0.68	3.41	206	4.04	542	5.03	1076
				3992		7264		11 514
SE Asia								
Thailand								
Poultry	638	0.51	11.00	43	12.49	105	14.75	199
Pork	301	0.18	5.19	21	5.43	31	5.76	44
Beef	272	0.18	4.69	11	4.91	17	5.21	25
				75		153		268
Philippines								
Poultry	371	0.45	5.54	59	6.19	94	7.18	147
Pork	760	0.47	11.34	121	12.75	197	14.87	312
Beef	200	0.87	2.99	19	3.70	43	4.90	83
				199		334		542

Food security in Asia

Table 12.5 Projected additional meal requirements to meet Asia's livestock feed demand in 2005 (cont.)

Country	Con. 1995	Income elasticity	Alternative growth scenarios to 2005					
			No growth		Moderate growth (3%)		High growth (7%)	
			Cons. Per capita	Add. meal required	Cons. per capita	Add. meal required	Cons. per capita	Add. meal required
	1000 tons	*per cent*	*kg/person*	*1000 tons*	*kg/person*	*1000 tons*	*kg/person*	*1000 tons*
Malaysia								
Poultry	661	0.38	33.05	115	36.33	169	41.15	249
Pork	225	0.46	11.25	39	12.61	62	14.66	96
Beef	86	0.82	4.30	9	5.27	19	6.86	35
				163		**250**		**379**
Indonesia								
Poultry	747	0.47	3.93	84	4.42	154	5.15	260
Pork	671	0.24	3.53	75	3.75	107	4.06	152
Beef	392	0.71	2.06	27	2.46	62	3.10	119
				186		**323**		**531**
Other SE Asia								
Poultry	333	1.07	2.66	50	3.46	130	4.86	271
Pork	1803	0.66	14.40	272	16.95	528	20.97	933
Beef	30	0.71	0.24	3	0.29	6	0.36	10
				325		**664**		**1214**
Total Meal				**5212**		**9820**		**16 122**
Less China				1220		2556		4608

Source: Base year data from ERS, USDA (1998).

5. EAST ASIAN DEMAND FOR VEGETABLE OILS

Global consumption of vegetable oils over the past decade has increased from 48 million tons to 73 million tons – a 50 per cent increase. Most of this increase on the demand side has been associated with income and population growth within developing countries where rates of growth exceed those in developed countries.

Not only are population and income growth higher in most developing countries, the response of vegetable oil consumption to increases in income is also greater. In most of the developed countries, consumption of calories from fats and oils is near saturation. This leaves only the much smaller non-food industrial uses – soaps, cosmetics, plastics – as the major source of growth. For developing countries where large populations have a low per capita caloric intake, fats and oils are an inexpensive source of additional calories as their incomes rise. In addition, income growth leads people to increase their consumption of processed foods which rely heavily on vegetable oil.

Figure 12.3 shows the relationship between per capita income and per capita consumption of vegetable oils for 91 countries. The demand for vegetable oil increases at a decreasing rate as income rises as shown in the plot. East Asian countries are labelled along with a few others for reference. Note that some of the key Asian countries – China, the Philippines, and Indonesia (labelled CHI, PHI, IDO on the plot) – are still on the lower end of the curve where we can expect additional income growth to have a significant effect on vegetable oil consumption.

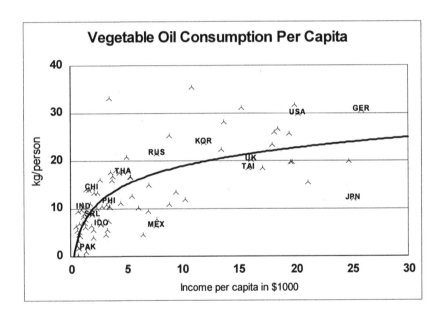

Figure 12.3 The rate of increase in vegetable oil consumption declines as income increases.

Source: World Bank (1996a) for Income and ERS, USDA (1998) for consumption.

Comprehensive time series data for vegetable oil prices for each of the East Asian countries in this study are not available. We therefore use cross-country estimation, using per cápita income and per capita vegetable oil consumption for 15 Asian countries to determine the response of vegetable oil consumption to income. We use a dummy variable to distinguish between the response of high-income countries (Japan, Taiwan, Korea, and Singapore) and low and middle income countries make up the remainder of the sample.[2] The procedure yields an income elasticity of 0.036 for high-income countries and an elasticity of 0.51 for the low and medium countries. We use these income elasticities to generate the increase in vegetable oil demand to the year 2005 for alternative income scenarios as shown in table 12.6. For East Asia, we use the same tree income growth scenarios as for the protein meal projections and an extrapolation of historical population growth. For the rest of the world, we assume that both population and income growth are the same as historical levels. We do not examine alternative growth scenarios for the rest of the world for two reasons. First, our focus is on the East Asian protein meal and oil balance. Second, it makes no sense to assume that all

Table 12.6 Vegetable oil consumption projections to 2005

	1995 population millions	1995 per capita consumption kg/person	Change in total vegetable oil consumption		
			No growth 1000 tons	Moderate growth (3%) 1000 tons	High rowth (7%) 1000 tons
World	5601	12.5	12 252	14 137	18 641
NE Asia	190	16.2	163	198	245
Japan	125	15.9	60	83	112
S. Korea	44	13.0	54	80	70
Taiwan	21	24.7	49	55	63
China	1191	7.9	1194	2935	5655
SE. Asia	457	12.5	1071	2182	3919
Thailand	58	9.6	58	159	317
Philippines	67	7.2	117	215	367
Malaysia	19	23.6	124	221	371
Indonesia	190	17.8	584	1235	2254
Other SE Asia	122	6.7	188	352	809
East Asia	1838	9.9	2427	5315	9819
World less East Asia	3763	13.8	8822	8822	8822

countries of the world could simultaneously achieve any but the No growth targeted growth rate.

Income growth has a significant impact on the additional demand for vegetable oil in all the lower income East Asian countries, but, as expected, only a very small effect on demand in the high-income countries. For the Northeast Asian countries — Japan, South Korea, and Taiwan — even the oil demand increase for the High growth scenario represents only an 8 per cent increase over the 1995 base vegetable oil consumption level of 3 million tons. For China and Southeast Asia, however, the difference between the No growth and the High growth scenarios is a factor of three. As a result, East Asia accounts for only 2.4 million tons (or about 25 per cent) of the world's additional 12.2 additional vegetable oil requirements given a No growth scenario for the region compared to a 9.8 million ton requirement of the world's 14.6 million tons for the High growth scenario. In absolute terms, income growth in China is the most important factor affecting additional vegetable oil demand in 2005.

6.   THE SUPPLY — DEMAND BALANCE IN 2005

Both the protein meal and vegetable oil demand projections show a wide range between the No growth and the High growth scenarios. This section will compare these projections in demand with the supply capabilities of the region and the world. Then we will look at the regional and global balance for the meal and oil market and draw implications for the region.

A projection of future meal and oil supply availabilities must begin with an analysis of each of the major oilseed production trends for each of the study regions and the world. Because each of the oilseeds has a different oil and meal extraction rate, we need to know how much of each oilseed is likely to be produced in 2005. The ideal approach for projecting oilseed production would be to develop a set of country models with information on own and competing crop prices, farm policies, and resource availabilities for each of the major producers of each of the major oilseeds. This goes far beyond the scope of this chapter and, if we focus primarily on major regional aggregations, trend analysis will closely approximate the projections of a more detailed modelling effort.

Table 12.7 shows the historical and projected changes in production of

Food security in Asia

each of the major oilseeds in the major producing countries of Asia and the world total. The rest-of-world projections are the residual after subtracting Asian production from the world total. The projections capture current trends in area expansion and yield growth and extend them to the year 2005. (The equations on which these projections are based are shown in appendix table 12.A1.)

Table 12.7 Supply projections for major oilseeds to 2005 (million metric tons)

	Production		10-Year increase		Proj 2005 increase	
	1985	1995	1985 to 1995	Proj.1995 to 2005	Meal equiv.	Oil equiv.
WORLD						
Total	135.3	184.0	48.7	48.5	34.5	15.4
Soybeans	97.0	123.6	26.6	34.5	26.9	4.8
Rapeseed	18.7	34.6	15.9	7.2	4.3	1.7
Sunflower	19.6	25.8	6.2	6.7	3.2	1.3
Palm Oil*	8.1	15.6	7.5	7.6		7.6
NE Asia						
Total	0.9	0.3	−0.6	0.0	0.0	0.0
Soybeans	0.9	0.3	−0.6	0.0	0.0	0.0
China						
Total	17.8	24.6	6.8	6.7	4.0	1.6
Soybeans	10.5	13.5	3.0	3.3	2.6	0.6
Rapeseed	5.6	9.8	4.2	3.2	1.9	1.2
Sunflower	1.7	1.3	−0.4	0.2	0.1	0.1
SE Asia						
Total	1.6	2.4	0.8	0.0	0.0	6.9
Soybeans	1.4	2.3	0.9	0.0	0.0	0.0
Sunflower	0.2	0.1	−0.1	0.0	0.0	0.0
Palm Oil*	6.2	13.4	7.2	6.9		6.9
Rest of World						
Total	115.0	156.7	41.7	41.7	29.9	6.6
Soybeans	84.2	107.8	23.6	30.8	24.4	4.3
Rapeseed	13.1	24.8	11.7	4.0	2.4	0.4
Sunflower	17.7	24.4	6.7	6.5	3.1	1.2
Palm Oil*	1.9	2.2	0.3	0.7	0.0	0.7

Note: *Not included in the oilseed or protein meal totals.

Source: ERS, USDA (1998) TIMESERIES Program.

To avoid confusion, palm oil which is reported on a crude oil basis, is not included in the oilseed or protein meal aggregations. Data on production levels in 1985 and 1995 and the increase in that ten-year time span are shown in the left three columns of table 12.7 to serve as a basis for evaluating the projections. We can see, for instance, that the projected increase in world oilseed production of 48.5 million tons by 2005 is about the same in quantity terms as the increase from 1985 to 1995. A larger share of the increased oilseed production, however, is expected to come from soybeans in the place of rapeseed. This will result in greater protein meal availability and less oil production than would be the case if rapeseed maintained its share of world production.

Asia has very little to contribute to additional global oilseed production with all of its 6.7 million ton increase coming from China. For vegetable oils, however, Southeast Asia is projected to contribute almost half (6.9 million tons) of the world's increase in oil supplies of 15.4 million tons and China is expected to add another 10 per cent (1.6 million tons) to the world total. Overall, the supply projections show that the dominant oilseeds — soybeans and palm oil — will provide an even greater share of the meal and oil needs, respectively, in the future.

Table 12.8 compares the oil and meal demand projections from the three scenarios presented in the previous sections with the production trends shown in table 12.7. The top nine rows show the supply—demand balance for the three East Asian regions which are summarized in the East Asia total. The Rest of World production of meal and oil comes from table 12.7, the consumption of meal is based on a trend projection and the consumption of oil projection is from table 12.6.

These results highlight the result that has been becoming more and more apparent from the start, that is, all regions in East Asia will face a significant added deficit in protein meal in the next decade. As the balance for East Asia shows in table 12.8, our projections indicate that the region will have an added protein meal deficit of 600 000 to 11.5 million tons of protein meal in 2005 depending on the rate of economic growth. The production—consumption balance for the rest of the world, given current trends, is projected to produce an additional surplus of 7.4 million tons of protein meal with most of this coming from the United States, Argentina, and Brazil. This surplus is sufficient to cover East Asia's added protein meal requirements for the No growth and the Moderate growth scenarios, but is 4 million tons short of filling East Asia's needs for the High growth scenario. This suggest that as East Asia's aggregate income growth begins to exceed a rate of roughly 5 per cent, it will begin to put pressure on the world's ability to supply protein meal to the region. Markets will, of course, adjust as growing demand puts upward pressure

on prices, which will bring about supply and demand adjustments and
assure a global balance. Nevertheless, these projections are useful in
showing the impact of income growth on global oilseed markets.

It is worth mentioning here that the Asian demand estimates are on the
conservative side. We have projected the demand for only the three major
feed uses of protein meal and have assumed efficient feeding technology.
Also, Rest of World consumption is held within its 20-year trend. The
ability of global surpluses to address Asia's deficit in protein meal, if
anything, is slightly optimistic.

*Table 12.8 Oilseed meal and oil supply – demand balances (quantity
change from 1995 in 1000 metric tons)*

	Growth scenarios for meal			Growth scenarios for oil		
	No growth	Moderate (3%)	High (7%)	No growth	Moderate (3%)	High (7%)
NE Asia						
Consumption	272	832	1673	163	198	245
Production	0	0	0	0	0	0
Balance	−272	−832	−1673	−163	−198	−245
China						
Consumption	3992	7264	11514	1194	2835	5655
Production	4601	4601	4601	1907	1907	1907
Balance	609	−2663	−6913	713	−928	−3748
SE Asia						
Consumption	948	1724	2935	1071	2182	3919
Production	0	0	0	6910	6910	6910
Balance	−948	−1724	−2935	5839	4728	2991
East Asia						
Consumption	5212	9820	16122	2428	5215	9819
Production	4601	4601	4601	8817	8817	8817
Balance	−611	−5219	−11 521	6389	3602	−1002
Rest of world						
Consumption	22 435	22 435	22 435	8822	8822	8822
Production	29 887	29 887	29 887	6599	6599	6599
Balance	7452	7452	7452	−2223	−2223	−2223
World balance	6842	2234	−4068	3162	−1378	−3226

The regional balance for vegetable oil is the reverse of protein meal at low levels of income growth. East Asia has a net surplus of vegetable oil for export to the rest of the world under the No growth and Moderate growth scenarios. However, under the High growth scenario, demand for vegetable oil within the region exceeds the region's current production trend and there are not East Asian surpluses to address the Rest of World projected deficit of 2.2 million tons.

Table 12.9 shows the global land adjustments that would be required for each of the four major oil crops to bring the World balance to zero. These are calculated using the yields and oil and meal extraction rates from table 12.1. In the protein meal column for the No growth scenario, for example, it would take a 5.6 per cent reduction in soybean area to eliminate the projected 6.8 million ton global surplus in protein meal; it would take a 10.5 per cent reduction in rapeseed area to achieve the same result, and so on. These data give a rough idea of the level of global production adjustments implied in each of the scenarios.

The table overstates the adjustments for each crop, of course, because all oilseed crops would adjust simultaneously to market forces. Also yield increases (not included in the calculation of future area adjustments) would diminish increases in area adjustments by perhaps 10—15 per cent and minor oilseeds would pick up some of the rest of the adjustment. The value of table 12.9 is that it shows that an increase in global area planted would be required beyond current trends, in order to meet the additional oilseed product demand associated with a high level of sustained East Asian economic growth over the 1995—2005 period. Vegetable oil requirements result in much greater relative area adjustments.

Table 12.9 Area adjustments implied by world meal and oil balances (quality change from 1995 in 1000 metric tons)

	1995 area harvested	Growth scenarios for meal			Growth scenarios for oil		
		No growth	Moderate	High	No growth	Moderate	High
World balance		6842	2234	−4068	3162	−244	−4634
Area adjustments	Mil Ha	*Per cent of 1995 world area harvested*					
Soybeans	61.7	−5.6	−1.8	3.3	−11.4	−5.0	11.6
Rapeseed	24.1	−10.5	−3.4	6.2	−12.8	−5.6	13.0
Sunflowers	20.7	−22.0	−7.2	13.1	−24.8	−10.8	25.3
Palm Oil	8.0	0.0	0.0	0.0	−10.0	−4.3	10.2

7.   TRADE CHOICES

Finally, consider the trade issue facing the region — and individual countries within the region — of whether it should import the products directly or build crushing capacity to fill meal and oil requirements by crushing of imported seeds. There are an infinite number of direct import and domestic crush combinations which are possible but we will consider only the three key alternatives — (1) build crush capacity to meet meal requirements and use trade to settle the oil balance; (2) build crush capacity to address oil needs and use trade to settle the meal balance; (3) build no additional crush capacity and use trade to settle both meal and oil balances. The first two alternatives favour the countries which produce and export oilseeds; the third alternative favours the countries which export the products.

The cost of each of these three alternatives will depend on the level of future oil and meal requirements, the type of oilseed crushed, and the prices of oilseeds, protein meals, and vegetable oils. Soybean crush produces large quantities of meal while rapeseed and sunflower seed crush produce relatively large quantities of oil. Using the oil and meal extraction rates from table 12.2, we can convert the meal and oil requirements for each of the three growth scenarios into seed equivalents to determine the crush capacity needed and the volume of seeds required for each oilseed. The seed volume multiplied by the appropriate world price will generate the oilseed import cost for crush.

This analysis of the trade choice will focus on the issue from a regional perspective. That is, we will assume, for the purpose of illustrating the choices facing country planners, that East Asia will first seek to fill its requirements from within the region. When regional sources of vegetable oil, protein meal, and oilseeds have fulfilled regional requirements, the remaining balance will be imported or exported depending on whether the region is net surplus or net deficit. If there is a net positive balance for meal or oil — that is, a need to import — then the issue is whether to import seeds and crush or import the product.

Table 12.10 shows the annual trade costs and revenues for each of the three trade alternatives for the region's projected change in protein meal and vegetable oil balances shown at the bottom of table 12.8. Negative values in the table represent export revenues. All costs are calculated using representative world prices from May 1996 of $350 for oilseeds, $300 for protein meal, and $530 for vegetable oil. We did not differentiate prices by oilseeds because the differences are not large and we want to focus attention on how differing extraction rates affect costs.   Before we discuss the implications of table 12.10, we will first explain the calculations.

The first two alternatives, which are the two crushing options, show the difference in costs associated with each of the three major traded oilseeds for each of the three income growth scenarios. For alternative 1, East Asia would fulfil all its net requirements for protein meal by importing seeds and extracting the meal. This means that the region would not incur any costs for importing meal but it would incur the cost of purchasing seeds (top three rows). The crush, however, will result in the production of vegetable oil which, it turns out, will exceed the region's oil requirements for all three oilseeds and for all three income growth scenarios (hence, the negative entries in the 'Oil cost/revenue' rows). When these surpluses are exported at world prices, they generate revenue which reduces the net total cost. The vegetable oil revenues shown for alternative 1 are those resulting from crushing the increase in oilseed imports and do not include export revenues generated from vegetable oil surpluses which are already present in the region. These are shown in the last column of table 12.10.

Table 12.10 Comparison of importing alternatives to fill Asia's meal and oil requirements (million $)

	Alternative 1 Crush for meal[a]			Alternative 2 Crush for oil			Alt. 3 import products	Sales of regional surplus
	Soybeans	Rapeseed	Sunflower	Soybeans	Rapeseed	Sunflower		
Seed cost								
No growth	271	356	445	0	0	0	0	0
Moderate	6161	8112	10 140	0	0	0	0	0
High growth	15 838	20 854	26 067	4144	1296	1201	0	0
Meal cost/revenue								
No growth	0	0	0	183	183	183	183	0
Moderate	0	0	0	4172	4172	4172	4172	0
High growth	0	0	0	8872	10 058	10 231	10 725	0
Oil								
Cost/ revenue								
No growth	-74[b]	-205	-276	0	0	0	0	-3386
Moderate	-1679	-4668	-6295	0	0	0	0	-1581
High growth	-3571	-11 254	-15 438	0	0	0	746	0
Net total cost								
No growth	197	151	169	183	183	183	183	-3386
Moderate	4481	3444	3844	4172	4172	4172	4172	-1581
High growth	12 267	9600	10 629	13 016	11 355	11 432	11 471	0

Notes: [a] Oil revenues are from crush of imported oilseeds and do not include vegetable oil surpluses from domestic production (shown in column 8).

[b] Negative numbers represent export revenues from exportable surpluses.

The costs for alternative 2 are calculated in the same way as the costs for alternative 1 with one key exception. East Asia has a net surplus balance of vegetable oil for both the No growth and the Moderate growth scenarios (see table 12.8). Thus, there is no need to import oilseeds to extract oil for these two scenarios. Crush for oil becomes a viable option only for the High growth scenario. For alternative 2, all or most of the costs of the three growth scenarios are associated with the expense of importing protein meal.

The last alternative — import the meal and oil products as needed — is calculated as simply the net positive protein meal and vegetable oil balances multiplied by their respective world prices. We do not differentiate imports by oilseed because we have assumed uniform protein meal and vegetable oil prices. As with alternative 2, there is no need to import vegetable oil for the No growth and Moderate growth scenarios.

There is actually very little difference in the net total cost of the three alternatives. Crushing rapeseed for meal (alternative 1) is cheapest ($151 million for the No growth scenario) and crushing soybeans for meal ($197 million for the No growth scenario for alternative 1) is the most expensive representing about a 25 per cent difference in costs. These differences would hardly compensate for other costs and factors which have not been taken into consideration. All the alternative 1 options for the Moderate and High growth scenarios result in substantial quantities of additional vegetable oil which must be exported. For a region which already is projected to export $3.4 and $1.9 billion in vegetable oil for the No growth and Moderate growth scenarios respectively (see column 7), this represents a substantial addition to the region's surplus. Also, the quantities of rapeseed and sunflowerseed required for crush for the Moderate and High growth scenarios of alternative 1 (8.6 and 19.2 million tons, respectively, for rapeseed and 10.8 and 24.0 million tons, respectively, for sunflowerseed), far exceed the projected additional availability of 7.2 million tons for rapeseed and 6.7 million tons for sunflowerseed shown in table 12.7. The only feasible option for alternative 1 is to crush soybeans.

The costs for alternative 2 and alternative 3 differ only for the High growth scenario because the region would not import any oilseeds for oil extraction when it has a surplus balance of oil. Again, only soybean meal is likely to be available in sufficient additional quantities to meet the increase in demand associated with the Moderate and High growth scenarios. Rapeseed meal has limitations on the animals to which it can be fed.

The cost calculations in table 12.10 ignore the fixed costs associated with the construction and depreciation of crushing facilities. With only a

25 per cent difference in costs between the cheapest and most expensive options, the inclusion of crushing facility cost will make the import option (alternative 3) look relatively more attractive.

This review of trade options has not specifically addressed the role of palm oil in the regional protein meal and vegetable oil balance. Yet, it is the large and growing exports of palm oil from Southeast Asia which has shaped the region's oilseed requirements. Import of high oil content seeds, such as rapeseed and sunflowerseed for domestic crush, may address some of the region's protein meal requirements but they end up contributing more to the region's vegetable oil surplus. This story will differ, of course, for individual countries and some may choose to crush imported rapeseed and sunflowerseed but this will just increase the palm oil availability for export to the rest of the world. The region's strong demand for protein meal and net surplus of vegetable oil ultimately means that the region needs to import protein meal or import and crush soybeans.

8.   DISCUSSION

The results of this analysis — that income growth in Asia will lead to a growing deficit in protein meal and a shrinking surplus in vegetable oil — are not surprising but the magnitude of the demand for protein meal relative to vegetable oil were not anticipated. This result suggests, as indicated above, that production of palm oil and soybeans actually complement one another. Before we draw the implications for Asia's future food requirements, a brief review of some of the major assumptions and decisions and their effect on the analysis will help put the results into perspective.

*   The protein meal projections are based on an incomplete set of animal feeding activities in East Asia. Consumption of farm-raised fish, dairy, lamb, ducks, and other animal products will increase as incomes rise, which will increase feed requirements. The omission of these animal feeding activities means that we have understated feed requirements on the input side and, to a smaller extent (because many of these animal protein sources from backyard production and marine catch are already included in consumer diets), overstated consumption of beef, pork, and poultry on the demand side.
*   We have assumed only one feeding technology for increases in animal products. This does not preclude the existence of many different feeding methods, including traditional backyard production throughout Asia. The analysis is based on the premise that adequate additional

quantities of animal products will only be forthcoming in the next decade if efficient feeding methods are employed. To the extent that feeding technology in Asia turns out to be less efficient, we have understated the quantity of feed required to meet consumption demand.

- We have largely ignored the contribution of the lesser oilseeds including cottonseed, peanuts, coconut, etc. Although these are not widely traded for crushing use, they are a significant source of protein meal and oil in some countries, especially China, accounting for roughly 20 per cent of current oilseed production. These will make some contribution to oilseed needs but only cottonseed is widely used for protein meal and any increase in the land area planted to cotton in China will be limited.

- We have treated all protein meals and vegetable oils throughout most of the chapter as if they can be easily substituted one for another. This is far from the case in practice. Imperfect substitution, of course, will increase the total requirements. However, price differentials reflect the quality and availability differences for all of these oilseed products and we expect these prices to allocate the scarcest oilseeds and products to their most efficient use. At the aggregate use level, substitution at the margin, based on premiums and discounts for quality differences, should be sufficient to clear all markets.

- We have chosen to only look at East Asian income growth scenarios and the effect on consumption. We have not looked at alternative growth scenarios for countries outside East Asia and we have not looked at alternative production scenarios — either within the region or at the global level. This limits the scope of the analysis but also allows us to focus on the most important factor — the role of income growth in determining the consumption of oilseed products.

A more sophisticated detailed analysis of East Asian protein meal and vegetable oil markets might yield results which are slightly different in magnitude, but the major conclusions would likely remain the same. Both the protein meal and vegetable oil markets are very sensitive to changes in income growth with future demand for meal relatively stronger than the demand for oil. China with its huge population, dominates the demand projections for the region particularly for protein meal. The strong demand for protein meal suggests further development and expansion of the oilseed crushing industry, especially in China. It seems likely that countries in the region will build crushing capacity for soybeans with the objective of meeting protein meal requirements and importing the balance of their vegetable oil needs. This will favour the trade of soybeans and palm oil.

9.   CONCLUSIONS

The regional economic crisis triggered by the devaluation of the Thai baht in July 1997 has changed dramatically the expectations of Asia's economic performance for the next decade. A moderate average annual growth rate of 3 per cent for the region would have seemed very pessimistic in 1996 and a decade of no growth would have been unthinkable for most of the key countries in the region. Yet Japan, the largest economy in the region, will struggle to post even a 1 per cent rate of growth for the five years to the year 2000 and Indonesia, despite its 8 to 9 per cent growth in 1995 and 1996, will be fortunate to begin the millennium with an expanding GDP. If the economic crisis persists or spreads and brings with it new social upheavals in the region, the economic prospects for the region may be closer to the No growth scenario than to the High growth scenario. The key country in the regional and global oilseed balance is China. A sustained economic expansion at levels close to its 7 to 9 per cent growth of the past decade will certainly result in a tightening of global oilseed markets, particularly for protein meal. The relatively stronger projected demand for protein meal should lead to a narrowing of the spread between oil and meal prices if there are no offsetting demand trends in the rest of the world. This will favour soybeans with their high meal content over oilseeds with high oil content.

This chapter has shown that, whatever is the outcome of the Asian economic crisis, the Asian food security issue related to oilseeds is closely tied to economic growth. The income-associated changes in the demand for oilseeds and products is a microcosm of the broader change in food consumption patterns in Asia. Rising incomes will shift demand away from traditional staples, such as rice and other food grains, and put pressure on the production systems associated with more income-sensitive commodities, particularly animal products and the feedstuffs required to produce them.

NOTES

[1]   There is a growing aquaculture industry which depends on manufactured feeds but comprehensive cross-country data make analysis of consumption and production in this industry very difficult. In addition, marine catch still provides the greatest share of fish consumption in most countries in the region.

[2]   The estimated equation:

$$LPCFOOD = -2.241 + 0.510\ LPPPGNP + 0.036\ DUM$$

where *LPCFOOD* is per capita consumption, *LPPPGNP* is per capita GNP and *DUM* is cross-product dummy and *PPPGNP*, where 0 = low-income countries 1 = high-income countries.

REFERENCES

Castaneda, J. and M. Giordano (1995), 'Palm Oil Prospects for 2005, ERS', USDA, Staff Report Number 9518, Washington, DC.

Chow, C.S. (1993), 'Forecast of Malaysian, Indonesian and World Palm Oil Production and Future World Demand for Palm Oil and Other Oils and Fats', PORIM Report G(183).

Economic Research Service (ERS), USDA (1998), 'Agricultural Commodity Supply-Utilization Statistics in TimeSeries', electronic files at [http://www.mannlib.cornell.edu/data-sets/international/93002 /]

FAOSTAT (1998), 'Electronic database of the Food and Agricultural Organization' (FAO), at http://apps.fao.org/lim500/nph-wrap.pl? Livestock.Primary&Domain.

LMC International Ltd. (1997), 'The Impact of Tariffs and Export Taxes on Crushing and Refining Margins', *Oilseeds, Oils and Meals*, January.

Pasquali, M. (1993), 'Prospects to the Year 2000 in the World Oilseeds, Oils and Oilmeals Economy: Policy Issues and Challenges', Proceedings of the PORIM International Palm Oil Congress, Kuala Lumpur.

PORLA (Palm Oil Registration and Licensing Authority) (1997), Palm Oil Statistics, 1996, Ministry of Primary Industries, Malaysia.

World Bank (1996a), *From Plan to Market: World Development Report 1996*, New York: Oxford University Press.

World Bank (1996b), *Global Economic Prospects and the Developing Countries, 1996*, Washington, DC.

Table 12.A1 Equations estimated for production projections [a]

	1995 production mmt	Estimated production equations		
		Intercept	Trend coefficient	Estimation period
WORLD				
Total	184.0			
Soybeans	123.6	16.93	3.45	1983 to 96
Rapeseed	34.6	−0.87	0.72	1976 to 96
Sunflower	25.8	3.28	0.67	1976 to 96
Palm oil	15.6	−9.5	0.78	1981 to 97
China				
Total	24.6			
Soybeans	13.5	3.03	0.32	1986 to 96
Rapeseed	9.8	−1.67	0.32	1982 to 96
Sunflower	1.3	0.71	0.02	1979 to 96
SE Asia				
Total	2.3			
Soybeans	2.3	1.12	0.04	1988 to 96
Palm oil	13.4	−9.46	0.69	1982 to 96

Notes: [a] Equations estimated of the form $Y = a + b\,T$ where $T = 1$ in 1964; $T = 2$ in 1965, etc.

Index

accreditation, 193
additives, chemical, 215, 216
Afghanistan, 15
Agcaoili-Sombilla, M., 85
age, 220–21, 221–2
agricultural trade *see* trade
agriculture, 2
   China, 4, 19–34
      labour, 19–20, 21, 23–9
      policy bias against agriculture, 19,
         21–3
      policy options, 27–9
      position in the national economy for
         Japan and South Korea, 120–21
      research, 16, 55–7
      rice in Asia, 36–7
   Singapore
      phasing out inefficient/pollutive,
         191–2
      unsubsidized and fully commercial,
         191–4
   wages, 43
agrotechnical parks, 192, 194–6
almost ideal demand systems (AIDS)
   rice imports and Taiwan, 171–7, 178
   urban and rural China and Japan, 6,
      94–101, 105, 110–18
Alston, J.M., 94
ASEAN Free Trade Area (AFTA), 5,
   61–81
   comparative advantage and intensity of
      agricultural exports, 66–72
   impacts and measurement problems,
      73–7
   role of agricultural trade in Taiwan and
      ASEAN, 63–6, 67
Asia
   demand for protein meals and
      vegetable oils *see* protein meals;
      vegetable oils
   economic crisis, 255
   population and income for major East

Asian countries, 235
rice economy, 4–5, 35–59
   importance of rice, 36–8
   policy and research, 55–7
   supply and demand in 2010, 45–53
   trade and sustaining food security,
      53–5
   trends in demand, 38–41
   trends in supply, 41–5
Association of Southeast Asian Nations
   (ASEAN), 5, 61, 62, 193–4
   intra-ASEAN trade, 66, 67
   role of agricultural trade, 63–6, 67
   see also ASEAN Free Trade Area
Australia, 165, 167–70, 172, 173–6, 178,
   179

Balassa, B., 68
Baldwin, R.E., 143
Bale, M.D., 154–5
Ballance, R., 68
Bangkok Declaration, 61
basmati aromatic rice, 169
beef
   import liberalization in Japan, 6–7,
      131–2
   protein meal demand, 236–7, 238,
      239–42
   Singapore and imports of, 193
   see also meat
Belize, 224
Berndt, R.E., 173
binary-ordinal probit model, 209–12,
   217–23
Blanciforti, L.R., 171
Bouis, H., 88, 91
Braun, J.V., 198
Brown, L.R., 20, 84, 92
Buse, A., 94–5
Buzby, J.C., 208

Cai, F., 21, 24, 26

calorie intake, 52, 53, 54
  trends in Japan and South Korea, 121–3
calorie self-sufficiency rate, 125–6
capital intensity, 26–7
Carter, C., 22, 24, 26
cereals *see* grain
chemical food preservatives/additives,
  215, 216
Chen, T.J., 143
Chern, W.S., 84, 85–6, 88, 92, 93
Chernobyl disaster, 134
children, 220, 221
  malnourished, 52, 53, 54, 84
China, 51, 169, 229, 235
  demand-side factors, 5–6, 83–118
  urban–rural income gap, 4, 19–34
    abundant agricultural labour, 23–7
    policy bias against agriculture, 19,
      21–3
    policy options and implications for
      grain markets, 27–9
  vegetable oils and protein meals, 230,
    233, 240, 245, 254, 255
    demand projections, 246, 247, 254
cholesterol, 216–17
Christensen, L.R., 173
collectivization, 25
commune system, 25
comparative advantage, 66–72, 77
consumer surplus, 154–7
consumption
  grains in China and Japan, 89–92
    grain vs meat, 92–3
  Japan and South Korea, 120–26
    trends, 121, 122
  levels in Asian countries, 36
  per capita income growth and grain
    consumption, 39
  reducing in wealthy economies, 15
  rice import issue in Taiwan, 146–57
  Singapore, 186–8, 189, 190
  see also demand
contingent crisis, 11, 12–13
contingent valuation methods (CVM), 208
  see also willingness to pay
Cook, S., 26
cooperation, international, 16–17, 56–7
Corden, W.M., 157
cottonseed, 254
Cragg, J.G., 211
Cramer, G.L., 94

Crook, F., 19, 23
crushing capacity, 250–53, 254
currency crises, 85, 134
cyclical crisis, 11, 13–15

dairy beef, 132
David, C.C., 45
Deaton, A.S, 94, 171
decoupling payment mechanism, 180
demand
  allocation and rice imports in Hong
    Kong and Singapore, 7–8, 163–83
  Asian demand for vegetable oils and
    protein meals, 9, 229–57
  for rice in Asia, 38–41
  projections for rice, 127–31
    Asia in 2010, 45–53
    in Japan, 6, 127–9
    in South Korea, 6, 129–31
demand control programs, 136
demand-side factors, 5–6, 83–118
  econometric analysis, 93–101
    model, 94–7, 98
    regression results, 97–101, 110–18
  food security issues, 84–5
  grain as an inferior good, 87–92
  grain vs meat, 92–3
  income elasticities in China and Japan,
    101–4
  puzzle of income elasticity, 86–93
domestic market, 126–32
domestic production capacity, 16, 136
domestic stockpiles, 12–13, 135–6
double hurdle model, 211
Duncan, R.C., 84
dynamic trade effects, 73

economic development, 6–7, 119–40
  food consumption and self-sufficiency,
    120–26
  food security issues, 133–6
  impact of agricultural trade
    liberalization on domestic market,
    126–32
  and position of agriculture in the
    national economy, 120–21
economic growth
  agriculture's contribution in ASEAN
    and Taiwan, 63–4
  and Asia's demand for vegetable oils
    and protein meals, 235–55

slow and rice economy, 49, 50, 52–3
economic integration, 73–7
see also ASEAN Free Trade Area
educational attainment, 220, 221
efficiency
  agriculture in Singapore, 191–2
  feeding technology, 239–40, 253–4
Engel functions, 101–2
environmental protection, 56
Evenson, R.E., 47–8
expenditure elasticities
  demand-side factors in China and
    Japan, 93–4, 99–104
  rice import competition and demand
    allocation, 172, 173–7, 178
  see also income elasticities
export promotion, 188–91
export regulations, 135
exports
  AFTA and Taiwan, 65–6
    export intensity, 66–72, 77
  Singapore, 199–200, 201
    export promotion, 188–91
  see also trade

Fan, S., 20, 85
farm price, 146–54
fats, saturated, 216–17
feed–meat conversion ratios, 239–40
feeding technology, 239–40, 253–4
  see also protein meals
Fei, J.C.H., 25
fertilizer use, 45
filter design for WTP, 209
Fischer, K.S., 36
fishery products, 69–72
Flavin, C., 20
food crises, 1, 3–4, 11–17, 134
  contingent crisis, 11, 12–13
  cyclical crisis, 11, 13–15
  Malthusian crisis, 11, 16
  political crisis, 11, 15
food poisoning, 215, 216
food quality *see* quality of food; food
  safety
food reserves, 12–13, 135–6
food safety, 8–9, 205–27
  measuring willingness to pay, 207–9
    empirical results, 217–23
    survey design and sample data,
      213–17

    theoretical framework and
      estimation procedure, 209–12
food security, 1–3, 194
  fallacy or reality, 3–4, 11–17
  issues, 84–5
  Japan and South Korea, 133–6
  and national security, 16–17
  policies, 134–6
  and self-sufficiency, 2, 8, 196–8
forestry products, 69–72
Forstner, H., 68
Foster, W.E., 158
free trade area *see* ASEAN Free Trade
  Area
French, H., 20
fresh food, 194, 195, 197
Fu, T.-T., 209, 220–21, 222, 223
fully commercial farming, 191–4

Gao, X.M., 94
Garcia, P., 169
Gemma, M., 127
General Agreement on Tariffs and Trade
  (GATT), 62, 124, 135, 141, 150
  Uruguay Round *see* Uruguay Round
  see also World Trade Organization
general equilibrium approach, 73
  analysis of food trade in Singapore,
    196, 197
genetically modified organisms (GMOs),
  3
Germany, 134, 135
Gerpacio, R.V., 44
Global Trade Analysis Project (GTAP)
  database, 69
Goldstone, J.A., 21
Good Agricultural Practice (GAP)
  program, 207, 209
Gorman, W.D., 132
government purchase, 146–54
governors grain bag responsibility
  system, 23
grain
  demand in urban and rural China and
    Japan, 6, 86–106
    econometric analysis, 93–101
    grain vs meat, 92–3
    income elasticities, 101–4
    inferior good, 87–92
    import liberalization and food security,
      13

policy in China, 22–3, 27–9
self-sufficiency rate in Japan and
    South Korea, 125–6
supply and demand in China, 20–1
US embargo on Soviet Union, 15
see also rice
grain bag responsibility system, 23
grain markets, 27–9
Grant, W.R., 87
Green, R., 94, 174
Greenshield, B.L., 154–5

Haddad, L., 91
Hahn, W.F., 95, 105
Hammitt, J.K., 209, 220–1, 222, 223
Heckman, J.J., 210
Heien, D., 95
Herrmann, R.O., 209
Higuchi, T., 121
Hong Kong, 2
    rice imports, 7–8, 163–83
        import allocation aids model, 171–7
        relative reliability, 165–71, 179
Hossain, M., 36, 44
household registration system (hukou),
    21
household responsibility system (HRS),
    25–6
Houthakker, H.S., 73
Huang, C.H., 206
Huang, C.L., 221, 222, 223
Huang, J., 20, 88
Huggan, R., 37
Hussein, M.A., 40
hydroponically grown vegetables (HGV),
    8–9, 207–24

IMPACT model, 5, 45–53
    Asian rice market under baseline
        scenario, 49, 50
    baseline assumptions, 47–9
    effect of slow economic growth on the
        rice economy, 52–3
    intersectoral linkages, 47
    rice and food security, 52
    structure, 45–6
    trade performance by country, 49–51
import allocation aids model, 171–7
import substitution, 188
imports, 135
    ASEAN, 65–6

Japan, 124
    beef import liberalization, 6–7, 131–2
    rice, 163, 165, 177–8
    policy choice of rice import issue in
        Taiwan, 7, 141–61
    rice import competition and demand
        allocation in Hong Kong and
        Singapore, 7–8, 163–83
        import allocation aids model, 171–7
        relative reliability, 165–71
    Singapore's food security strategy,
        193–4, 196, 197, 198–200, 201
    South Korea, 124–5
        rice, 163, 165, 177–8
    trade choices for vegetable oils and
        protein meals, 250–3
    see also trade
income
    and demand for vegetable oils and
        protein meals, 235–55
    farm household incomes, 37, 38
    household incomes and grain
        consumption in China and Japan,
        89–92
    per capita and grain consumption, 39
    urban–rural income gap in China, 4,
        19–34
    and WTP, 220, 222
income elasticities
    Asian demand for protein meals, 236–7,
        238
    Japan and China, 85–106
        econometric analysis, 93–101, 110–18
        grain as an inferior good, 87–92
        grain vs meat, 92–3
        puzzle of, 86–93
    see also expenditure elasticities
India, 51, 169–70, 176–7
Indica rice, 164
Indonesia, 51, 255
    currency crisis, 85
    palm oil, 232–3, 234
industrialization, 21
inferior goods, 87–92
Ingco, M.D., 84
inspection, 193
interest groups, 144–5
international cooperation, 16–17, 56–7
International Monetary Fund (IMF), 124
    Food Cereal Import Facility, 14
international trade theory, 142

intersectoral linkages, 47
investment, 47–8
irrigation, 42–3, 45
Ito, S., 87, 127

Japan, 6–7, 51, 119–40, 229, 245, 255
  demand-side factors, 5–6, 83–118
    passim
  food consumption and self-sufficiency,
    120–6
  food security and food crises, 3–4,
    11–17 *passim*
  food security issues, 133–6
  impact of beef import liberalization on
    domestic market, 6–7, 131–2
  projections of supply and demand of
    rice, 6, 127–9
  rice imports, 163, 165, 177–8
  Simultaneous Buying and Selling
    (SBS) system, 164
Japanese Beef Market Access
  Agreement, 131
Japonica rice, 164, 179–80
Jiangsu Province, China, 94, 95–6, 98,
  99
Johnson, D.G., 15
Johnston, B.F., 25
Jorgenson, D.W., 25
Josling, T.E., 78

Kako, T., 127, 130
Kanai, M., 87
Korea, North, 51, 134
Korea, South, 6–7, 51, 119–40, 229, 245
  food consumption and self-sufficiency,
    120–6
  food security issues, 133–6
  projections of supply and demand of
    rice, 6, 129–31
  rice imports, 163, 165, 177–8
Krenin, M.E., 73
Kunimoto, K., 68

labour
  agricultural labour force in ASEAN
    and Taiwan, 64
  China, 19–20, 21, 23–9
    abundance of agricultural labour,
      23–7
    scarcity, 43
  labour productivity, 120

land
  China, 28–9
  global adjustments needed for
    vegetable oils and protein meals,
    249
  scarcity, 42–3
  Singapore, 186, 187
Lardy, N.R., 21, 23
Laspeyres index, 172, 173, 174, 175, 177
Lee, J.O., 125
Leu, G.-J.M., 188
Lewis, W.A., 25
Li, E., 93–4
Li, Z., 21
liberalization of trade, 56, 141, 185
  implications of Singapore's strategy
    for other East Asian economies,
    196–200, 201
  Japan and South Korea, 124–5
    impact on domestic markets, 126–32
  Taiwan, 61–2
Liesner, H.H., 68
limited access, 7, 142, 145, 147–59
Lin, J.Y., 21, 25
linear approximate almost ideal demand
  system (LA/AIDS), 171
  China and Japan, 93–101, 105, 110–18
linear expenditure system (LES), 93
Liu, J.-T., 209, 220–21, 222, 223
Liu, M.S., 143
livestock, 12–13, 69–72
low-income developing countries, 205
Lunven, P., 40

Mad Cow Disease, 193
Magee, S.P., 73
Malaysia, 51, 232–3, 234
malnutrition, 52, 53, 54, 84
  see also undernutrition
Malthusian crisis, 11, 16
Marshallian elasticities, 172, 173–7, 178
Mayes, D.G., 73
McMillan, J., 21
meat, 220
  demand for protein meals, 236–7, 238,
    239–42
  demand in urban and rural China and
    Japan, 6, 91, 93–4, 99, 103–5
  grain vs meat, 92–3
  imports in Singapore, 193
  self-sufficiency rate in Japan and

Korea, 125–6
see also beef
Mellor, J., 25, 87
Meng, C.L., 210, 212
migration of labour (China), 24, 26–7,
    27–9
military crisis, 134
minimum access (MA) rice imports,
    127–8, 130–1
Misra, S.K., 221, 222, 223
Mitchell, D.O., 84
Mori, H., 132
Moschini, G., 95, 105, 142, 171–2, 173
Muellbauer, J., 94, 171
multiplier analysis, 147–54
Murray, T., 68
Myanmar, 49

national security, 16–17
Naughton, B., 19, 21
neoclassical economic theory, 142, 143
newly industrial economies, 205–6
non-grain agricultural products, 69–72
non-staple foods, 2

occupational structure, 39–40
oilseeds, 9, 229–57
    Asian demand for protein meals, 235–42
    Asian demand for vegetable oils, 242–5
    major oilseeds, 231–4
    supply–demand balance in 2005, 245–9
    trade choices, 250–53
oligopoly, 135
organically grown products, 207
Oshima, H., 25
Otsuka, K., 45
Ott, S.L., 221, 222, 223

Paasche index, 172, 173, 174, 175, 176
Pakistan, 51
palm oil, 231–4, 246–7, 249, 253, 257
Pandya-Lorch, R., 39, 135
partial equilibrium approach, 73–7
partial observability, 210–11
peacetime food crises, 134
Peng, T.-K., 87
Perez, N.D., 85
perishable food, 194, 195, 197
Perkins, D.H., 87
pesticides, 206–7, 208–9, 213–17, 221, 222
    see also willingness to pay

Peterson, E.W.F., 87
PFC calorie ratio, 123
Philippines, 51
pig farming, 192
    see also park
Pingali, P., 44, 56
Pinstrup-Andersen, P., 39, 84, 135
Poirier, D.J., 210
policy, 56–7
    China
        policy bias against agriculture, 19,
            21–3
        policy options, 27–9
    food security policies, 134–6
    policy choice, 7, 141–61
        multiplier analysis, 147–54
        order of political preference, 157–9
        theory of, 143–5
political crisis, 11, 15, 134
political economy, 142–3
political preference, order of, 157–9
political preference function (PPF),
    143–5
political support rating, 157–9
pollution, 191–2
population growth, 40–1, 235
    Singapore, 186, 187
pork, 236–7, 238, 239–42
    see also meat
potential production capacity, 16, 136
poultry, 236–7, 238, 239–42
    see also meat
poverty, 3
preservatives, chemical, 215, 216
pressure groups, 144–5
presupposition effect, 209
price elasticities, 171–2, 173–7, 178
price supports, 180
prices, 84, 220–1
    control in China, 22
    cyclical crisis, 13–15
    rice imports
        Hong Kong and Singapore, 169–70,
            171–2, 173–7, 178
        Taiwan, 146–54
    Singapore, 199
private stock change, 146–54
processed products, 40
producer's price, 146–54
producer's surplus, 154–7
production

potential production capacity, 16, 136
rice in Taiwan, 145–57
scarcity of resources, 42–3
Singapore, 186–8, 189
world rice production, 165, 166
see also supply
productivity, 120
protein meals, 9, 229–57
Asian demand for 236–42
income elasticities, 236–7
projections, 237–42
major oilseeds, 231–4
supply–demand balance in 2005, 245–9
trade choices, 250–53
public opinion, 133–4, 136

quality of food, 3
rice, 40, 103–4, 164, 169, 179–80
see also food safety

Randall, A., 208
Ranis, G., 25
rapeseed, 232–4, 246–7, 249, 250–53
passim, 257
rationing, 136
Rausser, G.C., 158
reliability of rice imports, 165–71, 179
research, 16, 55–7
resettlement practices, 191–2
resource availability, 42–3
retail price, 146–54
revealed comparative advantage (RCA),
68–9
rice, 2–3, 4–5, 35–59, 229
ASEAN and Taiwan, 69–72
and the Asian economy, 36–8
demand in Japan, 89, 90, 103–4
emerging trends in demand, 38–41
emerging trends in supply, 41–5
import competition and demand
allocation in Hong Kong and
Singapore, 7–8, 163–83
projections of supply and demand
Japan, 6, 127–9
South Korea, 6, 129–31
quality of, 40, 103–4, 164, 169, 179–80
research and policy, 55–7
supply and demand in 2010, 45–53
sustaining food security through trade,
53–5
Taiwan

econometric model of rice market,
145–54
import issue, 7, 141–61
world rice market, 54–5
world rice production, 165, 166
risk, 208–9
perceptions of, 213–17, 220
Robertson, D., 62
Rosegrant, M.W., 20, 42, 47–8, 85, 135
Rozelle, S., 20, 22, 26
rural households, 95–106, 110–16
rural–urban income gap, 4, 19–34

Sabin, L., 26
Saeki, N., 124
safety, food *see* food safety
salt, 216–17
Samuel, S.N., 93–4
saturated fats, 216–17
Sawada, M., 87
Sawada, Y., 87
Schmidt, P., 210, 212
Schwartz, A.N.R., 73
sea lanes, closure of, 12
self-interest approach, 143
self-sufficiency, 53–4, 85, 180
China, 22–3, 27–8
food security and, 2, 8, 196–8
Japan and South Korea, 120–26
agricultural trade and, 124–5
declining trend, 125–6
Singapore, 186–8, 189
Shephard's lemma, 171
sickness, 220, 222
Sicular, T., 85
Singapore, 1–2, 8, 185–203
export promotion policy, 188–91
food production, consumption and
self-sufficiency ratio, 186–8, 189,
190
implications of strategy for other East
Asian economies, 196–200, 201
measures to ensure adequate and safe
food supply, 188–94
rice imports, 7–8, 163–83
import allocation aids model, 171–7
relative reliability, 165–71, 179
unsubsidized farming, 191–4
welfare analysis of food security
strategy, 194–6, 197
slow economic growth, 49, 50

Food security in Asia

effect on rice economy, 52–3
social-concerns approach, 143
social welfare *see* welfare
Sombilla, M., 85
Soo, K., 206
Soviet Union, grain embargo on, 15
soybeans, 231–4, 246–7, 249, 250–3
    passim, 257
specialization, 224
staple foods, 2–3
Starke, L., 20
static trade effects, 73–7
statistical modelling, 3
Sterngold, A., 209
stockpiles, 12–13, 135–6
Stoll, J.R., 208
Stone's price index, 94, 95, 171–2
storable food, 194, 195, 196, 197
subsidization of agriculture, 28
substitution, 254
    rice imports in Hong Kong and
        Singapore, 174–5, 177, 179
sugar, 216–17
sunflowerseed, 232–4, 246–7, 249, 250–53
    passim, 257
supply
    and demand for vegetable oils and
        protein meals in Asia, 245–9
    projections of rice supply, 127–31
    Asia in 2010, 45–53
    Japan, 127–9
    Korea, 129–31
    of rice in Asia, 41–5
    Singapore's measures to ensure,
        188–94
supply control program, 180
supply-side policies, 135–6
surplus labour, 23–7
Svendsen, M., 42
Swinnen, J., 143, 144
Switzerland, 135, 136

Taipei, 209, 213
Taiwan, 2, 51, 165, 229, 245
    demand for food safety, 3, 8–9, 205–27
    food security and food crises, 3–4,
        11–17 *passim*
    implications of AFTA on agricultural
        trade between Taiwan and
        ASEAN, 5, 61–81
    comparative advantage and export

intensity, 66–72
    role of agricultural trade, 63–6
per capita consumption, 121, 122
rice import issue, 7, 141–61
    analysis of economic effects, 145–54
    experience of Hong Kong and
        Singapore, 163–4, 177–81
    order of political preference for
        policy scenarios, 157–9
    policy choice theory, 143–5
    welfare analysis, 154–7
Tangermann, S., 78
tariffication, 7, 142, 145, 147–59
Taylor, J.R., 24
technology, 44–5
testing, 193
Thailand, 49
    Hong Kong and Singapore's rice
        imports from, 164, 167–70, 172,
        173–7, 178, 179
Tobata, S., 17
Tornqvist index, 172, 175
township and village enterprises (TVEs),
    26–7
trade, 1–2
    ASEAN Free Trade Area and, 5, 61–81
    choices and Asia's demand for
        vegetable oils and protein meals,
        250–53
    liberalization *see* liberalization of trade
    policy choice and Taiwan, 7, 141–61
    rice, 53, 165, 166
        performance by country, 49–51
        sustaining food security through
            trade, 53–5
    role in Taiwan and ASEAN, 63–6, 67
    Singapore and food security through,
        8, 194–6, 198–200, 202
    see also exports; imports
trade creation (TC), 73–7, 78
trade diversion (TD), 73–7, 78
trade-oriented self-reliance, 194–6, 198–
    200, 202
transportation routes, cut-off, 12
Tweeten, L., 84, 86, 87
Tyers, R., 144, 145

undernutrition, 35, 39–40
    see also malnutrition
United Kingdom, 193
United States (US), 165, 208

food concerns, 215–17
grain embargo against Soviet Union, 15
Hong Kong and Singapore's rice imports from, 7–8, 164, 168–70, 173–7, 178, 179–80
longshoremen's strike, 12
Unnevehr, L.J., 169
unsubsidized farming, 191–4
urban households, 95–106, 117
urban–rural income gap, 4, 19–34
urbanization, 39–40, 47
Japan and China, 88–9
Uruguay Round, 62, 135, 141, 163, 185, 198
Japan, 127
South Korea, 130
tariff reductions, 151

vegetable oils, 9, 229–57
Asian demand for, 242–5
major oilseeds, 231–4
supply–demand balance in 2005, 245–9
trade choices, 250–3
vegetables, safe, 8–9, 205–27
Verdoorn, P.J., 73, 74
Viner, J., 73
Vision 2020 Project, 84
Vollrath, T.I., 68
Vousden, N., 143

wages, 43
Wagyu beef, 132
Wailes, E.J., 94

Wan, C.W., 209, 218, 220, 221, 222, 223
Wang, C.S., 209, 218, 220, 221, 222, 223
Warland, R.H., 209
Warley, T.K., 78
water, 42–3, 45
Webster, A., 68
welfare
analysis of Singapore's food security strategy, 194–6, 197
rice imports in Taiwan, 154–7
Wessells, C.R., 95
willingness to pay (WTP), 8–9, 207–9
for HGV in Taiwan, 209–24
world agricultural markets, 135
rice, 54–5
World Food Crisis 1973–74, 13–14, 134
world rice production, 165, 166
World Trade Organization (WTO), 2, 61, 125, 135
see also General Agreement on Tariffs and Trade
Wu, Y., 93–4

Yang, D.T., 21, 26
Yang, M.H., 151, 157–8
yields, 41–2, 44
Yumkella, K.K., 169

Zee, F. van der, 144
Zhong, F., 24, 26
Zhou, H., 21, 26
Zhou, K., 24
Zind, T., 220
Zulkifly, Hj. M., 194